# Hollywood's Small Towns

## An Introduction to the American Small-Town Movie

by Kenneth MacKinnon

Campanelli 84

The Scarecrow Press, Inc.
Metuchen, N.J., & London 1984

**Library of Congress Cataloging in Publication Data**

MacKinnon, Kenneth, 1942–
    Hollywood's small towns.

    Bibliography: p.
    Includes index.
    1. Cities and towns in motion pictures. 2. Moving-
pictures--United States--History. I. Title.
PN1995.9.C513M3 1984    791.43'09'09355    83-27113
ISBN 0-8108-1678-4

7073802

## ACKNOWLEDGMENTS

I should like to thank Jim Cook of the British Film Institute Education Department for help with the initial stages of this book and Kevin Brownlow of Thames Television Ltd. for advice on Appendix B.

A small part of Chapter 1 of this book and much of Chapter 9 are based on a project prepared for the University of London Diploma in Film Study in 1978. I am grateful to the University of London Department of Extra-Mural Studies for its permission to include this material.

Gratitude is owed also to small-towners Joan and Frank Grant and city-dwellers Thomas Milburn, Jane and Bob White, alike, for encouragement which has been every bit as important as the more formal help acknowledged above.

# CONTENTS

Introduction                                              1
Archetypes                                               27
Utopia                                                   47
Home Is the Hunter                                       67
Alien                                                    97
Misfits                                                 113
Epitaph                                                 125
Resurrection?                                           141
A Delineation of the Genre                             151

Appendix A:   The American Small-Town Movie
              as a Genre                                175
Appendix B:   Small-Town Movies Before 1940            183
Appendix C:   A Selection of Small-Town Movies         191

Selected Bibliography                                   199

Index

[v]

# 1. INTRODUCTION

Small towns were for many years the staple of the
American cinema. Most audiences were small-town
folk, and wanted to see slightly idealized versions of
themselves. Thus the popularity of the happy families,
the Hardys and the Joneses: thus Our Town, The Human Comedy, Ah Wilderness, The Music Man and The
Dark at the Top of the Stairs. The darker side of
small-town life was shown in The Chase, Kings Row,
Peyton Place and The Invasion of the Body Snatchers.... [1]

This brief entry in Halliwell's Filmgoer's Companion represents the most sustained examination discoverable in the
entire British Film Institute book library of that "staple of
the American cinema." It explains little. Were most audiences of small-town movies "small-town folk"? Increasing
urbanization has not coincided with any diminution of the
small-town movie's importance. Moreover, despite the increasing necessity in the 'seventies, if not before, to recognize the youth of the movie audience as common denominator
rather than any such division into urban and rural audience
as Halliwell implies, some of the most commercially successful movies of that decade, notably American Graffiti, Carrie
and The Deer Hunter, are recognizably small-town.

An analysis of the genre is long overdue, particularly
in light of its phenomenal popularity from the earliest days
of cinema to the present day, but, before there can be useful consideration of it, some account of the small town in
American culture in much broader terms than the cinematic
should be attempted, if only to dispel the notion offered by
Halliwell that the raison d'être of the small-town movie is
small-town inhabitants' wish to see themselves idealized.

Even a cursory examination of the political and sentimental connotations which the term "small town" carries with
it in American thought and of the significant place that the

1

small town has taken up in American literature and drama
would suggest an importance well beyond itself.   Perhaps
that examination may suggest clues as to the popularity of
the small-town subject, its perennial appeal for highly industrialized twentieth-century America, an appeal that may be
explicable in terms of the common experience and, more particularly, common aspirations of the American people, whether
rural or urban.

## The Small Town in American History[2]

To understand the place which the small town occupies in
American public sentiment, we need to return to its beginnings
in the east coast colonies.   The English settlers arriving in
the New Land attempted to revitalize the dream, long lost in
England, of an ideal village amidst the wilderness.   New England's towns were set up by a powerful Puritan minority impelled by the desire to realize utopian ideals of community,
to create in these towns a society bonded together by the ties
of Christian love.   At the heart of the town was the church.
Indeed, the most significant innovation of all, the town meeting, which fostered those democratic ideals that found expression in the Revolution, was simply the church congregation
reconstituted for the secular business of managing the town's
affairs.   The planners of these early New England towns
aimed at producing tight, homogeneous communities.   Thus,
the number of families was limited to between forty and fifty,
in the belief that the town thus reached its ideal size.   A
form of egalitarianism operated in the town, which discour-
aged extremes of wealth and poverty.   Modesty, simplicity
and decorum were the hallmarks of the utopian community.

Yet, even at its inception, there were strains within
the system.   Because the community had at its center the
church and because the love and charity which the town sought
to embody was Christian, individualism or defiance of the
community seemed tantamount to blasphemy, a rejection of
God.   Unquestioning conformism was positively valued as a
proper attitude to what could ultimately be argued as a divinely
ordered community.

A move away from the ideals of the "covenanted" utopian town is evidenced as early as 1686, in Dedham, where
the minister's wages had to be raised by taxation.   Loss of
confidence in the avowed ideals of Christian charity seems to
be indicated, too, by the growth of litigiousness and gossip as,

presumably, means of releasing the tensions engendered by
the confinement of individuals within close families and in
communities themselves confined to a modest number of families.

        By the late seventeenth century, sharp rises in the
birthrate produced larger families and accelerated population
growth.   This gave rise, as the limited land resources proved
insufficient, to problems within towns, problems which were
solved in different ways.   One method was the foundation by
younger, discontented townspeople of new towns on the old
model, or their emigration to the frontier.   Another was a
move away from farming to trade, which inevitably hastened
the transition from communality to individualism.

        While, then, the New England community ideal was
always under stress, an appreciation of it is profoundly important for an understanding of the attitudes of even present-
day Americans to the notion of the small town.   It was, after
all, an ideal which was in part and for some time realized.
Among the achievements of the New England covenanted town
was the evolution in town government from an oligarchy of
freemen to a limited democracy, and the conduct of economic
planning by the town meeting.   While some historians might
be less impressed by the apparent workings of the town and
might deduce that there was still an invisible oligarchy operative, nevertheless such class distinctions as did exist within
the town were considerably less rigid than in the Mother
Country, and the possibility of upward mobility lightens even
the gloomier picture of oligarchy within the town.   It was,
too, from the self-confidence of the New England towns that
resistance to the colonial administration was most effectively
expressed in the 1770s and that finally rebellion was insti-
gated as their autonomy was usurped.   Moreover, the ideal,
if only partially realized in its true setting, continued to live
during the westward expansion, and to become an important
aspect of the spirit of America.

        Significantly, it is the image of the ideal, rather than
its realization, which ensures the place of the small town in
the American imagination.   In the actualization, with its imperfections and compromises, of the Christian utopian ideal,
however, can be found a possible basis for all the uncertain-
ties about, and even attacks on, the fundamental concept of
the American small-town community which we find in American literature and drama.   We have already noted that the
promotion of community as an expression of God meant the

suppression of individuality.  We may further note another,
related offshoot of the theocracy that some might discern the
utopian town to have been--the plethora of hierarchies,  in
church, school, family,  all inimical to dissent or even questioning of their existence.  There is, too,  the fear of strangers and all that lies beyond the town, the "wilderness" on
to which the Puritan townsfolk projected their fears.

Although the war against the British crown seems
now to be the climax of the New England communities'
achievements,  it marks the natural end to them.  No longer
could the covenanted town restrict itself to local issues.  Inevitably,  it has become part of a larger national scene,  with
its parties and factions wiping out the homogeneity so beloved
of the New England town.  Yet,  small-town traditions long
survived the death of the small town as focus of government
and even found a new lease on life as American settlers
pushed farther West,  into the wilderness whose exclusion
the Puritans had grouped in their towns to achieve.

We must not misrepresent the role of towns built
during the westward expansion.  They were largely products
of their promoters' acquisitiveness,  and only those towns
founded by religious groups had any communal purpose.

By 1880,  the frontier was moving still farther,  to the
West itself.  In this final stage of expansion, towns were
built simply to exploit different natural resources,  and no
overall identity for towns (no general concept of them) was
created.

The latter half of the nineteenth century was a period
of particularly rapid change for the United States,  a time
during which its agricultural isolation and strongly marked
regional differences were eroded.  As the continent was
spanned (in 1869) by the railroads,  as communications became multifarious and easier with the introduction of elec-
tricity,  the telephone, telegraph and typewriter,  the small
community which had provided for itself and enjoyed relative
economic autonomy increasingly gave way to the city,  at
least in the sense that marketing was rendered more complex and standardized,  controlled from outside by the advent
of standard packaging,  brand name advertising and mass dis-
tribution.  Moreover, between 1870 and 1900 there was a
marked shift of population from small towns to cities.  A
more centralized, urban, industrialized America with a growing awareness of an international role rendered the small
town marginal.

From the opening years of the twentieth century, the
processes of urbanization and centralization accelerated. The
homogenization of America begun by the railroads continued
with the building of long highways in the wake of the invention and marketing of cars, so that towns linked by highways,
as once by railroads, became increasingly like one another,
despite the considerable distances often separating one town
from another. Depopulation of rural areas continued. The
Depression of the 1930s, the two world wars, the Korean
War and the Cold War, all demonstrated the dependency of
the small town, its apparent insignificance and possible irrelevance when the concept of nationhood required emphasis
and demonstration, when solidarity and cohesion were of
primary importance. Moreover, the countryside and small
towns underwent a different sort of hazard after the Second
World War when many were swallowed up as suburbs and
became perforce part of the city.

In the late 'sixties and early 'seventies, the small
town enjoyed a minor comeback. Disillusion about even the
suburbs of cities encouraged the back-to-the-land movement
espoused by young Americans who felt themselves the vic-
tims of the upheavals of the 'sixties. A hunger for community and for a simpler life close to the soil took hold of
a sizeable minority of the nation, and the utopianism of New
England enjoyed a modest revival as the beauty of smallness
was rediscovered. Paradoxically, this move to the countryside can be explained in part by the similarity by this time
of the small town to the city. Salary disparities between
city and town had narrowed, and the small-town way of life
was not unlike that experienced in the city, except that the
latter was associated more closely with higher taxes, crime
and traffic congestion.

The visible death or, more accurately, translation of
the small town in the twentieth century has not resulted in
its dismissal from the American imagination. Rather, to
judge by the intensity of interest in the small town in novels, popular magazines, the theatre, cinema and, later,
television, America remains fixated on it. Perhaps it is
the very forces of centralization that contribute most to the
survival of the small town, not so much on the landscape of
America as in the minds of Americans, as an ideal, the embodiment of a wish.

> The community in which we had been brought up and
> the education ground into us were ordered, self-
> contained, comprehensible, while this new society was

incoherent, without fixed aim, and without even a pretence of homogeneity.  We were like pond fish who had been flooded into a river.[3]

## American Conceptions of the Small Town

It may be nostalgia for the pond that helps to explain the publication in 1972, some fifty years after Sinclair Lewis's best-selling satirical onslaught on small-town America, Main Street, of such a paean to rural life as Donald S. Connery's Small Town.  His reason for choosing provincial life as his subject is a belief that the small community may act as antidote to the impersonality of modern American life.  Connery, living in a New England village which he finds considerably more democratic than his former suburban home and attracted by its cohesion and ethnic and cultural harmony as well as the notion of the town meeting as basic cell of the American system of government, appears a more recent and articulate spokesman for the nexus of inchoate and largely unexamined notions of themselves which certain celebrated studies of American communities uncovered in the townspeople.

Robert and Helen Lynd undertook two investigations of a medium-sized American town, Muncie, Indiana--in the mid 'twenties and then mid 'thirties.  Middletown, A Study in Modern American Culture deals with the impact of industrialization on this community, and particularly with the mental defenses erected by the townspeople.  Middletown in Transition principally considers the effects of the Depression on the external reality and self-perception of the town.  In the first volume the Lynds record, in area after area of the town's life, the decline of autonomy and self-sufficiency, with, for example, the influx of mass-produced articles and the homogenizing effects of advertising and mass-media entertainment, accompanied by the increased tenacity of the dominant middle class's beliefs in the solidarity and democratic principles of the town and the strenuous promotion of civic loyalty and patriotism.

The tension between social reality and Middletown's self-image practically reaches a breaking point during the Depression.  Working-class families in particular, already on the periphery of town society, and markedly less affected by the apparent ethos or avowed principles of the town, become increasingly aware of the fragility of its ostensible

autonomy. Because of new attitudes toward the federal government, especially in connection with relief funds and pro-
grams for the unemployed, there is an increasing acceptance
in all sectors of town society of the paramount importance of
national, rather than local, affairs, because both the origins
and solution of the Depression appear to be at the national
level. Paradoxically, however, the Lynds observe the increasing awareness of Middletown's dependence on centralized government as strengthening the isolationism already
discerned in the middle class. The vastness of the problem of national recession steers the townspeople towards
private business and self-blinkering in order to survive the
onslaught of disquieting and heretofore avoidable reality.

    With further disruptive factors, particularly the Sec-
ond World War and the Korean War, threatening the towns'
shaky belief in their independence and value (as repositories
of grass-roots democracy), there is a widening of the divide
between social reality and town self-image, according to Vidich and Bensman's Small Town in Mass Society, an early-
'sixties study of the medium-sized upper New York state
town of Springdale.

    The defences that they [Springdale residents] have
    erected against this sense of powerlessness took the
    form of a reaffirmation of the very same values that
    were denied by their reality. [4]

The reality which Vidich and Bensman discover in Springdale is that it is undeniably part of, not distinguished from,
mass society. The ubiquity of the mass media, the extent
of cultural importation into Springdale (75 percent of the
population being immigrants to the town), the professional
class's ability to link Springdale with larger society by over-
seeing political institutions, the force of federal and state
regulations and laws, the fact that many industrial workers
are employed outside the town, working on products geared
to a national market, combine to suggest that there is no
indigenous culture, no possibility of understanding Springdale's nature in isolation from New York state or the United
States in general. Yet, there is a generalized set of beliefs, themselves founded on a belief in the town's autonomy
or self-selective dependency, easily discoverable in Springdale, embracing the notion that the basic traditions of American society, freely expressed individualism, grass-roots
democracy and decency, are preserved in the small town.
This vision of local society is strengthened by stereotypical

images of the cities, whereby their size is linked with impersonality, their values deemed anti-Christian and anti-American because of the corruption of urban politicians and labor leaders, their churches and universities deemed out of touch with the spiritual lessons apparently taught by life in the country. Thus, such little effect as the city is believed to have on the small town is thought to produce those few problems to which the town admits, the city therefore being a useful counterimage against which the town's values may be defined and by which any failures of the town can be explained. Such mass-circulation periodicals as the Saturday Evening Post cater to the flattering sense of Americanism enjoyed by the Springdaler, its artwork and stories or articles frequently paying tribute to the quiet, healthy, family-oriented rural life. 5

In short, Vidich and Bensman conclude that there are two apparently contradictory but simultaneously operating dimensions of social control in Springdale, the maintenance of belief in small-town ideology together with the maintenance of a social system which adapts local affairs to the demands of mass society.

While, then, the American community sociologists have repeatedly discovered a set of small-town beliefs which would correspond with actuality only if America had ceased developing about 1860, most of them recognize the value of these beliefs as a factor in social cohesion and a means to the community's less painful adjustment to wider social reality. More interesting still is the possibility that the small town's popular image has been highly important for city-dwellers and for Americans in general. Peter Schrag argues that, from the time the West was tamed up to the late 1960s, a collective fantasy of Americanism, embodied above all in the White Anglo-Saxon Protestant or WASP stereotype, has given validity to American history and that the legend is the more fiercely promoted as the actuality dies. 6

Not surprisingly, American literature and drama in part reflects, and in part occasions the wider society's perennial fascination with small-town values. For at least a century, the small town has provided American writers[7]--many of them writers of international celebrity--with a subject which they never tire of exploring, as they seek to determine whether or not it is the healthful, nurturing community which the Puritan utopianists of the seventeenth century dreamed that they were establishing.

Some writers attempt merely to document the American small town at a particular period or geographical area. Even if their selection of material inevitably betrays the writers' attitudes to the apparent subject, there seems to be no manifest intention to buttress, or to attack, what might be termed the small-town myth of the caring, democratic, decent community. The principal point of, for example, Edward Eggleston's The Hoosier School-Master (1871) or of the three novels[8] which earned Willa Cather her reputation as "the historian of Nebraska" seems to be the desire to record regional experiences.

Most writers, however, subscribe to one of two dominant traditions--the romantic or the realistic.

Sarah Orne Jewett's Tales of New England (1879), Margaret Deland's Old Chester Tales (1898) and Edward Arlington Robinson's books of poems[9] all suppress their writers' evident awareness of the unhappiness engendered by small-town codes of conduct in the interests of promoting small-town virtue. Many writers of the romantic tradition offer far more glowing and optimistic accounts, however. Edward Westcott's David Harum (1898) depicts not only a community of unqualified warmth but promotes the rural philosopher, a character which later makes appearances in much of the fiction purveyed by such mass magazines as the Saturday Evening Post, Liberty and Collier's ... fiction which sought to depict the small town as a sanctuary of goodness and kindliness, a more fundamentally American place than the new urbanized, industrialized America. Booth Tarkington's fictional Plattville is described as "one big, jolly family."[10] Zona Gale calls another fictional town Friendship Village. The more the town adapted to the ways and technological advance of the twentieth century, the more writers insisted on closeness to the land and its freedom from changes affecting the nation at large.

The 'thirties, almost certainly because of the influence of the Depression, saw a revival of the small town's prestige in popular sentiment. Treatment of it was markedly less realistic, after the acerbic commentaries offered mainly in the 'twenties. Even Sinclair Lewis, the supreme satirist of the small town, produced in 1938 The Prodigal Parents, a novel which attempted to heroize the middle-class businessman of the small town, and completed his conversion to the wisdom of small-town simplicity in times of complexity and national doubt in Home Town (1940).

Although the myth of American self-realization in the
small-town ethos continues beyond the 'thirties, with such
writers as William Saroyan (particularly in The Human Comedy of 1943), the apotheosis of the small town occurs most
evidently and influentially in Thornton Wilder's play, Our
Town (1938).

Our Town concerns life in Grover's Corners, New
Hampshire during the opening two decades of this century.
As if to universalize this town, Wilder indicates that no
conventional scenery or props are to be used in the production.    His principal themes are the dawning of love, the
marriage and finally the separation by death of two young
inhabitants, George Gibbs and Emily Webb.    Where such
novels as Sinclair Lewis's Main Street (1920) discern absurdity or, at most, pathos in the ambitions and accom-
plishments of the small town, Wilder positively celebrates
them, suggesting that more abiding values are enshrined
outside the cities of America.    Though Grover's Corners
is a hotbed of gossip, though the events of town life are undisguisedly petty, the play seems to invite its audience to
share the point of view of its characters, and not to judge
them by the standards of the city.    No more potent celebration of the small town as embodiment of the best in
American life has been produced by any American play-
wright to date. 11

Alongside the literary and, to a much lesser extent,
dramatic tradition which has fostered belief in the small
town as repository of the fundamental American virtues,
there has been a counter-tradition which discerns the emptiness of provincial life--the philistinism, conformism and
spitefulness underlying the veneer of small-town warmth.
Much of the work of E.W. Howe, Hamlin Garland and Harold Frederic attempts to uproot the notion of rural closeness to a beneficent nature and to emphasize that the anomie affecting America at large is particularly destructive in
a small, enclosed and literally impoverished society.    Even
Mark Twain, despite the gentleness and apparent affection
for small-town inhabitants demonstrated in The Adventures
of Huckleberry Finn (1885), reveals the meanness of spirit
and emptiness of Mississippi village life, a life which Huck
flees on the raft.

The most concerted attack on the village myth came
later, however, from a group of writers of the teens and
'twenties of this century, largely, but not exclusively, based

during their writing lives in Chicago, who appeared to be identifiable in terms of their "Revolt from the Village," as their movement was described in 1920 by the critic Carl Van Doren.

The seminal work now seems to be the best-selling volume of poetry written by Edgar Lee Masters, the Spoon River Anthology (1915). In it, two-hundred forty-four poetic monologues are offered, in the form of epitaphs, through which tortured, wasted lives are revealed and the repressiveness and hypocrisy of a town are indicted. So powerful was the image of small-town meanness of spirit in Masters' poetry that it could even be thought to have created a myth of its own, that of the small town as force of repression.

In 1919, Sherwood Anderson's Winesburg, Ohio covered similar ground, showing thwarted lives and apparently identifying the cause of suffering as the narrowness of small-town existence. Although the mellowness of Anderson's memories of adolescence informs his treatment of Winesburg's inhabitants and softens his picture of the town itself, it is hard to conclude, with Malcolm Cowley, that it is "... a celebration of small-town life in the lost days of good will and innocence."[12] Rather, it is a compassionate exploration of the sufferings of certain deviant, often specially gifted, characters in a community with little tolerance for misfits. Anderson is aware of writing about a community in transition, of recording the loss of the church's social and intellectual centrality due to the technological revolution, improved communications, mass-produced newspapers and magazines. If he is a pessimist about the advent of mass society, it is impossible to conclude that his novel belongs in the tradition of nostalgia for the preaching of rural values. The book ends with the departure of the book's central character, George Willard, from Winesburg, indicating the symbolic self-uprooting of Anderson himself.

When Sinclair Lewis's Main Street was first published in 1920, its subsequent effect on the world of American letters and its considerable international celebrity combined to suggest greater originality than the novel could fairly claim. Main Street could not have owed its shock effect to its castigation of a provincial town's mediocrity, of its unwitting cruelty, boorishness and complacency. Rather, it is the trenchantly satirical tone of the work, with its egalitarian puncturing of the crusading heroine's ambitions for the town as well as its blanket ridicule of America itself under the more

specific exposure of the town's foibles, that must have
startled its readers.   If the small town had heretofore suggested a subject worthy of serious contemplation, whether it
was bathed in the sunlight of pastoral romance or it lamented
(with Sherwood Anderson) the death of mute, inglorious Mil-
tons in too cloddish earth, Main Street holds up what Lewis
believed to be American's image of themselves to international scrutiny and finds it laughably false.   In such an atmosphere of self-delusion do Babbitts spring into life.   When the
denizens of the town are so self-satisfied and dull of wit, the
essentially American sense of educative mission which his
heroine feels can appear as absurd as the town itself.   The
first three words indicate that his satire is directed well beyond the individual town:

> This is America--a town of a few thousand, in a re-
> gion of wheat and corn and dairies and little groves.
>     The town is, in our tale, called "Gopher Prairie,
> Minnesota," but its Main Street is the continuation of
> Main Streets everywhere.   The story would be the
> same in Ohio or Montana, in Kansas or Kentucky or
> Illinois ... Main Street is the climax of civilization
> .... 13

"The Revolt from the Village," because, above all,
it included best-selling works on the subject of the small
town, helped to fix the image of the American small town
as chiefly that of an outwardly respectable, complacent society under whose surface repression and ill-concealed
scandals seethed.

However, after Main Street, which argues the irrelevance of the small town and its ostensible values in a society homogenized and brutalized by technological progress and
which overtly criticizes the images of small-town life purveyed by popular fiction, writers taking this as their theme
either have to amplify Lewis's vision, concentrating on the
ugliness and hypocrisy of the small town, or to seek new
justification for the promotion of the small-town ethos.   The
two small-town novels most popularized by the cinema in
their respective decades, Henry Bellamann's Kings Row
(film version released in 1942) and Grace Metalious's Peyton Place (film version released in 1957), adopt different
strategies to justify their focussing of interest on provincial
society.

Bellamann sets his 1941 novel in the closing years of

the nineteenth century, shortly before the period of rapid
industrial and technological change whose aftereffects are
described in Main Street.  The nostalgia suggested by the
choice of period by a novelist writing shortly before America entered the Second World War is mirrored by the nostalgia of certain older characters in Kings Row.  Indeed,
most of the novel concerns the passing of the older families, a largely ex-European provincial aristocracy, under
irresistible economic pressures.  Like Lewis, Bellamann
reveals the class divisions of the little community, its den-
igration of certain inhabitants by reason of nationality or religion, and the characterlessness of the town's appearance
is indicated, in terms reminiscent of Lewis's criticism of
Gopher Prairie:

> Looks like every town its size from Ohio to Kansas....
> You can't tell by looking around if you're in Indiana
> or Iowa.  Looks like any town--and just as ugly. 14

Nevertheless, the tone of Bellamann's novel is far
from satirical, the plot far from a record of the town's
failings or the disappointments of a would-be reformer.
Instead, it is peopled by decidedly bizarre characters swept
along by forces that they little understand and cannot control.
One doctor is a sadist who persuades certain patients to un-
dergo surgery without anaesthetic, to gratify his appetites,
another has an incestuous relationship with his daughter and
may have murdered his wife to remove any obstacle to it.
As in Winesburg, Ohio, the author--or rather his spokesman hero--appears to feel compassion for his tortured de-
viants and to believe that the repressive conformity of the
town partly explains the violence with which instinct erupts.

Having exposed the ugliness of Kings Row, its non-
descript architecture and its stultifying prejudice, Bellamann
does not, however, have his hero turn his back on the place.
Much of the novel is an attempt, instead, to explain the importance of the place to him.  Dr. Tower, the newcomer
with the darkest secrets of all, suggests the permanent appeal of the small town in an early passage of the novel in
which he uses conceptions of man's relation with the universe in a pre-Galileo world as an analogy.  He believes
that the church was justified in opposing discoveries which
dislocated the relationship between God and man because
"what was really threatened was the happiness and peace of
all mankind. "15

Towards the end of the novel, when the hero has returned from studying in Vienna and sees anew the shabbiness
and provinciality of his home town, he expresses the para-
doxical importance of it:

'I'm not exactly in love with Kings Row, not with the
town, or the way it looks, nor any places in the town,
nor the people that live there.  But I'm attracted to
all the stages of being that I went through right
here.'16

Bellamann's contribution to the history of the small-
town novel is in part the tendency to hyperbole, to the
heightening (to the point of self-parody) of contrast between
respectable, placid surface and hidden appetites or unspoken
desires, whereby an ostensibly unremarkable town contains
more horror than the house of Atreus knew, where death is
usually violent, passions febrile and morbid, social control
warped and malignant.  More important are the suggestions
that small-town life is not so much absurdly anachronistic
and redundant as a sort of adolescent stage in the growth of
the American, prompting, though not fulfilling, dreams of
community and idealism, and that the town is more than the
sum of its people or its buildings, that there can be an almost mystic bond between the site and those growing up on
it, a feeling of oneness with the soil which curiously echoes
that more European form of intimacy between man and terrain celebrated by, for example, certain of Leni Riefenstahl's films of the 'thirties.

An unkind judgment of Grace Metalious' Peyton Place
(1957) would be that it is a rewriting of Kings Row minus
its introspection and philosophizing.  Although the period is
different, covering the late 'thirties to early 'forties, there
are obvious similarities.  Like Kings Row, Peyton Place is
constantly abuzz with gossip, lives are ruined by innuendo
and whispered prejudice.  Like it, too, Peyton Place has a
placid appearance belying its inhabitants' secret turmoil,
their subjection to dark, inexplicable passions.

One aspect of her novel that distinguishes it from
Bellamann's is that Metalious chooses to locate her story of
small-town life not in the middle West of Sinclair Lewis but
in a particularly attractive New England town, set in harmonious relation with the woods and hills of the surrounding
countryside.  Moreover, the running of the town is seen to
involve demonstrably greater participation of the townsfolk

than elsewhere, although this impression is modified in practice.

Where Bellamann's hero finally recognizes his revulsion from the narrowness and anachronism of the town's values and also, simultaneously, his abiding links of sentiment with, not people or buildings, but place, Metalious' heroine appears to learn ultimately that the town is not special, but simply one community among many similar:

> 'You wonder too much about Peyton Place,' said Mike. 'It's just a town, Allison, like any other town. We have our characters, but so does New York and so does every other town and city.'[17]

In novels such as Kings Row and Peyton Place, there is a move away from the literary conflict up to the 'thirties, of whether a writer is to depict the small town as a force for good or evil, to a questioning of the significant place of the small town in the American imagination, and therefore of the intense concentration by American writers upon it.

One way of comprehending the interest in the small town may be to note that it is seen as a sort of microcosm. This indeed is the lofty claim of Main Street. [18]  Another is that the small town may be taken metaphorically, to stand for the past, for youth and dreams, as in Kings Row and throughout such novels as John Updike's Rabbit, Run (1960) and Couples (1968), or Lisa Alther's Kinflicks (1977).

Finally, in Richard Brautigan's Trout Fishing in America (1967), the reality of the agrarian myth is itself held up to question. In this novel, a young man tries to find a place where he may go trout fishing, and then tries to find a pastoral setting where he and his family may be independent and liberated. He fails, and concludes that this sort of pastoral dream is indeed merely a dream.

### The Small Town in American Movies

The foregoing analysis of the prominent place of the small town in the American imagination may well suggest that the popularity of the small town as subject or at least setting of numerous Hollywood movies has little to do with pleasing the rural population (Halliwell's suggestion--see p. 1) or diverting attention from wider national issues to what would tradi-

tionally be conceived of as escapist entertainment. A more
likely hypothesis is that the small town is enshrined as a
storehouse of American values, thanks to the memory of the
New England covenanted town and its ostensible ethos and
that, as America becomes more aware of cultural hetero-
geneity and the American sense of nationhood becomes increasingly attenuated, the small town increasingly becomes
a focal point for the creation of American identity. It may
well be that, America's self-image being capable of equation
with small-town values, an examination of the small town in
the national imagination, whether to confirm, deny or merely explore its workings, is an attempt to examine the national psyche. There is no intention to suggest that America's
self-image is explicitly or consistently enunciated in, for example, the subject of this book, small-town movies, or that
the writers and directors of small-town movies are necessarily conscious of any such enterprise (although Lillian Hellman and Arthur Penn seem fully conscious of such an under-
taking in The Chase, for example). The present hypothesis
does at least suggest reasons for the waves of small-town
movies at particular periods of crisis for the American nation.

        The fact that genres are created in Hollywood to ex-
ploit fields that seem profitable or popular in other media
doubtless plays an important part too. The fondness of apparently all sectors of the American reading public for
small-town fiction, whether it be Mark Twain, Bellamann,
Metalious or the Saturday Evening Post, the creation in the
theatre of a classic by Thornton Wilder and the fascination
of two of Broadway's most celebrated playwrights, Tennessee Williams and William Inge, with the small town, help
to explain Hollywood's abiding interest in the small-town
subject.

        Peter Schrag, chronicling the genesis and evolution
of the WASP ethos, believes that Hollywood plays a key part,
bolstering WASP values whenever reality threatens to break
through. "Where the schools and the farm and the shop
failed, the movies came to the rescue."19 It is the movies
that the bulk of this study treats, from Chapter 2 onward,
in an attempt to isolate the various structures recurrent in
the small-town genre, 20 to illustrate by reference to what
may be argued to be typical small-town movies the uses to
which the small-town movie puts its subject, and to sub-
stantiate the accuracy of the belief held by students of the
small town, that it is of far greater emotional relevance to

Americans, be they urban, suburban or small-town, than it could reasonably be supposed to be, given its marginality in political and social terms.

Before the study can be entered into confidently, some questions need to be answered, some explanations of the study's scope given.

## What Is a Small Town in American Movies?

The sought definition of "small town" is for the movie small town. Generally, and certainly for such towns as New York, Washington, D.C. or Los Angeles, for example, some sort of interconnection between American geographical data and cinematic locale in Hollywood cinema may be understood. There is an implicit reference from, say, the New York of the screen to the actual city, so that the movie set in New York need expend little or no effort, whichever aspects of the city are required, on establishing that this is a major northern city, a port, a commercial center, a sophisticated metropolis, a teeming concrete jungle, with considerable urban problems, including those connected with successive waves of immigration. Admittedly, the selection from all these given aspects depends on subject and treatment, with the Manhattan chic underlying such works as Blake Edwards' Breakfast at Tiffany's (1961) or Woody Allen's Annie Hall (1977) sited in the more fashionable Central Park area, Fifth Avenue or the Village, and those movies centering on poverty, social tensions, juvenile crime (from the comparatively gentle "Dead End Kids" series through the musical West Side Story [1961] to Frankenheimer's The Young Savages [1961]) tending to restrict their ambit to the West Side, the lower East Side, the Bronx or, more narrowly, Spanish Harlem; and, moreover, the image of New York for the outside world has been largely created by Hollywood. Nevertheless, the essential point remains, that New York does not have to be entirely created (though it must in a measure always be re-created) as a fictive entity, with certain associations, but that there is an obvious relationship between the real town and the cinematic town in New York-based movies.

With towns which are small, there must be a far more tenuous assumed relationship between fictive and factual, the obvious point--that extra-American knowledge of individual small towns is practically nil--being underscored by the frequent use of different names even for movies shot

in real small-town locations.  Thus, Madison, Indiana becomes Parkman, Illinois in Some Came Running; Camden,
Maine becomes Peyton Place; Archer City, Texas is Peter
Bogdanovich's Anarene; the Georgia small town of The Member of the Wedding is represented by Colusa, California; and
even a relatively major town, such as Cincinnati, Ohio, is
to be taken as Boone City in The Best Years of Our Lives.

This latter example encourages the tentative conclusion that individual small towns in Hollywood movies have
no resonance of the sort analogous to that of New York or
Los Angeles in the movies and that such associations as are
imported into individual small towns seem to be those created by an amalgam of elements much less to do with actual
American small towns than with manifold literary descriptions and repeated cinematic treatments.  It also suggests
that the definition of "small town" has much less to do with
smallness of area or population than might at first appear.
While the actual identity of Boone City might elude most
Americans and practically everybody else outside the United
States, the location shooting and particularly the aerial views
of the town suggest a large industrialized area with wide-
ranging residential neighborhoods, which in turn suggest a
city-size population.  Yet, British reviewers of the movie
in 1947 seemed to take Boone City as closer to a small
town than a city (see p.  70).

Because there is no useful label for the provincial
large town, the unrecognizable city as opposed to the me-
tropolises that have gained individual identity both through
factors independent of Hollywood and also because of American movies, the term "small town" must be treated with
generous elasticity in the movie context.

A definition in negative terms is easier than a positive summation.  The small town in movies is not a metropolis, not one of the great urban centers whose image and
architecture have been absorbed by the cinema-going public
of all continents.  Instead, it is a large, medium or little
town which, although possibly located (cinematically) in a
state and exhibiting variations of population or architecture
indicative of certain broad geographical or cultural areas--
the Middle West, the Deep South, New England--possesses
a certain autonomy in respect of its identity, or rather has
its identity created by only or very largely cinematic means.
As in literature, it is frequently the case that one small
town, albeit geographically located, stands for all small
towns, or the small-town mentality in general. [21]

## What Is a Small-Town Movie?

If the above is acceptable as an exposition of the usage of
the term "small town" in a filmic context, it may be easier
to defend the term "small-town movie." The rationale for
the creation of this category would base itself on the fact
that there are a number of Hollywood movies which are not
only set in small towns, as defined above, for the totality or
major part of their action, but in which town denizens relate
significantly with (in reaction against or acquiescence with) a
town ethos, real or imagined. Some of the more obvious
examples of these movies are named after the town (Kings
Row, Peyton Place), begin or end with all-inclusive, frequently aerial shots of the town (Peyton Place, Picnic, Best
Years), or contain sequences in which a character withdraws
from and contemplates the town from a distance (Allison
MacKenzie and Norman Page looking down on Peyton Place
from her secret place on the hillside, Sonny in The Last
Picture Show watching the town lights from his stationary
vehicle after he has made love to Ruth Popper). While the
small-town movie may center on a tiny fraction of the town's
population, the significant factor is whether there is a sense
of the town's influence on that fraction, whether the characters relate beyond their immediate house or family environment in terms of action or self-image. The Member of the
Wedding, for example, seems to qualify for consideration as
a small-town movie because, despite the fact that its action
is largely confined to the kitchen and backyard of one house
and that only two brief excursions are made into town, the
heroine, Frankie, repeatedly blames her frustrations on life
in this town and sees her salvation in getting out of it, and
it is the racial hatred of the town that disunites the family
of Berenice, the black cook.

Categorization is usually easy enough based on the
criteria suggested, but there are difficult borderline cases,
as there would be for any category which one might choose
to set up. One of the most difficult in this case is Vincente Minnelli's Meet Me in St. Louis (1944). Minnelli himself saw St. Louis in terms of a small town. "I remembered
everything I could of the small town where I was brought
up.... But it was set in an earlier period, with American
Gothic architecture and so on."22 Moreover, St. Louis was
taken by some critics quite unequivocally to be a small
town.23 Yet, there are at least two problems about taking
the movie as small-town. First of all, there is the simple
point that St. Louis is thought to be a city within the film
itself, even if it is a much more caring, protective place

than New York is deemed to be.  When the family is informed by the paterfamilias that it must move to New York,
the mother of the family remarks regretfully, thinking of
the impersonality and size of New York City, "Not that St.
Louis isn't big but it doesn't seem big out here where we
live." This remark would lead one to conclude that the
family inhabits a suburb of a city which has all the warmth
and cohesion of a small town, rather than that it actually
lives in a small town.  The other problem is that Meet Me
in St. Louis is so precisely, and repeatedly, localized within an actual city where the World's Fair actually did take
place in 1903, whereas the small town in the small-town
movie seems normally to stand for myriad other small
towns.  Ultimately, our decision depends on whether we are
sufficiently impressed by the feel of the movie, particularly
the visuals and atmosphere of family-within-a-larger-family,
to deny the information on the soundtrack and afforded by
our knowledge of American geography.  Is a movie which
treats an actual, identified American city as a small town
a small-town movie?  This writer's judgment is that it is
not, although there are undeniably reasons why others might
come to a different conclusion. 24

     Fortunately, categorization is seldom as difficult as
this.  Another Minnelli film, Father of the Bride (1950),
may be excluded, for example, because its concerns are
entirely those of the extended family, not the locality (which
is expressly termed "surburban"), and because the family's
activities take place in New York City to which Stanley, the
father, commutes daily.


## Methods

The peculiarly important place of the American small town
in the American psyche now having been demonstrated and
the terms of reference of the proposed analysis now having
been outlined, it should be possible to move on to detailed
consideration of the American small-town movie.

     In the eight chapters which follow, the aim is to open
up the vast but almost totally neglected field of the small-
town movie to generic analysis.  A glance at what is merely
the selection of small-town movies constituting Appendix C
should indicate the range and sheer numbers of movies in
this area.  When the large quantity of publications on such
recognized genres as, say, the Western or musical is borne

in mind, it ought not to be surprising that this first step in the analysis of a genre is highly selective.  No doubt, for every movie selected for special consideration by this writer, a quite different choice might be made by another researcher in this field.  No doubt, the movies picked as specially valuable for their typicality may seem less representative to certain readers than quite another set of choices. Another book, adopting an encyclopaedic rather than a selective approach, might well adopt a diachronic, rather than the present synchronic, method, a method which is particularly useful in that it permits juxtaposition of movies separated by, in some instances, several decades, to illustrate the recurrent nature of certain small-town movies' concerns.

However, the present introductory study's contention will be that, there being a limited number of recurrent themes and dominant structures discernible even in such an enormous number of individual examples, the close study of even a few of the movies ought to expose principles of organization and initially covert conceptions of the meaning of the small town common to considerably more small-town movies.  Therefore, the sense of the repressiveness of the small town is exemplified in Kings Row, Picnic, or Carrie, in this study, but it could well have been so exemplified by close consideration of Beyond the Forest, Storm Warning, All I Desire, All That Heaven Allows, Splendor in the Grass, or the 1981 release, The Raggedy Man, to name but six from a potential total of many more.  The hope of the study is that analysis of one or two particular examples of a certain kind of approach to the small town in movies may serve to illuminate scores of similar movies.

## Notes to Chapter 1

1. Halliwell's Filmgoer's Companion, 6th edition.  Hart-Davis, MacGibbon Ltd., 1977, p. 667.

2. The principal source for this section is Richard Lingeman, Small Town America:  A Narrative History 1620-The Present, G. P. Putnam's Sons, New York, 1980.

3. Henry S. Canby, The Age of Confidence, quoted in John W. Dodds, Everyday Life in Twentieth Century America. B. T. Batsford Ltd., London, 1965, p. 52.

4. Arthur J. Vidich and Joseph Bensman, Small Town in

Mass Society, revised edition, Princeton University
Press, Princeton, New Jersey, 1968, p. ix.

5.    Interestingly, it is exactly the same counterimage of
      the inner city which helps to validate life in the sub-
      urbs, despite their more visible dependence on the life
      of the city.  While the most spectacular population shift
      in the 'forties and 'fifties is the move from city and
      country to the suburbs, it is the romantic ideology of
      the small town which is grafted on to the outer city.

6.    Peter Schrag, The Vanishing American (U.S. title, The
      Decline of the WASP).  Victor Gollancz Ltd., London,
      1972.

7.    The principal sources for this section, apart from the
      books themselves, are David M. Cook and Craig G.
      Swauger (editors), The Small Town in American Liter-
      ature, 2nd edition.  Harper & Row, New York, 1977,
      and Richard Lingeman, ibid.

8.    O Pioneers! (1913), The Song of the Lark (1915) and
      My Antonia (1918).

9.    The Torrent and the Night Before (1896), The Children
      of the Night (1897) and The Town Down the River (1910).

10.   Plattville is so described in his The Gentleman from
      Indiana (1899).

11.   Few subsequent plays set in American small towns of-
      fer such reassurance or suggest that compensation for
      the mediocrity of provincial society's taste is to be
      found in the town's proximity to the elemental and its
      inhabitants' knowledge of eternal verities.  William
      Inge normally depicts his small towns sympathetically
      but suggests the inhibitions engendered by provincial
      values and the narrowness of the small-town mind.
      Picnic, The Dark at the Top of the Stairs and Come
      Back, Little Sheba balance the warmth of the commun-
      ity with its restrictiveness and complacency.  Tennes-
      see Williams, concerned in such dramatic works as
      Orpheus Descending and Summer and Smoke with con-
      trasting images of repression and freedom, decay and
      potency, seems to find a useful metaphor in his small
      communities, offering images of disintegration or of
      stasis.

12. Malcolm Cowley in Sherwood Anderson's, Winesburg, Ohio. Viking Press, New York, 1964, Introduction.

13. Sinclair Lewis, Main Street. Cape, London, first published in Great Britain, 1921, reissued 1973, Foreword.

14. Henry Bellamann, Kings Row. Cape, London, 1941, p. 382.

15. Ibid. p. 211.

16. Ibid. p. 437.

17. Grace Metalious, Peyton Place. Frederick Muller, London, 1957, p. 413.

18. William Faulkner, too, appears to treat Yoknapatawpha County as an exemplar in miniature of life in the South and also as an illustration of the human condition in general.

19. Peter Schrag, Ibid. p. 39.

20. That there is a small-town genre seems to require little argument, though it is expressly mentioned as such comparatively late in its lifetime. Belated recognition occurs only in 1971 in the course of several reviews of Peter Bogdanovich's The Last Picture Show, and even then this tentatively identified genre, far from being analyzed, is scarcely christened. Pauline Kael (New Yorker, October 9, 1971), for example, contrasted Picture Show with "earlier films of the genre, such as Kings Row and Peyton Place" and then proceeded to think in terms of melodrama, while Jim Pines (Time Out, Issue 109, March 17-23, 1972) felt that it vacillated between two genres, the western and another which he variously termed "provincial" or "rural" drama.

21. The studio publicity departments' claim for both The Member of the Wedding (George Lait, Director for Publicity, Columbia Studios, Production Notes, 1952) and To Kill a Mockingbird (The Rank Organization World Film Distribution--UK Division, 1962: "The only way of restoring the faithful image of Maycomb was to build the little town in the Universal Studios") that no existing town could be found to represent the

southern small-town locations demanded by these prop-
erties, suggests that even the conception of the look,
the physical image, of the southern town is prior to
contact with real southern towns, and that diversion to
California or resort to studio set will be encouraged
when the actuality fails to match the pre-existing conception.

The interchangeability of the small-town location,
the generalized quality of the particular movie small
town, may explain why Alan Lovell, in his book on Don
Siegel, makes the curious error of describing Santa
Mira as "a typical small mid-western town" when he
deals with Invasion of the Body Snatchers (Alan Lovell,
Don Siegel:  American Cinema, British Film Institute,
revised edition, p. 22).  The movie makes it clear that
the setting is California, but nothing about the appearance of the town underlines the location in that state.

22.  Richard Schickel, "Vincente Minnelli" in The Men Who
     Made the Movies.  Atheneum, New York, 1975, p. 257.

23.  "St. Louis, c'est la petite ville de province familière
     et protectrice, grande famille au sein de laquelle ...
     la petite communauté des Smith"--St. Louis is the
     homey, protective, provincial small town, a large
     family at the heart of which [is] the little Smith com-
     munity.  (Marion Vidal, Vicente Minnelli, Editions
     Seghers, Paris, 1973, p. 51)

24.  Perhaps the reason why Meet Me in St. Louis remains
     a difficult case is that movies set in the suburbs of
     cities deliberately take on the look, and therefore share
     the charisma, of the small-town movie.  There are
     many thematic and iconographic elements in the suburb-
     set movie which are shared by small-town movies, the
     principal divisive elements usually being the absence of,
     or markedly lesser importance of, the sense of belong-
     ing--or equally of not belonging--to a community out-
     side the family domain, and the greater mobility of the
     suburb-set movies' characters.  John Frankenheimer's
     All Fall Down (1961) relates its characters almost en-
     tirely to the family although the location of the major
     part of the work, despite being named as Cleveland,
     Ohio, looks and feels remarkably like a small town.
     Conversely, in certain sequences of Invasion of the
     Body Snatchers (Siegel), the regular lines of identical
     houses seem more appropriate to a suburb than to the

small town in which the film purports to be set. It
would require another study altogether to explore the
reasons why the image of suburbia is so frequently related by Hollywood to that of the small town, but community sociologists have already traced the process by
which middle-class suburbanites have abandoned the
anonymity of the inner city in part to attempt--and
fail--to create an atmosphere redolent of the small
town, which is itself viewed in terms of communality.
(See especially Maurice R. Stein, The Eclipse of Community. Harper & Row, New York, 1964, pp. 293 ff.)

## 2.   ARCHETYPES

Today, the Hollywood film most generally taken to be the
small-town movie par excellence would surely be Peyton
Place (1957), partly for intrinsic reasons--an epic-length,
big-budget filming of a notorious best-selling novel centering on a New England town--but more significantly because
it generated, apart from the 1961 movie Return to Peyton
Place, a popular long-running television serial which launched
the careers of Mia Farrow and Ryan O'Neal.   Nevertheless,
just as Grace Metalious's book owes an obvious debt to Henry
Bellamann's novel, Kings Row, so too it is known that John
Michael Hayes, when writing the screenplay for Peyton Place,
consulted Casey Robinson's Kings Row screenplay. 1   Before
Twentieth Century-Fox filmed Peyton Place, Warner Brothers'
Kings Row must have seemed the definitive small-town movie.

The director, Sam Wood, and set designer, William
Cameron Menzies, of Kings Row had already worked together
on the filming of Sol Lesser's most distinguished property,
the Wilder play Our Town.   Despite the theatrical prestige
of the latter work and Warner Brothers' delaying of Kings
Row's release for several months after its completion due
to nervousness about its reception so shortly after Pearl
Harbor, it was Kings Row which proved the more popular
enterprise, however.   Perhaps the import of the film was
less unflattering to America at a time of national crisis
than the studio imagined.   It would be foolish to over-
interpret the appeal of the movie to one of its stars, Ronald Reagan, although the choice of a line of his from this
film as the title of his 1965 autobiography, Where's the
Rest of Me?, is at least interesting.   It may be slightly
less foolish to detect some significance in Sam Wood's willingness, albeit as a contract director, to direct both Kings
Row and Our Town, in the light of his vehement political
views.   Wood had been an extremely busy but scarcely in-
dividualistic or distinctive director in the 'twenties and 'thirties and, despite his work on such celebrated films as A

27

Night at the Opera (1935) and Goodbye, Mr. Chips (1939),
nobody has to my knowledge ever argued for Wood as auteur.
The choice of Wood by Warner Brothers on the basis of his
efficient direction of Our Town was presumably of far greater moment in 1941 than his personal sentiments about the
project.   Nevertheless, he must by this time have already
become passionately anti-Communist and right wing, in that
only three years later he founded and became first president
of the Motion Picture Alliance, an organization dedicated to
the extirpation of supposedly Communist elements in the film
industry.   Possibly the turn-of-the-century setting, the celebration of a period when the American dream must have
seemed less anachronistic, would help to explain the appeal
of the Kings Row project, despite the novel's disquieting portrayal of provincial America.

---

The movie seems to divide into two parts of unequal length.
The earlier, shorter part covers the infancy of the chief
characters and those moments of it charged with social or
psychological relevance.   While the primary focus is upon
the children, inevitably their adult relations play a significant part in that it is their behavior which largely shapes
the future pattern of the children's lives, even if this movie
credits an unusually generous share of this process to hered-
ity.

    The two doctors in town, Dr. Tower and Dr. Gordon,
each have a daughter.   Cassandra Tower, being the child of
a recently arrived family with what the town believes to be
dark secrets, is a social outcast at school, while Louise
Gordon, the progeny of a doctor secure in town favor, appears popular among her peers.   The hero of the film,
young Parris von Eln, brought up by a grandmother guardi-
an of aristocratic, European background, is emotionally
drawn to Cassandra but aware of problems beyond his understanding in her home.   This section of the film ends
with two disturbing sequences.   First, Parris and his best
friend, Drake, encounter a young boy, Willie Mackintosh,
crying in front of a house.   He sobs out the information
that the doctor is with his father and is to operate on his
leg ulcers without chloroform because (ostensibly) of his
father's heart disease.   Dr. Gordon (Charles Coburn) is
glimpsed shutting an upstairs window.   At the sound of
terrible screams from within, the boy bangs on the front
door in anguish, while Drake and Parris flee home.   Then,

in the next sequence, Cassie tells Parris through her tears that she is no longer allowed by her father to attend school. "Maybe I'll stay at home like Mama does all the time." After she runs off, Parris's face is held in close-up.

The second, longer part of Kings Row deals with these same characters' early adulthood.

Parris (Robert Cummings), preparing for the study of medicine with the help of Dr. Tower (Claude Rains), falls in love with Cassie (Betty Field), while Drake (Ronald Reagan) spends his summer happily philandering. Through Dr. Tower, Parris is introduced to psychiatry, and, after his grandmother's death and the shock of learning that Dr. Tower has committed suicide after killing Cassie to save her from dementia praecox, he leaves for Vienna. Drake, rejected by the Gordons in his bid for Louise's (Nancy Coleman) hand in marriage, falls in love with Randy Monaghan (Ann Sheridan), daughter of an Irish railroad section boss. Financially ruined by the defection of a local banker, Drake takes a job with Mr. Monaghan on the railroad and is involved in an accident. Dr. Gordon, to thwart his daughter's continuing interest in Drake, amputates his legs. Parris returns to help his friend, now voluntarily incarcerated in the Monaghan household, and liberates both Drake and Louise from their psychic pain by revealing the truth concerning the amputation. Drake bursts out laughing. "That's a hot one, isn't it? Where did Gordon think I lived? In my legs?" Drake returns to reality, while Parris finds a new love in a recently arrived Austrian girl.

———

One of the most noticeable features of Kings Row is that, though the title gives promise that the town itself will be the subject and though immediately after the credits the camera pans to the town sign advertising the ostensible goodness of Kings Row, there is little sense of the town as an entity. Instead, a number of houses and natural settings with their own actual and metaphorical geography represent all that need be known of the town. The population, of some 8,000, is indicated on the railroad station sign, and though we may thus imagine its probable size we are never permitted knowledge of the town's shape, boundaries or layout, by, say, an overhead shot. The fragmentation of the town, explicable at the most basic level as a consequence of the studio's decision to use its Burbank sound stages, is still remarkably appropriate to the schematism of the film,

whereby the novel's scope, temporal and spatial, and discur-
siveness have been systematically pruned not only to isolate
moments in time and individual houses and woods in the locality but to invest them with levels of meaning and to suggest "probable or necessary" connections between these superficially discrete units.    In other words, what André Bazin would discern as disrespect for spatial integrity, inter-
ference with what he conceives to be nature's essential ambiguity, is operative everywhere in Kings Row, from the decision to construct a town from separate studio sets to the
harnessing of natural phenomena (thunderstorms, sunshine,
shadows) to overall meaning.

So permeated is the movie with antitheses, repeatedly underscored by visual contrasts or parallelisms, that it
seems today like a structuralist's paradise.    Since many of
these contrasts reappear in scores of other small-town movies, as might be expected of a movie identified as an archetype, it ought to be illuminating to isolate examples.    While
they will inevitably be separately discussed here, there is
much overlapping and therefore economy in their use in the
movie itself.

Possibly the most striking and suggestive antithesis,
one which is an epitome of a contrast that seems to make
an appearance in every small-town movie, a contrast that
may explain the entire narrative of certain small-town movies, appears in the opening sequence, immediately after the
credits:    this is the opposition of wishful ideal and practice,
of old-time idealism and present malfunction.    Kings Row
opens with a shot that could have appeared in John Ford, of
a horse-drawn wagon against a skyline which takes up two-
thirds of the frame.    Korngold's triumphant music wedded
with this image suggests pioneering connotations, an American memory of braver, freer times.    The wagon approaches
behind the credits and at their end enters town to vanish,
although memory of that image and its intimations of a passing epoch is invited in the sequences involving the older families of Kings Row.    As the wagon leaves the frame, the
camera pauses at the town sign, with its optimistic message, "A good town.    A Good clean town, a good town to
live in, and a good place to raise your children, " a message immediately called into question by the scene to which
the camera continues its interrupted pan.    Outside the school,
a lonely-looking girl is being ridiculed by other children.
We later learn that she is Cassandra Tower, and that at the
center of her tormentors is Louise Gordon, the more socially successful doctor's daughter.

If the town is indeed a good place to raise your children, then, it would appear, it is so only for certain sections of town society. The town sign promises a beneficent influence that ought to be all-embracing. The rest of the movie is devoted to the demonstration of division, of a town riven by social differentiation on a multitude of criteria. The refusal of the movie to allow physical completeness to the town, its concentration on separate houses, separate work or leisure areas, its investing of gardens with accoutrements and residences with architecture so redolent of their owners' status or personalities that they acquire an almost Expressionist function, the revelation of "soul," indicates the vision of even turn-of-the-century small-town America as having lost its way.

By the end of the childhood section, the principal structures of the movie have all been introduced. The major division within the town is that between the materially secure (the Gordons, Towers) and the poor (the Monaghans). This, the most self-evident of the town's lines of demarcation, finds expression in that the railroad tracks, the most ubiquitous symbol of social division in small-town movies, are where Randy Monaghan chooses to leave Drake in the belief that he belongs uptown. Yet, there are divisions within divisions. If the Gordons and Towers are united in being well off, they are clearly differentiated in their social status within the town. The daughters of these remarkably symmetrical families each hold a birthday party on the same day. Cassie's is badly attended, by a few guests who sit miserably eating in a forbidding garden, while Louise's proves highly successful. It is interesting to see that the Gordons' garden is marked off by a low white picket fence, the frequent indicator of social well-being, actual or claimed, while the Towers' garden is surrounded by iron railings, the usual promise of a forbidding or dangerous residence in the American Gothic cinema. The interior too is unsettling, the flocked wallpaper of the front hall being heavily shadowed. In a movie so questioning of appearance and actuality, it is ironic, of course, that the salubrious, tree-lined street and home where the Gordons reside prove more terrifying and secretive than the conventionally threatening Tower home. [2] A further contrast is made between the thoroughbred and the arriviste families. If the Gordons are socially successful, Mme. von Eln, a woman deemed in the movie's terms more worthy of respect, reveals her disapproval, by implication, when she applauds Drake's decision to attend Cassandra's birthday party in preference to Louise's.

A wider division, signaled by the opening with the horse-drawn wagon disappearing into town, is between free spirits and the shackled or repressed. This seems to be the point of the inclusion of a scene in which Cassie forgets her humiliation at school by swimming in a pond with Parris, but more obviously in the sequence where Drake jumps over the picket fence, away from Louise's "sissy birthday party," to join Parris and Randy Monaghan in an icehouse, where they swing on iron rings in an exuberance of hitherto repressed youthful energy. 3 While Parris and Cassie enjoy freedom only infrequently and approach it tentatively, Randy seems, by virtue of her family's poverty, to embody it.

Finally, as if to indicate the double-sided nature of freedom, certain areas are beyond the children's, or even the town's, knowledge, and certain truths about instinct or appetite remain veiled. The freedom which Dr. Gordon abuses in order to satisfy his sadistic appetites is only one aspect of the madness which lurks in this superficially ordered town. Particularly interesting in this regard is the early appearance of the dark at the top of the stairs, the way that upper rooms are marked off as taboo areas, where madness or cruelty lurks, and from which children are excluded despite their desire, ultimately their need, to comprehend. Dr. Tower gently restrains Parris when he attempts to mount the stairs after Cassandra's birthday party to thank Mrs. Tower, glimpsed briefly at an upstairs window, Dr. Gordon locks a young boy out of his home as he performs surgery without anaesthetic on his hapless father in the upstairs room. The second exclusion may seem benevolent, the first ill-intentioned, until events prove the reverse to be true.

The final concentration of the childhood section on Parris, with the closeup of his face after Cassie's hysterical departure from him, seems to promise development of his role as intermediary, moving among all the worlds outlined above, with the gentlemanly concern and intelligence bred in him by Mme. von Eln. His success in this endeavor comes about, by the end of the movie, as the result of his training in psychiatry.

The practice of medicine plays a crucial role in this movie, but, until Parris's return from Vienna, medicine is linked above all with forces of repression. At one level, it constitutes a mode of social control. Dr. Gordon has played God, punishing those whom he deems wicked with operations

that result in fatal shock or paralysis. Finally, he succumbs to the temptation of ridding his family of the threat
posed to its respectability by Louise's desire for Drake and
renders him a cripple. Dr. Tower has used his medical
knowledge to decide the fates of those closest to him, con-
fining first his wife and then his daughter for their own
protection and finally eliminating Cassie when Parris's happiness is threatened.

Kings Row under the influence of its doctor guardians
has fallen ill. The theme of closeting, of hiding unacceptable truths in upstairs rooms, a theme further developed in
the later sections when Parris considers using his authority
to confine Louise when she wants to tell the truth, is taken
up in the presentation of the town itself. This is a community where the Towers came to hide from the world. It is a
burial ground. Louise's desire is denied because the town
requires its denial, Cassie avoids the thought of marriage
and self-fulfilment because her father denies her the right
in view of her illness. Yet, it is a burial ground where,
it is finally suggested, resurrection may still come about.

Psychiatry is, arguably, a branch of medicine concerned with liberation, even if medicine has been used as a
force of repression by its practitioners in Kings Row. That
this is the view of psychiatry advocated by the movie seems
certain on the evidence of several sequences. In one, Dr.
Tower, as Parris's tutor, describes psychiatry in terms of
therapy for the stress brought about by modern life. According to him, the strain of modern life ensures that "mankind is building up the biggest psychic bellyache" and the
cure for that bellyache is to be found in psychiatry even if
it is "maybe too big, maybe 100 years off." Moreover,
Parris takes up his Viennese studies in order to make Cassie's death meaningful and productive. His chance to prove
the efficacy and beneficiality of psychiatry comes when both
Louise Gordon and Drake are traumatized, Drake by the
loss of his limbs, Louise by the discovery of her father's
mutilation of Drake. That both have, as it were, departed
from life is indicated by their determined self-confinement
to their respective bedrooms and particularly by the turning
of their heads towards the wall. Louise is imprisoned
through dread of what she knows and cannot tell, lest she
be shut up in an asylum, Drake through ignorance of the
true significance of his accident. In this movie, truth liberates. Parris becomes aware that Louise must "relieve
her obsession by telling all she knows, or go insane."

Deciding to treat Drake as a patient rather than a friend, he informs him of Dr. Gordon's part in his mutilation, with the result that Drake rallies, determined not to yield the victory to his old enemy. Moreover, the physician must heal himself. Parris admits that, though he has lost his feelings for Kings Row, he loves the countryside, yet fears "meeting ghosts, " particularly at the pond and the old house. There is another close-up of Parris as he resolves to lay these ghosts. This he does by returning to his grandmother's house, where he meets the new inhabitants and falls in love with the daughter of this household whom at first sight he mistook for Cassie Tower.

The simple formula to which psychiatry is reduced here--of truth-telling, facing up to hitherto denied or unacceptable realities in order to achieve psychic balance-- becomes a common feature of small-town movies. The stress on facing up to experiences so that one may grow healthy and strong may explain why so many of these movies insist on having characters return "to face the town" or intimate that characters have returned because they have "found themselves" through some out-of-town experience. It is as if the town stands for the past, for accretions of guilt, particularly potent for adolescents who so often form the central focus of the small-town movies. If the town stands at some level for the past and some of the damage as well as the value that the past can represent, the emphasis on adolescence and on returning to the town, or not running away in the first place, is at least partly explicable in terms of popularized and diluted Freudianism.

At first viewing, an elegiac mood seems to dominate the movie, not only because of its opening with the disappearing wagon, but also because of the importance attached by the older citizenry to the death of Mme. von Eln. "When she passes, " says one of them, in reference to her, "how much passes with her--a whole way of life--a way of gentleness and honor and dignity. These things are going and may never come back to this world. " Yet, if the movie chronicles the last years of pre-industrialized society, the theme indicated in the quotation, of departing glory, is not dominant. There appears to be a suggestion that living in the past is a mark of illness, and that it is when Drake throws himself into business ventures and reasserts his masculinity by reducing his dependence on Randy that hope is generated within Kings Row. (It is impossible, incidentally, to ignore the irony that the actor playing Drake--

a character whose salvation depends on cutting off over-
dependence on maternal but ultimately deleterious help and
standing on his own two, albeit artificial, feet--seems lately
to have adapted the formula to restore the economic health
of an entire nation!)

Psychiatry, which was beginning to impinge increasingly on the awareness of the mass audience of the 'forties,
with movies such as Hitchcock's Spellbound (1945), affects
the meaning of the town vitally. Parris's equation of a patient's returning to sanity with his being home again is il-
lustrated in his own career and that of Drake. The accum-
ulation of disasters and of psychic detritus which Kings Row
represents to them by mid movie must be faced in order that
the characters may be free. When Drake turns his face to
the wall, he is completing the process of withdrawal already
begun in his decision to move south of the railroad tracks
and to stay within the Monaghans' bedroom. He has abandoned the struggle against the social prejudice represented
by the Gordons and has taken refuge in his disfigurement.
Parris's sojourn in Vienna increases his numbing awareness
of Kings Row's provinciality and, when he does return, he
seeks to evade the responsibilities placed upon him as a doctor by protecting Drake and therefore himself from reality.
Release for both characters involves facing distasteful fact.
Paradoxically, Parris is freed from Kings Row only when
he embraces its uglier aspects, suffering with and for his
friend. Drake may take his rightful place in town only when
he feels he can transcend its cruelties. Thus, the past is
a nightmare to be lived through afresh before the town can
become ordinary and unthreatening.

The sense of hometown as metaphor for all that can
blight youthful development appears stronger finally than that
of nostalgia for vanished graciousness. James Wong Howe's
photography, casting shadows over elegant interiors and re-
serving its closeups for youngsters facing adult anxieties,
underlines the point.

At a less personal level, it is tempting to see Kings
Row as an exploration of the coming industrialized age's relations with the past, the expression of a hope that the new
generation will find in a liberal European inheritance (Mme.
von Eln's bequest to Parris) and in its own untapped entrepreneurial energy (Drake) release from the enervating effects of social snobbery and outmoded middle-class conservatism, as represented by the Gordons.

Peyton Place deals with members of the local high
school's graduating class and those adults involved in their
lives--parents, teachers and the local doctor.

In the first part of the movie, the adolescents are
still at school. The central figure, since the movie is punc-
tuated by voice-overs from that character, may be taken to be
Allison MacKenzie (Diane Varsi), daughter of an attractive
dress-shop owner, Constance MacKenzie (Lana Turner), who
is thought to have married and been widowed in New York
City. Among Allison's friends at school are: Rodney Harrington (Barry Coe), son of the powerful local mill-owner,
Leslie Harrington (Leon Ames), who opposes Rodney's liaison with Betty Anderson (Terry Moore), the class siren
from a lower social stratum; Selena Cross (Hope Lange),
daughter of Constance MacKenzie's maid, Nelly (Betty Field),
stepdaughter of the school janitor, Lucas Cross (Arthur Kennedy); and, especially, Norman Page (Russ Tamblyn), a
mother-dominated, bookish recluse. The early school sequences center on the class's dismayed reactions to the ap-
pointment of an out-of-towner, Mike Rossi (Lee Philips) as
principal in place of their much-respected teacher, Miss
Thornton (Mildred Dunnock). Rossi, having rebuked the
school board, traditionally dominated by Leslie Harrington,
for its mean-ness in the matter of pay for school staff,
wins the respect of both Miss Thornton and her class. He
also, despite hesitancy and resistance on Constance MacKenzie's part, enters upon a relationship with her. Allison escapes from the tensions between herself and her mother and
from her shock at seeing Lucas Cross physically assaulting
Selena in their filthy shack-of-a-home to her secret place on
a hillside overlooking Peyton Place, a retreat to which she
invites Norman Page. Released from the town's repressiveness, Norman talks about his sexual problems and how he
sent off for a sex-instruction manual in a plain wrapper.
Allison admits to doing the same. "Everybody in this town
hides behind plain wrappers," they conclude. Allison's affection for him leads to a tender, chaste kiss.

A sense of community is suggested by the high school
prom, with Miss Thornton's brief address ("We're a small
town on a small spot on a great big map. Peyton Place will
be part of you forever. Make it great by honoring it.") and
the singing of "Auld Lang Syne." Tensions reappear immediately after it, however, with Constance's outraged rejection of Mike Rossi's love-making and with the rape of
his stepdaughter by Lucas Cross.

After graduation, the separate problems of the principal characters develop further.  Doc Swain (Lloyd Nolan)
refuses to perform an abortion on Selena, now pregnant with
her stepfather's child, but orders Lucas out of town.  The
miscarriage which results from a fall when Lucas vengefully
pursues Selena is recorded by Doc Swain as an appendectomy.
On Labor Day, Allison and Norman are mistaken for Betty
Anderson and Rodney Harrington, who go swimming in the
nude in a local pond.  Thus, when they return home, they
uncomprehendingly suffer vilification from their mothers.
To compound her suffering, Constance reveals to Allison
that her kindly dead father is a fiction, that she never married.  Running upstairs, Allison finds Nelly Cross' hanged
body in her closet.

In the next sequences, which detail events during Allison's retreat to New York, which coincides with Pearl Harbor, local boys enlist and leave for the war.  Rodney Harrington is killed, Leslie Harrington is reconciled with Betty
Anderson, whom Rodney had married despite paternal opposition.  Constance and Mike Rossi are also reunited.  Selena
Cross, to protect herself from the threat of further violence,
kills Lucas and, with her young brother, buries the body.

The climactic scenes of the movie concern Selena's
trial for murder.  On the train home, to appear in her defense, Allison meets a confident, masculine Norman Page
returning from the war.  On arrival, she refuses to see
her mother, but at the trial realizes that Constance's thoughts
on the witness stand concern her own troubled relationship
with her daughter, not the Cross family's problems.  As
each defense witness's testimony is rendered vague and
weak by the prosecution, Doc Swain at last reveals the
truth about Lucas Cross's violence towards Selena.  He
berates the town for its repressiveness.  "We're all prisoners of each other's gossip.  Our best young people leave
because they're stifled in Peyton Place....  We're a small
town but we're a prosperous one and we allow shacks to
stand.  We have six churches, but we don't practice what
they preach.  Our newspapers are used for wrapping gar-
bage.  We have failed as a community to watch over one
another."  The jury returns a verdict of not guilty.  The
courtroom is silent, some spectators smiling, some disapproving, but as Selena leaves the court with her boyfriend
Ted (David Nelson) the people massed on the court steps pat
her on the back.  Allison and Norman enter Constance's
house.  "We finally discovered that season of love.  It is

only felt in somebody's heart.   Right now, somebody is looking everywhere for it, and it's in you. "

———————

If the public expected on the appearance of the movie version as harsh a portrayal of the small town as Grace Metalious's novel promised or as Kings Row had in its darker
episodes suggested, it must have been surprised.   While
murder, suicide, rape and the casual malice of local gossip are retained from the novel, the film version has radically transformed the material.   The uncomfortably pat
moralism of Metalious's version, whereby, for example, the
over-privileged local Don Juan, Rodney Harrington, is killed
in a car crash with his latest conquest, after loose-living
Betty Anderson has ended up with an unwanted pregnancy is
replaced by more positive, if no less pat, resolutions.
Whereas the younger characters in the novel are impelled
towards fittingly unhappy destinies, as if their future were
already determined by their adolescent experience within
Peyton Place, the very achievement of growing up, as well
as external influences (the city, the war) liberates the potential within the young of the film version.   Thus, Rodney
and Betty, despite their nude swimming and their daring attitudes to drink and sex, are finally seen to be a conventionally decent couple with marriage on their minds; Norman
Page who in the novel is discharged from the army because
of emotional problems and yet presented to the town as a
hero by his mother, organizing his adult life as she did his
youth, becomes a paragon of all-American masculinity when
freed from Mrs. Page's influence in the film.   While Rodney in the movie dies in battle, in the novel his father has
used his influence on members of the draft board to keep
Rodney safely at home.

The differences from Kings Row are far more, however, than the movie's happy resolution of adolescent problems in adult life, something which, after all, the more
sombre Kings Row also ultimately offered.

The most striking change is in the visual presentation of the small town.  Peyton Place is as active in pur-
veying images of the town's organic qualities, its wholeness
and tactful integration with the natural world, its changes
with the seasons, as Kings Row was in fragmenting the town
and preventing an overall conception of it.  Peyton Place
opens with an aerial view of the town as the credits roll,

the sound track offering the serene, romantic theme music
later popularized by the television serial. A montage of
superior calendar art introduces the town to us in poster-
bright colors as a succession of CinemaScope vistas inviting
admiration for the natural beauty and architectural taste of
New England. The focal points seem to be the mill and the
church. The seasons' change is indicated by autumnal trees
giving way to snowscapes. "My name is Allison MacKenzie,"
a voice-over begins. "Where I was born, time was not told
by the clock but by the seasons--autumn, the time of bitter
regret, then winter ...," as the images illustrate the dominant seasonal weather. Throughout the movie, the Cinema-
Scope frame, filled with the natural beauty and architectural
simplicity of Camden, Maine, a typically decorous New England town in one of the least industrialized states, repeatedly offers the principal characters a sense of spaciousness,
freedom of movement and healthful influences on their young
lives.

In some ways, the apparent insistence on wholeness
and healthfulness may lead us to overemphasize the effects
of Peyton Place's visuals. We would be wrong, for example,
to conclude that Kings Row makes its houses and their surroundings bear a symbolic weight while Peyton Place does
not. The quasi-expressionist treatment of architecture and
terrain, to reveal the inner life of human beings associated
with them, is almost as evident in the later film.

For example, immediately after Allison's post-
credits voice-over has ended, we join the driver of an open
car in the countryside, asking the way to Peyton Place. It
is with the driver that we enter town and glimpse the topography of Peyton Place. Thus, at the railroad crossing, we
see the Cross family's filthy shack. Then, as the car enters a street of white clapboard houses, a sign indicates
that we are "Entering Peyton Place." At the simplest level,
that the audience should take the point of view of a visiting
outsider seems remarkably appropriate to its viewing situation, and it may seem as if there is nothing more to be
gleaned from the sequence than a first view of Peyton Place.
However, it is surely not accidental that the Cross family's
home is literally outside Peyton Place, since we officially
enter the town only after we have passed the shack. Selena
Cross attends the local school, Lucas Cross is that school's
janitor and Nelly Cross is Constance MacKenzie's maid. All
of them are part of town life, and yet are outside town. The
location of their home strongly suggests social marginality

and, in a movie which deals with repression and fear of
sexuality in the parental generation, it is singularly appropriate that the most sexually appetitive character, the most
contemptuous of bourgeois hypocrisy, Lucas Cross, should
live in an area which is deemed to be beyond the scope of
the town's recognition.

Again, Constance MacKenzie's home, the first residence glimpsed by the audience after the stranger has entered town, has the white picket fence and wholesome appearance which, as in the Gordons' residence in Kings Row,
represents social acceptability. When Allison runs to school
from her home, her route, all of which is recorded by the
camera, takes her past a number of areas which have special meaning for the community or which are green and
"natural." She runs past children on a swing, past lines of
washing, over grass and falling leaves, then past the cemetery, the Peyton Place hospital, and what looks like the town
hall, to arrive at the brick school. Allison, admittedly by
virtue of her mother's falsification of her out-of-town past,
occupies a secure position within town; its institutions are
for people like her and her mother. Significantly, after
Lucas Cross has been ordered out of town and Nelly has
committed suicide, Selena and her brother clean their formerly filthy home and, in the Christmastime sequence during which she kills Lucas, it becomes apparent that they have
attempted to produce the antiseptic look of the MacKenzie
residence as a means of aligning themselves with the community which formerly used their parents' services but re-
fused to acknowledge their place within it.

Therefore, the topography of the town in both movies
is often symbolic, though it is never merely symbolic. Why,
then, the apparent emphasis in the later movie on notions of
organic unity, of wholeness? Is this evidence of a disjuncture in style, certain sequences counteracting the tendency
towards stylization and symbolization in local topography? On
the contrary, it seems to be an attempt to take mere suggestions in Kings Row much farther. In particular, the small
town is being linked with the natural world in order to suggest that its best realization permits its inhabitants to feel
no conflict between small-town civilization and the natural
world. There certainly is a contrast between the two until
the town is finally purged by the experience of the trial (and
of big-city life as well as world conflict), but the visuals
and voice-overs from the beginning promise the resolution
which is finally offered, whereby the contrast between nature

and town is eliminated.  When Allison retreats with Norman
Page to her secret place outside town, clearly the town has,
for her, excluded the serenity which she finds in New England's countryside.  When Rodney and Betty, Allison and
Norman, escape from Peyton Place to swim at the local
pond, they are again indicating the repressiveness which
they believe to exist in town.  At its worst, Peyton Place
denatures its young; at its best, in the final moments, it
brings the town back into harmony with nature, creating
what Allison names "the fifth season, of love."

While the young are blighted in Kings Row by parental
snobbery or cruelty, there is no clear or sustained suggestion that the young are somehow "natural" even if the older
generation are repressive, and therefore implicitly anti-
natural, 4 elements in each community.

Just as all events outside town in Kings Row are reduced to comparative insignificance, Vienna being a mere
caption on a snowy exterior, so Peyton Place refuses to follow Allison to New York, or, for that matter, Rodney, Ted
and Norman to the Second World War.  New York is somewhere "out there," a place of moral chaos from which wom-
en return shaken and afraid or, as with Allison, toughened
and refreshed.  Reality is only in the small town.  The point
of Norman's war experiences as a paratrooper seems to be
to equip him to free himself from his mother, the point of
Allison's publishing career to grant her an (unspecified) understanding of her hometown.  (That the Second World War
becomes a survival course for the young male small-town
inhabitant should, incidentally, help us to understand why
The Deer Hunter is almost certainly misunderstood if it is
interpreted as a film "about" Vietnam [see pp. 83ff.].)

Just as this movie seems to create the notion of
youngsters' and town's (at its best) special closeness to nature from hints in Kings Row and to extend the latter's attitudes to experience beyond the town limits, so Peyton Place
enormously augments its predecessor's basic, but concisely
expressed, dichotomy between ideal and practice.

The implied contrast between the town sign's sentiments
and town practice in the opening sequences of Kings Row is
reiterated all through Peyton Place, by means of juxtaposition of town institutions and extra-institutional conduct.  The
school performs a particularly important function in this
respect.  For example, after we have been invited to contrast

the Cross family's home with the MacKenzie's, we find that
Selena Cross and Allison MacKenzie are treated with equal
respect in a classroom run by Miss Thornton on obviously
democratic lines.   School practice is then immediately contrasted with the penny-pinching conduct of the school board.
As if the point needed underlining, Lucas Cross observes
drunkenly to Miss Thornton that teaching school is unimpor-
tant because as soon as the pupil leaves school he enters "a
dog-eat-dog world." The new principal professes belief in
"... two rules--I want the school to tell the truth and teach
a minimum of facts, a maximum of ideas." This reversal
of Gradgrind's educational philosophy is explained in terms
of the times through which they are living. "If war comes,
kids should fight for the ideas behind the facts." This as-
piration is indeed realized after Pearl Harbor and, to emphasize the link between school ideals and the town's war
effort, it is noticeable that Miss Thornton, Mike Rossi and
Doc Swain (a member of the school board) all turn up to
give encouragement to the enlisted young men.

     The climactic courtroom scenes are transformed into
a trial of the town itself when Doc Swain shifts the emphasis
from questions of Selena's guilt to the reasons for her secrecy.   This examination of the town's purported values in
relation to its practice is simply a more overt summary
variation of the film's method throughout.   Sequences centering on individuals' conduct are always bracketed by others recording, for example, a town celebration, a speech
concerning the ethos of Peyton Place, or some aspect of the
town's communal identity.   Thus, Miss Thornton's democrat-
ically run classroom, the church services, the high school
prom, the graduation ceremony, the Labor Day celebrations
and the preparations for war, all suggest a set of values
constantly alluded to and invoked.   These values, seldom
enunciated but rather assumed, seem to be identifiable with
those of grass-roots democracy and of decency and fair play.
They are, significantly, espoused largely by the young or
those vitually associated with the welfare of the young.

     Since the young are intimately associated with the
natural world this has the interesting effect of making democracy itself "natural" and healthful.   The schematism of
the movie is such that Peyton Place's youth is a symbol of
the small-town spirit at its best, while the majority of the
older generation, particularly of the parental generation, has
lost or betrayed it.   While, for example, Constance MacKenzie's New York affair has ended in hypocrisy and frigidity,

Allison uses her confidence in the ideals (though not the
practice) of her hometown to further her New York publishing career.  Her voice-overs are written, and indeed deliv-
ered, in an alarmingly cloying manner, with the reference to
"a fifth season, of love" being so kitschy that serious consideration of the film's central thesis is threatened.   This
seems to be, however, that the faith of the adolescents in
egalitarianism and comradeship is confirmed by the natural
world while parental evasion and selfishness are unnatural
importations or perversions.   The point emerges in the way
that Peyton Place itself is shot, its tactful architectural relationship with the natural environment which is incorporated
within rather than threatened by the township.   It emerges
most clearly, however, in those sequences where Allison,
after a mild contretemps with her repressed mother, runs
to school through grass and trees and past civic buildings,
and especially when she and Norman retreat to her secret
place on the wooded hillside overlooking the town, or to the
bathing pond.   In the secret place, they talk easily of their
growing sexual awareness and find that their fear is generated purely by the censorious attitudes of their parents, in
each case a single woman whose lack of male partner has
rendered her more possessive and prohibitive than protective
and caring.

      The serenity and beauty of the seasonal changes are,
in this movie, therefore more than a device to prettify melodrama.   Rather, this kind of visual is used by the director,
Mark Robson, to underline the movie's linking of the town
spirit with that of New England, to suggest a political ideology which is as beneficent and unsophisticated as the woods
and lakes of the countryside or the transitions from one season to another.   Small-town democracy because of the associations created by this movie becomes healthful and natural.
New York is defined simply by what it lacks and by its un-
reality and artificiality, a place from which home may be
serenely contemplated and assessed, an endurance test to
build and toughen character so that one may at last come
home to reality.

      Kings Row and Peyton Place, despite their fundamen-
tal differences of approach, including, incidentally, the elimination of all considerations of ethnic difference in the later
work, share certain preoccupations.   Apart from the reap-
pearance of doctors as agents of social control (Doc Swain
with his extra-legal decision to falsify Selena's medical record, his expulsion of Lucas Cross, and his dominant role in

the draft board and at the trial being an extension of the
paternalistic Dr. Tower), there are common ideas central
to both. Thus, the emphasis on facing truth, the unhealthi-
ness of such fictions as Constance has woven to protect her
past, the trauma to and eventual restoration of Allison effected by exposure to knowledge of her birth, and the feeling
that psychic balance is demonstrated by a return to the previously overpowering or threatening small town, are all to
be found in the earlier work too. Sexual health and maladjustment are linked in each with frank acceptance and evasion, respectively. Constance's falsification of her amorous
adventure in New York extends to an inability to accept her
daughter's sexuality, an inability mirrored in Mrs. Page's
attitudes. Norman, withdrawn and neutered by his mother's
demands, returns on the same train as Allison with a new
awareness of his virility. The expression of the healthy,
confident Norman is jarringly familiar in 'fifties melodrama.
His back-slapping heartiness of manner with his soldier bud-
dies has the bogus quality of the John Kerr character's final
appearance in Minnelli's Tea and Sympathy (1956), crewcut,
squarely dressed and flanked by wife and offspring, the word
"normal" writ large all over him. Nevertheless, the essential point remains, and echoes Drake's positive embracing of
life, even with its physical hardships, at the end of Kings
Row. Peyton Place, like Kings Row, also considers the
family in damaged and ideal form. Thus, the one-parent
families--the MacKenzies, the Pages, the Harringtons and,
in the peculiar sense that Lucas is not a blood relation of
the younger members of the family, the Cross's--all inflict
damage on the young. The idealized family, suggested in
the sexual stereotyping of submissive but sexually responsive
woman and assertive, dominant but caring male provider, is
promised finally, after the catharsis of the trial and the embracing of truth by Constance in the union of herself and
Mike Rossi, and in the return to the fold of a loving daughter, herself apparently to enter marriage with the newly
masculine Norman Page.

The nightmares are over, the young surmount their
problems, the older generation learns the rightness of its
youngsters' ideals and suffers into truth, and the tension between repressive civilization and beneficent nature is rendered illusory and unnecessary. Potentially, at least, the
small town at that final point of both movies earns its description: a good clean town, a good town to live in, and a
good place to raise your children. Doubts about the reality
of small-town values and thus about the reality of America's

fundamental view of her best self, apparently justified in the
darker passages of both movies, and the chastening of town
society at large, are ultimately, through the pain of the
characters dispelled when these values are retrieved and
made credible once more, at the points where they seem
most threatened. The town may cut off your legs, threaten
to commit you to an asylum if you speak the truth, relish
your discomfiture as you are put on trial for murder, but
when the mirror is held up to it and it can see the distor-
tion of the town code which it has perpetrated, the faith of
the young is validated in the town's sudden reversion to the
small-town ideals it had not till then realized it had forsaken.
The wider message seems to be that, at times when it loses
confidence in Americanism, the American people should have
the faith in itself and its institutions to see beyond the failures and compromises to the reality of an ideal which may
still be effective, given the commitment of all to it.

## Notes to Chapter 2

1. See John Cosgrove, 'Revisiting Kings Row,' Screen Facts
   no. 9, vol. 2, no. 3.

2. Hitchcock recognizes the connotations of the Victorian
   house of old-fashioned wallpaper and forbidden upstairs
   rooms when he uses it in contrast to a reassuringly
   modern motel, in Psycho (1960). Minnelli uses another
   in the Hallowe'en sequences of Meet Me in St. Louis
   (1944), though once more doubt is cast on the accuracy
   of (this time, childish) conclusions about its inhabitants'
   nature.

3. A similar sequence occurs early in East of Eden (1955),
   where the heroine and her boyfriend retreat to an icehouse to make love, and the James Dean character ex-
   plodes out of his painfully acquired "civilized" persona to
   hurl blocks of ice down the icehouse chute, this time in
   a paroxysm of uncomprehending frustration rather than a
   sense of release.

4. The unfettered lustiness of Lucas Cross could in other
   contexts make him the most natural-seeming of all, but
   in Peyton Place nature is always seen as serene and
   beneficent, never violent or destructive, connotations
   appropriate only to the less attractive adults' characters.

# 3. UTOPIA

The two films discussed in the previous chapter have so evidently assumed the appearance of definitive examples of the small-town movie that this may come erroneously to be wholly identified with melodrama or at least to be taken purely as a species of that genre. Thus, Pauline Kael, in a review of The Last Picture Show, states, "What makes Bogdanovich's film different from earlier films of the genre, such as Kings Row and Peyton Place, is an unexpectedly cool naïveté that carries conviction, so that the movie has the effect not of a slick, worked-up, raunchy melodrama about tangled lives but, rather, of something closer to common experience."[1] While there are manifold thematic correspondences between the Bogdanovich movie and Mark Robson's, for example (see pp. 127-28), the wide celebrity of the latter work may mask the fact that there are many small-town movies which are impossible to categorize as melodramas, just as, conversely, there are many melodramas which are impossible to consider small-town. Miss Kael's notion that there is a genre which incorporates all three of the films under consideration at that point in her review is interesting, her comparison of the Bogdanovich movie with only the small-town melodrama potentially misleading, though understandable, for, in the 'fifties at least, most melodramas do have small-town settings and most small-town movies are indeed melodramas.

The term "melodrama" is as casually employed in practice as the other Hollywood genre labels, but is even more elusive and difficult of definition than the rest because it has been seriously studied so comparatively late, no doubt in part because the traditional linking of the genre with the notion of "woman's picture" and therefore of a putative female audience has done it little good in patriarchal society. Fuller consideration of melodrama has followed in the wake of, or arguably been concomitant with, the growth of interest in the directors Vincente Minnelli and, particularly,

47

Douglas Sirk, the latter of whom is primarily associated, in
the 'fifties, with particular movies of that genre, though it
could also be claimed that he practically re-creates melodrama or marks it indelibly henceforth.  Kings Row is relatively isolated as small-town melodrama in the 'forties.
True, there is Wyler's The Little Foxes in 1941, Curtiz's
Mildred Pierce in 1945, King Vidor's Beyond the Forest in
1949, and such famous movies as Orson Welles's The Magnificent Ambersons, Hitchcock's Shadow of a Doubt (both
1942), Wyler's The Best Years of Our Lives (1946), Intruder
in the Dust (1949), which, though hard to identify readily as
melodrama in the sense in which the term might be used after Sirk, can be seen as related to melodrama at least in
their seriousness of tone, their concentration on familial relationships and, frequently, on female sexuality.  However,
in the 'fifties, the decade of Peyton Place and, indeed, well
into the 'sixties, the small town becomes the regular, the
almost inevitable, setting for melodrama.  We have, for example, Storm Warning and A Place in the Sun (1951), Come
Back, Little Sheba (1952), The Member of the Wedding (1953),
Young at Heart (1954), The Rose Tattoo and East of Eden
(1955), Picnic and All That Heaven Allows (1956), Written
on the Wind (1957), The Long Hot Summer, Some Came
Running and Home Before Dark (1958), The Sound and the
Fury and A Summer Place (1959), to name fifteen.

Brief consideration of the nature of melodrama should
make the appeal of the small-town setting patent.

Very broadly, cinematic melodrama appears to derive
from stage melodrama, which represents a democratization
of classical tragedy in that it invites a popular audience to
take seriously those issues which, because they are conceived
in essentially middle-class terms and concern the petits-
bourgeois, are traditionally deemed, in European theatre, to
be the concerns of comedy or, at best, tragi-comedy.  Fifth century B.C. Greek tragedy, dealing almost exclusively with semi-
divine and royal characters, treats its socially inferior characters merely as plot devices, as embodiments of the demos's
sentiment, or with some condescension as nature's gentlemen.[2]
When middle-class sentiment or preoccupations are permitted
to be the focus of Greek drama, it is in the context of New
Comedy rather than as a species of tragedy.  In more recent times, despite Arthur Miller's attempts to render
working- and middle-class concerns in terms of Renaissance
tragedy,[3] the chief dramatic form in which complicity is invited, sympathy extended, from a theatre audience for the

expressed emotional concerns of the lower-middle class or
working class has been melodrama.

Cinematic melodrama, taking bourgeois life as its
material and solemnly addressing its audience concerning
thwarted romances, disappointed lives, middle-class despair,
has at its center a concern with the family, whether nuclear
or extended. There is an implicit appeal in melodrama's
explorations of the family to a Platonic ideal of it, to a perfect realization of Family in which mother is maternal, "feminine" and faithful; the father, dominant, "masculine" and
protective; and the children, filial. Interestingly, if the
analysis of the movies discussed in Chapter 2 is credible,
a similar appeal to an ideal Small Town is made at a higher
or wider level in these melodramas, and, as we shall see,
in many others, so that at first glance it could appear that
there might be a case for seeing the small town itself as
macrocosm (standing for a still greater macrocosm, the
United States) to the microcosm of the small-town family.
Melodrama is largely a concerned exploration of the gaps
which inevitably open up when the ideal fails to be achieved.
Hence, the frequency of the damaged families, when one or
another component of them is dead or too dominant or sub-
servient, in Douglas Sirk, for example.

Melodrama, posing its questions and couching its solutions in predominantly bourgeois terms, takes the family as
an element which may be isolated from or marginally affected
by larger social forces. Since small towns in literature and
film appear to be communities in which families may have
meaning, which, in fact, one family may dominate, and since
small towns themselves are in American folk belief conceived
to be autonomous entities scarcely impinged on by mass society despite overwhelming evidence to the contrary, [4] the as-
sociation of Hollywood melodrama with the small town is
readily comprehensible.

Geoffrey Nowell-Smith, in a discussion of Minnelli
and melodrama, [5] takes the analysis further:

> In so far as melodrama, like realism, supposes a
> world of equals, a democracy within the bourgeois
> strata (alias bourgeois democracy) it also supposes a
> world without the exercise of social power. The ad-
> dress is to an audience which does not think of itself
> as possessed of power (but neither as radically dis-
> possessed, disinherited, oppressed) and the world of

the subject matter is likewise one in which only mid-
dling power relations are present. The characters are
neither the rulers nor the ruled, but occupy a middle
ground, exercising local power or suffering local pow-
erlessness, within the family or small town. The locus
of power is the family and individual private property,
the two being connected through inheritance. In this
world of circumscribed horizons (which corresponds very
closely to Marx's definition of 'petty bourgeois ideology')
patriarchal right is of central importance.... Notably,
the question of law or legitimacy, so central to tragedy,
is turned inward from 'Has this man a right to rule
(over us)?' to 'Has this man a right to rule a family
(like ours)?'

This inward-turning motivates a more direct psychological reading of situations, particularly in the Hollywood melodramas of the 50s.

If, then, the small-town setting has obvious attrac-
tions as embodying the "world of circumscribed horizons,"
it should nevertheless go without saying that the foundation
of a particular movie in such a world is not necessarily
proof that we are viewing a melodrama. Melodrama involves a "tone," attitudes of concern towards its clearly
identified conflicts, an ostensibly straight-faced and sober
treatment of love and death and family, with moments of
such "excess" that there is a threat to the fabric of the
work, a suggestion that it may not be able to contain its
subject-matter, and a resultant feeling that the resolutions
which inevitably end the movie are "unconvincing," in the
nature of the Greek deus ex machina rather than as a dramatically consistent dénouement. In Kings Row, the thun-
derstorm which accompanies the adult Cassie's surrender
to Parris's love-making, in Peyton Place the hysteria of
the confrontation between Allison and Constance MacKenzie
followed by the shocking discovery of Nelly Cross's hanged
body, threaten the credibility of the endings. If Parris's
decision to reveal the truth and the truths disclosed at
Selena's trial are conceived to be cathartic, the sheer speed
with which the catharsis proves efficacious in each case un-
dermines its reality. The space opened up by the psychic
and physical wounds inflicted on one generation by another
or by one class on another seems too deep for the familial
or societal institutions explored by the films to be so quickly restored to full strength. Both movies would appear to
be melodramas, with all the contradictions that Hollywood
melodrama can be discerned regularly to produce, but the

history of the small-town movie can never fully be told by a recounting of such work on melodrama as is available to us.

Even in the heyday of Sirk and Minnelli melodramas, there were (if rarely) small-town comedies, such as Rally Round the Flag, Boys! and It Happened to Jane in 1959, and musicals (The Affairs of Dobie Gillis, 1953; The Pajama Game, 1957). In the previous decade, the tone of the small-town movie is more regularly lighthearted, or free of "excess," as in Happy Land in 1942, The Miracle of Morgan's Creek (1944) or Little Women (1948).

However, to add further complexity to the analysis of melodrama, while even urban settings such as those for Imitation of Life (1958) or Where Love Has Gone (1964) may still keep the family as focus of attention and produce out of New York or San Francisco a "world of circumscribed horizons," several works which are obviously melodramatic are not only city-set but dwell primarily on questions of female sexuality, on the relations of the sexes, rather than on ideal-versus-particular family, as in, for example, The Best of Everything (1959), Valley of the Dolls (1967) or, more recently, The Other Side of Midnight (1977). It could well be argued that even here familial concerns are, if scarcely visible, to be assumed in that the problematic aspects of the heroines' relationships with men are viewed ultimately in terms of their nonfulfillment of the role of potential spouse or mother.

It has been suggested (p. 49) that melodrama implicitly compares the imperfect particular families which it takes as subject with a Platonic ideal, Family. While Plato's world of ideals is a world of absolutes and the purity and perfection of his concept of Family or, for that matter, Small Town would admit no alloy or defect, there is a period of Hollywood's history when it as closely approaches such a world as is conceivable in human terms. The cinematic contemplation of perfection implies a static drama of a kind that Hollywood could never embrace. It was fully capable, however, of celebrating the epitome of the best kind of middle-class family in the best kind of small community. This it did from the later 'thirties until the end of the Second World War, in a number of series lightheartedly extolling the virtues of such families and communities. Where melodrama may explore the occasionally vertiginous chasms between images of perfection and of actuality, these domestic comedies or "un-melodramatic family dramas" recognized the

possibility of space opening up between ideal and practice
only for the sake of dramatic suspense or narrative thrust
and eliminated all sense of its likelihood in these families
and settings by a dramatically appropriate, clearly resolved
ending affirming the abiding nature of the values for which
its protagonist stood.  Within the limits that a bourgeois
imagination might construct for itself and with the proviso
that the happy conditions reaffirmed in the dénouement must
be implicitly threatened and successfully championed in each
unit of the series, these films constructed the small town
as Utopia.

The doctors who play such crucial roles as arbiters
of town morality in small-town melodrama, Doctors Tower
and Gordon in Kings Row and Doc Swain in Peyton Place,
were enshrined before either of these films was made in a
series devoted to Dr. Christian of the mythical town of
Rivers End, Minnesota.  Jean Hersholt won the part of Dr.
Christian as a result of playing Dr. Allan Defoe (who de-
livered the Dionne quintuplets) in The Country Doctor (1936),
and played it first in a radio soap-opera serial in November,
1937.  The serial became popular, was moved to prime time,
and was extended from fifteen to thirty minutes an episode.
Dr. Christian survived as a radio character until 1953, but
his appearance on movie screens was limited to half a dozen
films between 1939 and 1941, the first of which was Meet Dr.
Christian.  These six movies represent the apotheosis of the
small-town doctor as kindly, philosophical, good-humored and
just, a view that leads directly to small-town doctor as, literally, God in the Henry King musical of the middle 'fifties,
Carousel.  In this latter film, the "star-keeper" who sends
the ghostly hero back to earth to repair the damage inflicted
on his daughter by her father's evil reputation, also plays
the village doctor who presides over the graduation ceremony on earth.  The hero notices the resemblance and questions his heavenly guide, who replies, "Many country doctors
look like him. "

That Dr. Christian was far more than a medical prac-
titioner, being a force for democratic justice in Rivers End,
is demonstrated by, for example, his second movie, The
Courageous Dr. Christian (1940).  This centers on the good
doctor's attempts to improve the lot of squatters in a shanty
settlement on the outskirts of town.  A young family from
their number is taken into his home when their shack burns
down until they can be housed with a wealthy widow, Mrs.
Stewart.  His appeal to the town council that a modern

housing project be financed for the sake of the squatters
meets with little enthusiasm. "These people are not like
us," says one of his audience. However, agreement is
reached on condition that Dr. Christian persuade Mrs.
Stewart to donate the vacant land which she owns for the
project. By a series of misunderstandings, Christian an-
nounces his success in persuading the widow, knowing
nothing of her conviction that he has by accepting her gift
also agreed to marry her. On the discovery of her mis-
conception, he puts social justice before personal dismay
and decides to go ahead with the marriage. Such little
enthusiasm as there is in town for the housing project
evaporates when a fight breaks out between a young squat-
ter and a local lad. Dr. Christian is accused of bringing
hoodlums into the community. When businessmen and
council withdraw their support, the squatters protest by
moving their shacks to Mrs. Stewart's vacant land. The
council reacts by declaring the shanty town a health men-
ace, and the police move against the squatters. Thanks to
an outbreak of spinal meningitis, however, the squatters
are quarantined and local citizens help Dr. Christian to
tend them. Much sobered by the thought of its reputation
had the poor been permitted to die without the town's help,
the council votes unanimously for the housing project.
Mrs. Stewart, content with her newfound "children" from
among the squatters, gives up her dream of marriage with
Dr. Christian.

The movie demonstrates the potential for good in the
small town. The squatters are misunderstood, it appears,
when they are labelled hoodlums, and as soon as a crisis
breaks out the town gentry rally round the hero, the fount
of the town's best impulses, and do what they always ought
to have done. Town prejudice is ephemeral and easily van-
quished by the patient kindliness of Dr. Christian, friend of
the poor.

A younger small-town hero, Henry Aldrich, is celebrated in no fewer than eleven films between 1939 and 1944.
Like Dr. Christian, Henry Aldrich achieved greatest longevity on radio, with a half-hour comedy program which always
opened with Henry's mother calling him and Henry's responding to her in his high-pitched voice. The genesis of Henry
Aldrich was, however, from Clifford Goldsmith's Broadway
play of 1938, What A Life! This play was itself made into
a movie in 1939, with Jackie Cooper playing Henry and Betty
Field co-starring as his girlfriend. The most regular Henry

in the series of Aldrich movies was, however, Jimmy Lydon
who took over from Jackie Cooper for the second movie, Life
With Henry (1941).   In some ways,  Henry Aldrich was the
B-picture equivalent of Andy Hardy.   "Some say Henry was
a kind of poor kid's Andy Hardy, " writes David Zinman. 6
"And, in fact, when you take a close look, it's amazing how
much alike they were.   They both lived in a small town.
They came from respectable middle-class families,  had their
own secondhand car.... "   Yet,  the less prestigious small-
town youth is more of an anti-hero than Andy Hardy,  always doing the wrong thing,  poor at football,  equally poor
at academic pursuits,  his voice breaking into falsetto under
stress.     Nevertheless,  the promotion of fair play and democratic principles which underlies The Courageous Dr. Christian reappears in such Aldrich comedies as Henry Aldrich
for President (1941).    Even if the presidency in question is
that of the class,  still,  a lesson in the rudiments of political decency is taught.

Centerville's rich boy attempts to win the class presidency by bribing the electorate with ice cream sodas or
brainwashing them with leaflets.   Moreover,  one of the
schoolteachers writes his speech for him and coaches him
in it.   Henry is expelled from school when it transpires that
two hundred phoney ballots have been cast.    Justice is
achieved when the printer of the phoney ballots is run to
earth by Henry,  and he learns that his rich rival organized
the cheating.   Henry,  for reasons too complex to bear repetition here,  is forced to pilot a plane back to Centerville on
discovery of the truth and his landing on the high school football field is witnessed by the whole town.

In Centerville,  as in Rivers End,  justice triumphs,
thanks to the town's interest,  ultimately,  in fair play.   If it
is momentarily diverted by social snobbery in the Dr. Christian movie or blinded to the truth by the trickery of Henry's
rival in the Aldrich movie,  once it has had time to consider
its attitudes,  the town always chooses the true American way.

By far the most celebrated of the wartime small-town
movies,  though,  is the Andy Hardy series.   It all started
with a low-budget comedy about what was conceived to be a
typical small-town family,  A Family Affair (1937).   Louis B.
Mayer welcomed the making of the picture as an antidote to
the Depression years,  since he believed that cinema patrons
wanted movies that showed "how 'nice' American life was. "7
It is interesting to note how Mayer implicitly equates America

at its best with the American small town. So hungry, apparently, was the public for the niceness that the Hardy family and hometown seemed to represent that 73 million dollars were grossed by the fourteen Hardy films made between then and 1946[8] and Mickey Rooney, who played Andy Hardy, became the United States' top box-office attraction.

The Hardy family consisted of Judge Hardy and his wife (played from the second movie of the series by Lewis Stone and Fay Holden respectively), their two children, Andy and Andy's older sister Marion (Cecilia Parker) and Aunt Milly (Sara Haden or Betsy Ross Clarke), the spinster schoolteacher who shared the family's home. The Hardys lived in the town of Carvel, with its population of 25,000, but were occasionally transported by the writers beyond the town boundaries to such localities as New York City, Washington, D.C., or the college (Wainwright) which Andy, like his father before him, attended. Wherever the particular movie was sited, the atmosphere was small-town, whether imported or not, since events were viewed through Carvel's eyes by its principal family.

Andy Hardy's Double Life (1942) was film number thirteen of the series, and may be regarded as a summation of the series' themes, since it dealt with Andy's last days in Carvel before his departure to Wainwright College. Consideration of this particular component of the series should offer some notion of the format and strategies of other Hardy movies of the period as well.

Double Life opens with the MGM lion giving place, briefly, to a family portrait of "Judge Hardy's family," while the credits roll, and opens with a sign indicating an auction sale for the "late" Andrew Hardy (here, as always, played by Mickey Rooney), about to leave for college. The town scenery is established as quintessential small-town, at least in the sense that elements of other studio-based small-town movies of the early 'forties, such as Kings Row and Shadow of a Doubt, are evident, particularly white wooden-frame houses with porches, mown lawns, picket fences, quiet, tree-lined streets.

Once the location, the principal characters and basic situation are thus adumbrated, the plot becomes noticeably episodic. The various strands of the narrative are tied up at the end of the movie. Nevertheless, this end is less dénouement than temporary finis to the latest incidents of

the Hardys' lives.  The only point made at the conclusion is
that announced in the film's opening--that Andy Hardy does
indeed set off from his home town to Wainwright College.
No loose threads must remain at his point of departure, but
this does not mean that unity of action has been maintained
throughout Double Life or even established in its closing sequences.   Rather, a number of incidents of no strongly probable or necessary interconnection occupy the bulk of the
film's running time.   Each of them illustrates some principle of the Hardys' familial conduct and therefore, since
the Hardys are regarded as one of Carvel's most respected
families, of the small-town code.   Thus, such unity as is
discernible has less to do with the albeit dovetailed incidents
than with the advertisement and, arguably, promotion of a
set of values espoused by Judge Hardy and his kinfolk.

  The principal situations on which the plot turns largely involve questions of integrity and mendacity or compromise.
Judge Hardy is called upon to decide a dispute concerning a
traffic offense between a widowed mother and a lumber company.   Although it is clear that his sympathies are with the
widow, the justice of the case is not.   In discussion with
Andy, the widow voices her fear that courts are for rich
people, to which he replies, "That's not true, Mrs. Steadman.   He wants to do what is right."   Although the legal
dispute is introduced early in the film and referred to
throughout, it is only near the end that the deus ex machina,
a piece of evidence proving the fault of the lumber company,
appears and permits human sympathy and legal propriety to
coincide.   Then, again, Andy intervenes on behalf of his sister Marion's boyfriend, in the hope of persuading Judge Hardy to show leniency for his drunk driving.   His father is im-
movable, however.   "If you take this like a man, you're lia-
ble to be one," he tells the accused in his own house.
"Court adjourned."   Not only does the condemned man accept the verdict, he reproves Andy and Marion for trying to
interfere on his behalf.   Another subplot, or rather strand
of plot, since there is no clear overriding narrative line,
concerns Andy's difficulties with the sale of his old jalopy
and the delivery of a new vehicle from New York.   Above
all, he must deposit twenty dollars in cash in the town bank
to cover a check for that sum, on which delivery of the car
depends.   Resisting the temptation to meet his difficulty in
raising the money by accepting a loan or gift from others,
he is rewarded by the happy surprise that his father has in-
dependently paid an allowance into the bank on his behalf.
His only other problem, playing no strikingly major part in

the movie despite the title, is to sort out his "double life, " the erroneous assumption by not only his regular girlfriend, Polly Benedict, but her undergraduate friend, Sheila, that he has proposed marriage to each of them.   When the mistake is explained and a confession made that he wants them both to write to him at college to impress the other boys, they both agree and kiss him.

The way that luck regularly comes to the aid of the pure in heart and unexpectedly happy solutions are offered to embarrassing but undeserved problems, never more improbably than in the rapid resolution of the double-life trouble, is underlined by the remark made at the point near the end where evidence proving the widow's innocence suddenly turns up.   "It just goes to show everything's wonderful. " Not only is virtue rewarded but such lessons are repeatedly drawn therefrom for the audience's benefit.   Domestic happiness appears nearly total but members of the Hardy family still seem to be compelled to remind each other redundantly of the blissfulness of their relationships.   Thus, Mrs. Hardy recalls fond memories of the child she took to kindergarten while Andy, now eighteen, offers paeans of praise for her tendance in his youth.   Judge Hardy, human enough despite his extreme moral rectitude to indulge in an exchange of slang with his son, is told by him solemnly that he is "the most wonderful father and judge that ever lived. "   This escalates, at the point of Andy's departure from Carvel, at the movie's end to enroll in his father's alma mater, to, "Dad, you're the most wonderful man that ever lived. "   Lest the banter between Andy and Marion be misunderstood to indicate antipathy, the movie's end also includes his surrender of his car to her, whereupon she obliges with "Andy, you're the best. "   The relations between husband and wife seem also to be a model of conjugal affection, though hardly intimacy, to judge by their twin beds and the Judge's blushes when he is gently teased.   "You're the finest wife a man ever had, " Mrs. Hardy is assured by her husband just before Andy leaves home.   With such perfect domestic relations-- Marion's admission to her erring boyfriend, "People don't like people because they're perfect, " sounds almost radical in this movie--it might seem slightly shocking that Andy does not want his father to drive with him to Wainwright College, until it appears in the closing sequences that he is merely afraid that the Faculty will feel that they owe favors to the son of a distinguished alumnus.

Along with obsessional demonstration and enunciation

of domestic happiness goes the ever-present fear of deviation
from social and sexual norms.    How else can the more frequent of the film's running gags be understood?    One of these
concerns Andy's introduction by his sister to the arts of what
is clearly intended to be housewifery.    One of his pals catches
Andy in the act of ironing a woman's slip and photographs the
event.    Later, having already been mortified by his mother's
reminiscences of his long golden curls and lace collar when
he attended kindergarten, Andy is "blackmailed" by his gang
who all possess a copy of the ironing snapshot.    His "double
life" proves to be occasioned less by sexual desire than by
his fear of looking inadequate before future fraternity members.    His regular girlfriend promises in the very first encounter with him to send "sizzling letters," and when his
"double life" is sorted out he has Polly's friend also guar-
anteeing a "bushel of hotsy letters."

        Dread of failure to match male and female stereo-
types permeates the comedy.    Thus, the visiting coed, a
psychology major, dismissed incredulously by Andy before
he meets her, with the remark, "A female brain?", proves
to be a glamorous young woman in a two-piece bathing suit
decorating the side of a swimming pool.    "You couldn't be
that intellectual goon," he compliments her at first sight.
She is, of course, but pains are taken in the movie to have
her apparent intellectualism outweighed by the conventional-
ity of her physical charms and the tameness of her concepts
concerning the relations of the sexes.    She ultimately lends
herself to the bolstering of Andy's uncertain machismo,
sportingly forgetting his potentially bigamous proposal of
marriage.    Marion's boyfriend, Jeff, takes his punishment
for drunk driving like a man, irritated that a girl had made
him look like a "crybaby" by interceding with Judge Hardy.
Even just before leaving for college, when he is unwilling
to board the train without saying farewell to his parents,
Andy is faced with the agonizing question, "Are you a man
or a pantywaist?"    Sadly, his parents arrive in time for
the audience to be denied the answer.    Nevertheless, it is
a question posed implicitly throughout the film, and indeed
the series.    The consequences of failure in the "man" department are alarming, but never revealed.    Even Judge
Hardy, bastion of democracy and the most publicly respected
member of the most prominent Carvel family, would receive
little sympathy if he relinquished the role by, say, suffering
a nervous breakdown, to judge by the family's anguished reactions when he is seen pulling a child's toy wagon along the
road.    Needless to say, he is absorbed in the legal problems

of the widow Steadman's battle with the Lincoln Lumber Company, but Andy's soothing tone and his anxious glances at neighboring houses when he meets his father in this state tell us a great deal about the precariousness of social tolerance in Carvel's middle classes.

Early in the comedy, Abraham Lincoln's profile can be discerned immediately behind Judge Hardy's. When the latter moves away, we discover that Lincoln has been used as an emblem for the Lincoln Lumber Company but the visual surprise of the perfect matching of the American archetype of honesty with the latter-day apostle of his creed has an element of seriousness in it, a promise that the American dream is alive and well in Carvel. (Lest this may seem too forced an interpretation, let it be recalled that in Andy Hardy's Private Secretary (1941), Judge Hardy states, "I know a man who was six foot tall at your age who split rails to earn a meager education. His name was Abraham Lincoln.") It is significant that, whereas Kings Row begins with an optimistic town sign which is then questioned in the rest of the movie, Andy Hardy's Double Life sets a confirmatory seal on the cosiness of the town at the movie's end. As Andy's train pulls out of the station, it passes a sign reading, "YOU ARE NOW LEAVING THE TOWN OF CARVEL. COME BACK SOON, WON'T YOU PLEASE?"

If Carvel was Utopia, it was Louis B. Mayer's conception of it, a specifically American Utopia, suggesting that fairness, equality before the law, respect for family life and for the traditional roles of the sexes, together with a generalized goodwill, were sufficient for the realization of perfect happiness. The chief families, the Hardys and Benedicts, headed by a judge and banker respectively, were unquestioned in their domination of the town. The poor acquiesced in the status quo because through the decency and humanity of such families their rights were assured. Such blacks as appeared were simple-minded, eyeball-rolling retainers, proud to serve the banker's family, for example, unthreatening because twodimensional. As America prepared to enter a world war, this set of images seems to have reassured the nation that traditional virtues were upheld and that society was stable.

In Spielberg's 1941 (1980), there are sequences, strongly reminiscent of Kubrick's Dr. Strangelove (1963), set in a Los Angeles cinema showing Walt Disney's Dumbo. Several servicemen and top brass are in the audience, and the latter become so absorbed in the vicissitudes of Dumbo's

life that the intrusion of news of a Japanese air attack on the
city is bitterly resented.   In the year 1941, Kings Row's release was postponed because of Pearl Harbor and American
audiences were granted the far more regular version of small-
town life as promoted in the small-town series in, for example, Universal's Deanna Durbin vehicle, Nice Girl?   In this
movie, based on a stage play, the three daughters of the local scientist are so charmed by a debonair bachelor scientist
visiting their father from New York that family life is temporarily disrupted and town gossip provoked.   One of the
daughters, bored by her fanatical car-enthusiast boyfriend's
assumptions of her fidelity and trustworthiness, arranges
that she drive the New Yorker back to his home to spend
the night alone with him.   She causes a scandal by arriving
back at dawn, apparently in pajamas and looking highly up-
set.   The dénouement concerns not only the unravelling of
mistaken assumptions about her morality and a restoration
of the town to its usual order, with the familiar romance of
heroine and car-enthusiast (echoed by the longer-lasting
courtship of the postman and the scientist's housemaid) reaffirmed, but a climactic scene in the town's public square
during which Miss Durbin sings to the local enlisted servicemen a patriotic air wherein she "pledges her heart to America."   Such scenes as these and another embodying a Fourth
of July celebration, as well as a twice-performed song about
the quiet virtue of the small town, indicate that beneath the
light, romantic-comedy surface a covert but easily decipher-
able message is being relayed to the audience, wherein American values, those for which the youth of the town has decided to fight, are linked with those reckoned to be rural,
while New York represents slick sophistication and dubious
sexual mores.

      The link between small-town decency and the Ameri-
can war effort in the Second World War is expressly enunciated in Peyton Place and may well explain the unparalleled
popularity of the cozy small-town world of Dr. Christian,
Henry Aldrich and the Hardys in the years immediately prior
to the entry of the U.S. into that war, and the apparent decline in the series' popularity almost immediately after the
fighting ended.

      It may seem a far cry from the relentless optimism
of, say, Andy Hardy's Carvel to Robert Mulligan's 1962 film
of Harper Lee's Pulitzer Prize-winning novel, To Kill A
Mockingbird.   For a start, the latter looks back some thirty
years to the very Depression from which the Hardys and

Aldriches seemed to offer an escape. Rather than a freshly
painted little model town with white picket fences, Mockingbird's setting (again studio-created) is a dusty township of
shacks and broken-down palings--Maycomb, Alabama in 1932.
While poor-white and black townspeople are relegated to the
margins of the Hardy family series, they are the primary
focus of Mockingbird since the movie centers on the trial of
a young black, Tom Robinson, for an alleged sexual assault
on a white woman, one of a poor-white family.  This latter
aspect is of no particular consequence in the Mulligan film
because all the families in town, including that of the lawyer on which it centers, are poor.  Social differentiation is
largely by relative degrees of poverty.  For example, at the
opening of the film, a farmer pays the lawyer, Atticus (Gregory Peck), for work undertaken on his behalf in kind since
he has no cash with which to discharge his debt, and we
learn that, though Atticus's family is poor, it is more com-
fortably off than the farmer's.  However, despite Maycomb's
unprepossessing appearance and the admission of racial in-
tolerance as a crucial element in the town's ethos, there are
close ties between Judge Hardy and Atticus and, thanks to the
charisma of the local lawyer, Maycomb takes on the appearance of a grubby, somewhat impoverished Utopia by the
film's climax.

The fact that the tale of the lawyer's fight on behalf
of Tom Robinson is told from a child's point of view in some
measure accounts for the beatification of Atticus.  Mockingbird begins with Elmer Bernstein's wistful piano music and
the opening of a child's jewel box and after the credits Kim
Stanley's voice speaks as the nostalgic adult version of Atticus's daughter, Scout, six years of age in 1932.  As she
remembers the heat and humidity of that summer, she continues, "There was no hurry, for there was nowhere to go,
nothing to buy and no money to buy it with.  But it was a
time of vague optimism:  Maycomb County had recently been
told that it had nothing to fear but fear itself."  The last
sentence seems sardonic.  We might expect a dissection of
Presidential optimism, a confrontation of official attitudes to
the Depression with sterner realities in such small towns as
this.  Instead, the movie seems to justify the "vague optimism" of the time, finding comfort in neighborliness and always, above all, in Atticus, who singlehandedly converts the
ugliness and disorder surrounding the children into exemplars
and subjects for homiletic discourse on civic duty.

The three youngsters who view and interpret the

incidents in the movie are Atticus's two children, Jem and
Scout, and a visitor from out of town, Dill. The reverence
in which Atticus is held is a child's reverence and the fragmented significance of certain key incidents reflects the partial nature of the children's experience of or access to these
incidents. Near the end, when the siblings cannot see prop-
erly because of darkness, confusion and the encumbrance of
the fancy dress in which they are attired, the audience is
permitted no clearer view of the attack on the children and
their rescue by an unknown benefactor than the children themselves could have had. If the tale is witnessed through the
eyes, and interpreted through the words, of infants, no irony
or distancing seems to be suggested. Scout as an adult has
in no discernible way modified her admiration of her father
or his attitudes.

The incidents which profoundly affect the children's
lives are their father's involvement in the legal defense of
Tom Robinson, and their own involvement with the mysterious Boo Bradley, a retarded man confined in an old dark
house which they have in their imaginations peopled with
monsters. The separate strands of the plot are brought together when the virulently racist Mr. Ewell, father of the
woman falsely claiming sexual assault, tries to harm Atticus's children in revenge for his defense of the alleged assailant and is himself stabbed to death by their rescuer,
Boo Bradley. Atticus's uncompromising stand on behalf of
Tom Robinson, despite his exposure to verbal abuse from
ignorant racists and threats to his children, is depicted as
a vital lesson in citizenship to the children.

There are others. When Scout attempts to avoid
school by suggesting that the teacher is incompetent, Atticus patiently explains that she too must be nervous on her
first day with a new class, and advises his daughter to attempt always to see things from other people's points of
view. A voice-over from the adult Scout commends his
wisdom in the matter. Shortly after, a rabid dog is shot
dead by Atticus. "Didn't you know your Daddy is the best
shot in this county?" the wondering children are asked.
Despite his remarkable skill, he uses it only when there is
no acceptable alternative. The film's curious title is drawn
from a speech in which Atticus recalls his learning as an
adolescent the wastefulness of violence. He believes that he
discovered it to be "a sin to kill a mockingbird ... because
it didn't do anything but make music for us to enjoy." When
he takes on Tom Robinson's defense, he warns his children

that there will be ugly talk about the family at school but
that they must not fight back.

The trial uncovers the truth about the alleged attack
on Mayella Ewell. Her desire for the young black has led
after a number of encounters to an attempted seduction which,
being discovered by her father, has been blamed by the pair
of them on the innocent Robinson. Atticus, like Judge Hardy,
believes in the beneficence of the law. In his oration for the
defense, he interprets the Ewells' behavior as an attempt to
rid themselves of guilt for the unspeakable offense involved
in a white woman kissing a black man. Yet, "In this country, our courts are great levellers. In our courts, all men
are created equal." His faith is misplaced, however. The
verdict is guilty, and Tom Robinson is shot dead when he
later attempts to escape from custody. A mockingbird is
killed.

Another lives, however. Boo Bradley, again a victim of prejudice, in that his spontaneous kindness is un-
noticed and his mental retardation and confinement to the
house are taken by the children as proof of his dangerous-
ness, causes, out of love for Scout and Jem, the death of
Mr. Ewell. The sheriff and Atticus conspire to protect Boo
from the consequences and decide to claim that Ewell fell on
his own knife. To do otherwise would be "like shooting a
mockingbird." Although the American judicial system is
shown to be ultimately as good as its ideals only when
American citizens on jury service free themselves of ignorance and prejudice, the guardians of law--the sheriff
and the lawyer--are at least vindicated in the dénouement
and the emergence of Boo Bradley argues for the rightness
of optimism, faith in the essential goodness of the human
heart.

Mockingbird does not wear its liberal heart on its
sleeve in quite the manner of the small-town series of the
'thirties and 'forties. Justice is not always capable of
achievement, there are vicious townspeople, innocence does
not always triumph. However, the Ewells are so patently
figures of liberal nightmare, so colorfully repellent, that
the audience is spared any implication in their attitudes.
Mayella in particular is so slatternly and stupid that she
could have been created in direct reaction to the opposing
stereotype of white womanhood in Birth of a Nation (1915).
On the other hand, the black characters are so noble in
their suffering, so generous in their reactions to their

oppressors and so humbly grateful to Atticus, that they seem
to have emerged from another sort of tradition--Gone with
the Wind (1939) or Showboat (1951).  These people deserve
sympathy because they are downright superior, in their sense
of inferiority, knowing their place, thankful for the consideration shown to them by a white American lawyer.  While Ewell
spits in Atticus's face, the blacks in the courtroom balcony
stand in silent respectfulness to honor him.  Ultimately, the
blacks of Maycomb are the mockingbirds, the pretty, melodi-
ous creatures who wish no harm.  If only white women could
cope with their desire for black virility, if only poor whites
could see that no possible threat can arise from such unas-
suming neighbors, if only the town would allow Atticus to run
it, Utopia could be realized, Depression or no Depression.

A footnote to this consideration of Hollywood's small-
town Utopias might be that Arthur Penn's The Chase (1966)
attempts to lay to rest forever the myths of Judge Hardy and
Atticus, of Rivers Bend and Carvel and Maycomb.  A Texas
town undergoes a night of violence in which it mercilessly
uses the runaway prisoner played by Robert Redford as
scapegoat.  The one bastion of democratic values, the town
sheriff, played by Marlon Brando, is so viciously beaten up
by the townspeople that no illusions can survive.  His answer is to leave town, abandoning any notion of its rescue.
Arguably, Lillian Hellman's creation of prejudice and ignorance is as unsubtle as anything in To Kill a Mockingbird,
particularly in the venomous hysteric portrayed by Miriam
Hopkins.  The apparent overkill in Hellman's writing and
Penn's direction can best be defended in light of the tradition dominating small-town portrayal for at least three
decades, a tradition which ultimately argues for the fundamental decency of the small town and therefore of America
itself.  Mockingbird would have been difficult to make in the
same way after the death of Martin Luther King.  It is impossible not to see a commentary in The Chase on recent
American history, particularly President Kennedy's assassination in Texas and Lee Harvey Oswald's demise under
police protection.  The law is no defense in this movie.
The notion of one man standing against the tide of aggres-
sion and cynicism is so romantic as to be risible.  Utopia,
like God and democracy, is pronounced dead.

Notes to Chapter 3

1.  Pauline Kael, New Yorker, October 9, 1971.  Cf. Jan

Dawson's linking of the Bogdanovich film with Peyton Place in Sight and Sound, vol. 41, no. 2, spring 1972.

2. The Nurse in Aeschylus' Choephori and the Watchman in his Agamemnon are good examples of the first two uses while the Peasant in Euripides' Electra illustrates the third point.

3. See, for example, Death of a Salesman and A View from the Bridge.

4. See p. 7-8.

5. "Dossier on Melodrama," Screen vol. 18, no. 2, summer 1977, pp. 105-119.

6. David Zinman, Saturday Afternoon at the Bijou, Arlington House, New Rochelle, New York, 1973, p. 386.

7. David Zinman, ibid., p. 369.

8. The attempted revival of the series in 1958, with Mickey Rooney's son in a starring role, Andy Hardy Comes Home, can scarcely be counted as part of the series.

## 4.  HOME IS THE HUNTER

The Second World War has ended.  Somewhere in the United
States, three men await transport back to their hometown.
On their arrival there, service rank is reversed in civilian-
life employment.  Row upon row of redundant planes stand
in the local airfield awaiting wrecking so that their material
may be converted into prefabricated houses.  The hometown's
attitudes seem unaffected by the war.  Only those who have
been at war are marked by it, and they, like the fighter
planes, must discover their peacetime relevance or suffer
destruction.

This summary of William Wyler's epic-length The
Best Years of Our Lives, made in 1946 at precisely the
period which the film seeks to explore, indicates the chief
focus of the film, the tension in America between the comparatively few with direct experience of warfare's physical
and psychic trauma and the majority on whose consciousness
the war has scarcely impinged and who expect demobilization
and reabsorption of servicemen to be simple.  The complacency of the small town and its significance as a force of
reaction and conservatism have seldom been more immediately conveyed, although the movie maintains a quasi-
documentarist stance of apparent objectivity, and its director is specifically praised by André Bazin, for example,
for his "democratic" approach to his material and his refusal to impose an a priori construction upon it.  According to Wyler, "... the picture came out of its period, and
was the result of social forces at work when the war ended.
In a sense, the picture was written by events and imposed
a responsibility, to be true to these events and refrain from
distorting them to our own ends."[1]

Tradition has it that the germ of the idea for the
movie was the impression made on Sam Goldwyn in the summer of 1944 by a newspaper account of war veterans returning to their dimly remembered homes, and that McKinlay

Kantor was commissioned by him to produce a literary treatment of this idea, which he did, in page after page[2] of blank
verse under the title Glory for me. Whatever the truth of
this account, Kantor is mentioned in the movie's credits as
the author of the novel on which the screenplay is based.

Wyler's concern with immediacy and the illusion, at
least, of actuality is indicated in, for example, his choice
of a nonprofessional handicapped ex-serviceman, Harold Russell, to play the part of the handicapped ex-sailor character.
Metro-Goldwyn-Mayer's publicity department played up the
concern of the director and cast with authenticity, in their
handouts on the making of the movie, providing such information as that three of the women players--Teresa Wright,
Cathy O'Donnell and Myrna Loy--purchased clothes that
seemed to them appropriate for their screen characters'
wear and became accustomed to wearing them for some
weeks before shooting began.[3] The stress by those concerned with the making of the movie on its contemporaneity
and sincerity, the reception of it by its most influential admirers as a particularly open and even-handed exploration
of post-war social problems, may combine to blind us to the
remarkably schematic nature of the movie's narrative and
the unusually painstaking selection of carefully observed detail to ease the viewer into the acceptance of certain positions on American society vis-à-vis the reabsorption of war
veterans.

The bare-bones summary of the movie in the first
paragraph of this chapter needs some fleshing out before
further exploration of it may illustrate the movie's covert
but detectable theses.

---

The narrative of Best Years proceeds through a number of
episodes, or, more accurately, stages in reintegration, of
the three principal male characters, beginning with that part
of the story where they are self-evidently outside their hometown of Boone City, returned from overseas but still awaiting a flight home. When their flight is called, Fred Derry
(Dana Andrews), an air-force captain, Al Stephenson (Fred-
ric March), an army sergeant, and Homer Parrish (Harold
Russell), a sailor, meet on the B17 taking them home and
strike up a friendship.

On arrival in Boone City, Homer hesitantly accepts

the attentions of his girlfriend Wilma (Cathy O'Donnell), embarrassed by the claw-like substitutes for hands which he
now has to wear. Al's return to his wife (Myrna Loy) and
children is heartfelt, while Fred is at first unable to locate
his wife who has taken a nightclub job and a downtown apartment during his absence.

Each of the veterans becomes aware of problems in
his return to domestic life. At home, Al finds that his son
is interested only in more technologically sophisticated warfare than that which he has just experienced and that his
daughter Peggy (Teresa Wright) has become an adult. Homer, nervous as his future in-laws discuss post-war economic
problems and the need for Homer to find a job, proves unable to hold a glass in his metal "hands" and runs out of his
parents' house. Fred, unable to make contact with his wife,
finds solace at a bar run by Homer's Uncle Butch (Hoagy
Carmichael). Here, the three men are reunited and Fred
meets Peggy.

Difficulties at work prove worse than the domestic
tensions. Fred, worried by his wife Marie's (Virginia
Mayo) apparent indifference to his return, is humiliated by
having to forget military rank in order to take employment
as a soda jerk and part-time assistant to a man who, before
the war, was his assistant. Al, welcomed back to the Cornbelt Trust Company and promoted to vice-president on the
basis of his war experience's relevance to the bank's deal-
ings with ex-GIs, finds his judgment questioned as soon as
he promises an ex-navy man without collateral a bank loan.

In the second sequence at Butch's bar, peacetime
priorities begin to thwart the friendship between Al and
Fred, and the latter is persuaded by Al to break off his
liaison with Peggy.

At the soda fountain, where Homer is visiting Al, a
customer questions the value of Homer's sacrifice of his
hands in a war which America was mistaken to enter. Fred
is dismissed for helping Homer to assault him.

Homer is at last reunited with Wilma when, showing
no revulsion at the removal of his artificial hands as he
prepares to go to bed, she tenderly helps him and embraces
him. Fred, however, finally separates from Marie when he
finds her with another, more prosperous, ex-serviceman.
Ignoring his parents' pleas, he heads for the airfield to catch

the first plane out.  In one of the rare "epic" shots of this
movie, there is an aerial view of legions of dismantled
planes lined up on the airfield as Fred walks among them.
He enters one of them and the camera moves to simulate a
flight takeoff while the engine noise on the sound track increases in volume.  Fred's trance is interrupted by a wrecker who jokes about the glamor that airmen enjoyed while he
was down with the tanks.  Fred's willingness to learn the
methods of turning plane material into prefabricated houses
wins him over.

The final sequence, which reunites the veterans, centers on Homer's wedding to Wilma in the front room of his
parents' house.  Al and Fred seem reconciled.  As the marriage vows are made, there is a closeup of Fred's face, then
Peggy's.  With great dexterity, Homer manages to maneuver
the ring on to Wilma's finger and kisses the bride amid general rejoicing.  Fred and Peggy, spatially isolated from the
other guests, kiss in the background.  Fred admits that he
has "no money, no decent place to live."  Peggy, however,
smiles and kisses him.

---

A movie of such visual inventiveness, such sophistication of
narrative technique (not to mention such sheer length) as
Best Years is in itself a worthy object of study.  The reader may nevertheless reasonably ask why it occupies a large
place in a book that selectively examines the small-town
movie.

Is Boone City, it may well be asked, a small town
in any case?  Certainly, the British reviewers of the period
seemed confused concerning the exact status of the town in
which the movie is largely set.  Bewilderment about the dimensions and nature of the town seems to have resulted in
multifarious descriptions of the same place and the same inhabitants.  Only C. A. Lejeune, in the Observer newspaper,
went so far as to use the epithet "urban," of the characters.
Other critics and reviewers, clearly less impressed by the
visuals which indicate a large, multi-faceted and socially
layered, therfore city-sized, locale than by an undefined
sense of something smaller, talked of Boone City as "a
modest town" (Dilys Powell in the Sunday Times), or "a
medium-sized American town" (Alexander Shaw in the Spectator).  Such various gradations abounded with, for example,
Elizabeth Frank using the term "small town" and Paul Holt
"little home town."

This bewilderment among critics about such an apparently basic and mundane point is unusually fruitful.
Metro-Goldwyn-Mayer was anxious to suggest the authenticity
of interiors by taking extreme care to ensure that credibly
modest dimensions were permitted for room sizes in the re-
constructions of houses on sound stages.  It was no less anxious to emphasize the reality of its Boone City and so took
very seriously the task of discovering an existing American
town to stand for the exteriors of Boone City.  Cincinnati,
Ohio was finally chosen for the aerial shots in the early
homecoming section of the movie and for certain exteriors.
Cincinnati is, and was then, no mean city.  How could it be
that a Boone City of Cincinnati's dimensions could be described as a "small" or "little" town?  The B17 flies over
outskirts for some considerable period.  The taxi taking the
ex-servicemen home from the airfield seems to cover considerable distance, moving from lower-middle-class suburbia
(Homer's parents' home) to an imposing "citified" brick residence of family apartments that would not have been unexpected in such an essentially urban movie as The Thin Man
(1934), then to a grimy neighborhood of trash cans, shacks
and railroad tracks.  When Al takes his family out on his
first night home, there is a distinctly urban montage of
drinks, jitterbuggers and café signs, to indicate the progress
of their revels.  Fred's wife, Marie, earns her living in a
nightclub and seems to be sufficiently anonymous in her downtown apartment to lead the life that she chooses, free from
her in-laws' knowledge.  How can such confusion on the part
of the critics be justified?  Either they have been unusually
careless and simply missed the signs that an urban community is being explored or their very attentiveness to the movie
has caused the confusion.  The latter seems the likelier explanation.

While some Americans, notably the inhabitants of
Cincinnati, might have recognized the true identity of Boone
City, it is evident that the filmmakers invited no such iden-
tification and in fact deliberately avoided the temptation to
set the movie in an existent and recognizable American city,
presumably because Best Years would have been an entirely
different movie, its power dissipated, if Americans and others could have identified the setting with certainty.  The important aspect of the setting is its imprecision.  Above all,
it is a hometown, with all the connotations that this word
conveys, not strictly a little hometown, as one reviewer
termed it, but a hometown with, therefore, the feel of a
small town despite all the visual evidence to the contrary.
If this analysis of critical confusion is acceptable, it sug-

gests at least one fascinating possibility, that "hometown"
and "small town" become, in the context of American popular art, interchangeable, that, paradoxically, the small town
in that context has therefore little to do with smallness of
dimensions or paucity of population.  The American small
town in American movies is thus not recognizable on the
basis of size, or, rather, lack of size, but on that of its
presentation--attitudes, sense of self-containment or tradition
--coupled with its being not readily identifiable as a particular city and not noticeably citified in architecture or, specially, in range of ethnic groups.

What, then, is the special appeal of the so-called
small town in a movie dealing with the return of American
veterans to their home?  An examination of the methods of
the film may help us to suggest the usefulness of such a
location for this particular story.

If we consider the homecoming sequences near the
start of the movie, a number of pointers to its overall
strategies are discoverable.  First of all, it seems remarkable that the three men thrown together by chance are
from each of the armed services--Homer from the navy, Al
from the army, Fred from the air force.  (Equally remarkable is the reversal of "rank" for the latter two, in that the
air-force captain was, and once again becomes, a soda jerk,
and a demoted soda jerk at that, while the army sergeant,
the most successful of the three in civilian terms, is further promoted on his return, so that the contrast is underlined with particular force. )  On the flight home, Al offers
the information that he has been married for twenty years;
Fred responds by saying that he was married for just twenty
days before he left for the war.  Homer then completes this
particular range of possibilities by indicating that he is not
yet married, just dating the girl next door.

The movie takes special care, on their arrival in
Boone City, to indicate the social milieu of these three
characters and permits details of setting and grouping to
signal, despite Bazin's contention of Wyler's freedom from
a priori construction of meaning, the differences between
these men's experience of civilian life.  Thus, Homer
alights from the taxi onto a street of trees and unpreten-
tious wooden-frame two-storied houses.  Al stops at an
imposing brick building and walks up a marquee-covered
entranceway to the desk clerk.  Fred dejectedly joins his
parents in the stratum of the other-side-of-the-tracks, the

world of the poor, working-class or down-and-out.   Each
return to the family is differentiated.   Homer, for example,
hesitates before leaving the taxi.   Then, his parents run to
hug him and Wilma comes through the hedge dividing her
house from his parental home.   He accepts his parents' embrace and stands stiffly unresponsive when Wilma holds him.
His mother cries.   A view from behind the screen door of
the homecoming scene underlines the suggestion of distance
and reserve.   The model nature of the family, warm and
supportive, to which Al belongs is signalled by the symmetry
and cohesiveness of the welcomers' positioning.   As Al is
taken into the apartment by his children--one son, one
daughter--they stand on either side of their father as he
walks down the corridor towards his wife.   At the moment
of total reunion, husband and wife embrace and son and
daughter are each granted a close-up.   Fred's homecoming
is more fragmented, our attention being drawn away from
the parents--Fred's dyed-blonde mother and hard-drinking
father--by the clearly visible train and cars moving in the
background and the irruption of train noise on the sound
track as Fred leaves on discovering that his wife has taken
a nightclub job and a downtown apartment.

In the face of all this evidence, it is impossible not
to conclude that these three individuals, far from being
"found, " carry a heavily symbolic weight as divergent types
of American manhood.   While they may be painstakingly
characterized and individualized, they are ultimately repre-
sentatives of social strata in American civilian life.   What
we are being offered is a study of Everyman, or, more accurately, of a triple-bodied EveryAmerican.   (At a time
when American cinema largely excluded racial, sexual and
social minorities from serious consideration except in movies which were marketed as "problem pictures" and when
women's concerns tended to be relegated to the sub-genre
of melodrama known as "the woman's picture, " it may be
anachronistic to deem it a study of EveryWASP. )   In its
time, it is difficult to see how a more all-encompassing
view of male America's social problems immediately after
the war could have been offered.

Now, to return to the principal investigation, the attraction of the so-called small town in a movie of this sort,
it is evident that these representative figures discover all
their problems, though not necessarily, it transpires, the
solutions to these problems, in a social setting.   Particu-
larization of locale might be fatal, since a movie about

"EveryAmerican" loses much of its point if there can be
comfortable responses to the problems posed by it, such as
that these social attitudes and conflicts are peculiar to the
big city.   The movie must concern an area that Americans
would accept as repositories of all that is best in American
aspirations, since these characters must be seen against a
background which is America herself.   America is not, it
seems, to be equated with, say, New York City but the more
modest small communities of the Boone City variety.   If the
three principal characters stand for all-American manhood,
Boone City stands for America.   The particular piece of evidence which might be cited to justify this account of the
choice of setting is the flight home in the B17.   This plane
trip suggests that America herself is under review and that
the township destination may bear the symbolic weight of the
"typically American community" which was discerned in
Boone City by one reviewer. [4]   At take-off, Homer, Al and
Fred sit in the nose of the B17 to "get a view of the U.S.A."
As they approach journey's end, the portentousness of the
descent to Boone City suggests something more universal
than the literal event.   At dawn, the men awaken and Homer
watches the sunrise.   In particular, the music on the soundtrack is stately and "nationalistic" in the manner that some
of Elgar could be loosely so called.   It is inappropriate to
a sentimental journey's end, highly appropriate to a proud
return to the heart of a country worth fighting for.

        The small town is furthermore attractive to Wyler
because it traditionally embodies continuity, resistance to
change, confidence in its own beneficent workings.   "The
old home town hasn't changed very much, " says one of the
veterans reassuringly after the plane has passed over the
town's golf club, high school and plentiful greenery.   In
Best Years, this conception of the value of changelessness
as well as the accuracy of belief in this town's unchanged
nature is consistently scrutinized.   Changelessness may be
all very well for Al, with his comfortable domestic life and
secure, financially rewarding job.   For Fred, it is what he
most dreads.   When he is reunited with his wife, she seems
unimpressed at first and then, on seeing his uniform and
decorations, excited and happy.   Later, Fred appears in
civvies, Marie begs him to wear his uniform for their night
on the town.   "Now you look like yourself, " she reassures
him, to his evident chagrin, when he dons his uniform.   Her
further remark, about their being able now to return to
where they started, only adds to his misery.

In any case, there is abundant evidence that change, rather than permanence, has become the rule. This sense of change is fostered not simply by, for example, Homer's loss of his hands since that misfortune seems to the responsibility of the war, and the initial signs are that the stability of the hometown can be used as a counter-balance against the social and personal upheavals attendant on warfare. (War itself, incidentally, has changed disconcertingly. This seems to be the point of the sequence where Al, whose reabsorption promised to be the least problematic, finds that he is in dispute with his son over, ironically, warfare. A new element enters the range of the film's concerns at this point--that the conventional fighting of the recent war, which is, interestingly, never explored from a moral or political viewpoint by the veterans even when an adverse interpretation of the war's advisability is offered later in the movie, is outdated by technological advance. Al, offering such souvenirs of the fighting as a samurai sword, finds his son's acceptance polite but cool, because he is more interested in discussion of Hiroshima and of the effects of radioactivity. Dispirited, Al talks of the necessity of international cooperation for survival.)

The hometown, appearances to the contrary, has changed considerably under the advances of capitalism within it. Early on in the movie, Fred, waiting for a flight home, is preceded in the allocation of plane seats by a businessman with golf clubs. This hint of peacetime priorities is considerably amplified later in the movie. When, for example, Fred tries to get his old job back, he finds that the drugstore he once knew has been taken over by the Medway chain. As he walks through the shop he has to pick his way past a multiplicity of product signs and counters, while one of the employees talks with another about the danger of having their jobs taken over by ex-servicemen. While Fred shows signs that he dreads returning to the same world that he once knew in Boone City, the changes overtaking the town can thus hardly offer him comfort. His pre-war boss is now a Medway employee, and, when he asks the manager for work, he finds that the best offer he can elicit is that he be a part-time assistant to his former assistant, the employee who foresaw danger in the return of ex-servicemen. Al, on the other hand, has been promoted as a result of his war experience to vice-president of the Cornbelt Trust Company. Reference is made by the president of the bank to the G. I. Bill of Rights, which creates a need for a man "who under-

stands soldiers' problems." Yet, Al finds his judgment
questioned when he promises an ex-navy man without collateral a bank loan to help him buy a farm.

At these points, the reality of American values seems
to be under attack or, at the very least, under scrutiny.
This scrutiny has a purpose beyond the ostensible examination of community. At first sight, the movie seems to sacrifice all consideration of the war and its justification for
the apparently sole purpose of this examination of small-
town values and their credibility. Yet, a closer reading
will reveal that, should American doubts about the country
in the guise of the generalized hometown be supported or
substantiated by the movie, the war's (assumed) justification
immediately crumbles. If American involvement in the war
is as morally right as all the principal characters seem to
take it to be, this is because what the characters believe
they were fighting for--in this movie, the fulfilment that they
believe can be theirs in the home country--is real and good.
The serious doubts that are raised about their perceptions of
home at times threaten the characters' confidence about this
war, which is tantalizingly unquestioned. Or almost unquestioned.

For most of the movie, the war is treated as a catalyst to an examination of civilian attitudes to ex-servicemen.
The scene where Fred's citations for bravery are read out
by Fred's father or that which reveals the majesty of the
fighter planes lined up on the Boone City airfield seems to
be free of all irony. Because the war is, then, a proud fact
which seems to require no interpretation or justification,
Wyler's inclusion of the sequence where a soda-fountain customer questions the usefulness of Homer's self-sacrifice is
all the more interesting. "For what did you sacrifice yourself?" he asks. His view of the war is that America was
pushed into it "by the radicals in Washington" when she
"should have fought the Reds." "I'm selling plain old-
fashioned Americanism," he objects when he is ordered out.
Homer's physical attack on the customer seems to be approved by Fred and to represent a statement that, whatever
may be wrong in America, the decision to fight was unques-
tionably right. What else is conveyed by the rescuing and
appropriating of the little American flag medallion by Homer
from a man who announced that he was selling "good old-
fashioned Americanism?" However, the quick dispatch of a
hostile interpreter of America's wisdom in entering the war
does not silence the questions that the sequence raises.

Until an outsider asks, nobody dares to question whether
Homer is reconciled to having lost his hands and, apparently, his happiness and dignity, in the fight. Moreover, Homer seems not to ask himself.

Fred comes temporarily much closer to renouncing
whatever reasons he had for gallantry in the war when he
asks his parents to throw away his citations, but his prov-
idential rescue so shortly after his loss of faith seems to
negate the gesture. Al's uneasiness about the general un-
willingness to honor governmental promises to demobilized
servicemen bubbles up and is expressed at the bank dinner
at which he is a speaker but the manner in which he wins
his hearers over to his point of view again negates the
doubts that underlie his speech. If the presumably fascistic
propagandist in the soda fountain is wrong about "good old-
fashioned Americanism," why is Fred immediately sacked
for, presumably, putting political principles before business
interests; why is such cynicism about the value of the returning veterans shown by those fearful for their jobs or
the bank's security; why is the businessman in the very
opening sequence given preferential treatment to the airman?

Since there is not even rudimentary political analysis
of the war, one might assume patriotism to play a highly
significant part. In the flight sequence, the beauty of rural
and small-town America is alluded to, and the pride of the
watchers, together with the solemnity of the score, suggests
at least nostalgia for the home country and a great deal
more about the principals' attitudes to the U.S.A.

Since the war is at this stage of little controversiality,
the weight of the film is concentrated in the treatment of the
veterans by a community. If this film had been set in New
York, Chicago or Los Angeles, say, the force would have
been dissipated since these cities do not traditionally claim
to represent community or an ideal setting for family life,
and the demobilized heroes would hardly expect the spirit of
competition or the need for material security as a basis for
a happy marriage to be waived or modified for their sakes.
While the swallowing up of Fred's original drugstore by the
Medway chain indicates an uncaring, commercialized side of
Boone City, it is the lack of impact from the war on what
might be expected to be a caring community that dismays
the returning veterans. It is this which is, however, finally
denied by the movie. The community does care, it would
seem, although evidence to the contrary could produce temporary uncertainty on the point.

If unquestioning patriotism be posited as the explanation of Homer's and Fred's stoicism about the war, the movie offers soothing reassurances to deny the significance of
the evidence of materialism, cynicism and isolationism in
the civilian population.   The fact that everything works out
well is a sign that the surface impression of civilians as
materialistic or selfish is only that, a surface impression.
Homer's parents are as self-sacrificing and generous-
hearted as he could hope, Wilma sincerely loving enough to
make her parents' hardheaded attitudes seem ultimately deviant.   Al, by the force of his personal integrity and rhetoric,
converts the bank to the policy of generosity to ex-servicemen
that the government had already promised.   Fred, disappointed in the shallowness of his wife, finds understanding
on his first night home and by a lucky accident is offered
the worthwhile job that he has despaired of acquiring in
Boone City.   The peacetime differences of class and opportunity are blurred and rendered nugatory by generalized
goodwill and decency.

Such fault-finding as there is seems to be inwardly
directed surprisingly often.   There is, for example, a sequence in which Homer, unemployed, works off his energy
in shooting practice in the garage, while his little sister
whispers to the local children about his affair with Wilma.
They try, once Homer and Wilma are together in the garage, to peep through the window.   Misinterpreting their
curiosity, Homer thrusts his hooks through the glass "to
give them a better look."   When Homer shocks his sister's
friends by smashing his artificial hands through the garage
window, it is Homer's mistaken assumptions that cause the
misery.   His treatment of his family and of Wilma turns
out to be entirely mistaken.   It is only he that holds back
from them, wrongly suspecting them of pity, while they run
to embrace him.   By learning to surmount his handicap, in
playing the piano with his uncle, and displaying his "manual"
skill at the wedding (this a demonstration of the player's
own acquisition of dexterity), he rids himself of all false
impressions of the attitudes of his loved ones.   Fred, too,
is clearly accused of negative thinking when he seeks to
jump on the first plane out of Boone City.   As so frequently in westerns and in small-town movies, the hero is told
that the rest of the world may be very much the same, that
he has to face his problems where he is, that escape to a
better place is a foolish dream.   What the result would be
if any of Homer's family had expressed revulsion or amuse-
ment at his handicap or if Fred had not been lucky enough

to get into conversation with the wrecker, it may be idle to speculate, but it reamins true that the solutions do not seem to arise organically from the "reality" observed, and that beneath the assurance of Goldwyn's small town lie some disturbing unanswered--and even unasked--questions.

---

Some thirty years after the making of Best Years, Michael Cimino's The Deer Hunter again explores the impact of war experience on three men from the same hometown. In the credits sequence of Cimino's movie, the financing studio is identified as EMI, so that in one sense it is a British film, but only from the limited (if crucial) perspective of budgeting. The cast, the settings, the sensibilities are peculiarly American.

Superficially, there are evident thematic and structural links between Best Years and The Deer Hunter. Apart from the concentration on three servicemen, there is the relegation of female characters to marginal or supportive status (so that women are given the audience's attention only in so far as their histories and attitudes relate to the heroes' fortunes), the significance for the men of homecoming, the equation of leaving town with irresponsibility (or even, in the later movie, with madness); the sense in which the United States itself seems to be epitomized by the town, and the location of key sequences in a friendly barroom. This said, the differences are more striking. Wyler's characters are of different social backgrounds, while Cimino's all work at the same steel mill, sharing the same pastimes and friends. Wyler's town is, to all appearances, wholly WASP with only one "ethnic" surname, Polish in fact, occurring in the sequence where Al offers the ex-navy man, Novak, a bank loan without collateral. Cimino's seems entirely composed of Russian immigrants with an apparently strong cultural cohesion, expressed in the rituals of the Russian Orthodox Church and the more mystical comradeship of the hunt. Whereas Wyler begins with the heroes' return, war ended, Cimino spreads his net wider to cover experiences before, during and after the men's entry into warfare. While Wyler's war seems relatively unexplored except in terms of its effects on the heroes' expectations of peacetime, it would seem that Cimino attempts some sort of statement about "his" war, although this question is at the heart of the controversy surrounding the later film and deserves fuller analysis. The Deer Hunter involves a much more contentious

conflict, far more widely and bitterly debated in America's
history than the Second World War--Vietnam.   Finally, Wyler's film ends as Cimino's begins--with a wedding.

Whereas Boone City was constructed from studio interiors and some soundstage streets intermingled with Cincinnati, Ohio exteriors, the American setting for The Deer
Hunter, Clairton, Pennsylvania, is an amalgam of a surprising number of steel towns.   In Cimino's words, "In order to
fully portray [sic] the little steel town in which the main
characters live, we literally had to create a town, because
invariably wherever we went, no one town had all the elements ... I decided to take a tremendous gamble and create
the ideal town from eight different towns."5   Thus, the fictitious town of Clairton is composed of shots of Mingo Junc-
tion, Struthers and Cleveland, Ohio, Weirton and Follansbee,
W. Virginia, Duquesne and Pittsburgh, Pennsylvania, while
the hunting slopes of the Alleghenies are in fact "played" by
the altogether more majestic Cascade Range in Washington
state.   The clash of realist and cinematic epic traditions is
evident in this latter substitution for the modest Alleghenies
and particularly in the "re-siting" of St. Theodosius' Russian
Orthodox Cathedral, appropriate to a town of Cleveland's dimensions and importance, in Clairton.   (Incidentally, the
Vietnam sequences were shot in Thailand.)

Cimino talks of three acts in his film, which he discerns as the town, the mountains and Vietnam. 6   Since dramatic acts are normally coterminous with chronological (in
terms of a play's performance in time, rather than "internal" dramatic time) segments of action, Cimino's analysis
is unhelpful, though it does offer some notion of the principal spheres of action.   If there are three acts, they are
surely, 1) the hometown rituals of the wedding and the hunt,
before the departure to Vietnam, 2) Vietnam, 3) the return
home. 7   The clarity of a plot summary of a movie as long
and complex as The Deer Hunter ought to be enhanced by
adherence to this division of the movie's action.

Act I Clairton before the three principals depart for Vietnam.

Michael (Robert De Niro), Nick (Christopher Walken)
and Steven (John Savage) are introduced along with other
workmates at the end of a week of work in the local steelworks.   Although it is the day of Steven's wedding, their
talk is of the hunt.   While wedding preparations are made
by the local womenfolk, the men drink and play pool in a

barroom owned by one of their friends, John (George Dzundas). One of the bridesmaids, Linda (Meryl Streep), after a violent assault upon her by her drunken father, is offered refuge in the house shared by Michael and Nick for the period of their absence.

The wedding service takes roughly five minutes of screen time, the wedding celebration four times as much. Cimino's inspiration for the epic wedding party would seem to be both Coppola's The Godfather (1971) and Norman Jewison's screen version of Fiddler on the Roof (1971). He alternates communal folk dances and inebriated choruses, speeches from the stage about the departure of Michael, Nick and Steven "to proudly serve their country" underneath a banner in which "God and country" are coupled, as if to indicate a synonym, with several revelatory vignettes or incidents. Michael skirts around the possibility of beginning a relationship with Linda, but it is Nick who finally proposes to her when she catches the bridal bouquet. Two incidents disturb the euphoria of the celebration. An uninvited Green Beret dampens the newly enlisted men's enthusiasm for Vietnam by his obvious contempt for their eagerness to get into action; a drop of red wine is spilled on her white gown by Angela, the bride, as she and Steven drain a good-luck cup.

Next morning, Michael, Nick and Steven go deer hunting in the mountains with some of their friends from town. Michael, who believes that the essence of the hunt is "the one shot," brings down a stag with a single shot. In the evening, the stag is brought home, tied to the hood of their car, by the seemingly drunken hunters. Inside the bar, John plays Chopin's Nocturne in G Minor. The men grow quieter and are photographed in a series of close-ups as they listen. After the piece finishes, there is a prolonged silence, finally interrupted by the sound of helicopter blades. . . .

Act II Vietnam.

The screen fills with the greenery of a Vietnamese village. Flimsy village huts are blasted, women and children huddled in an underground shelter, blown up by a hand grenade, as pigs root around in the undergrowth. A wounded woman and child emerge from the dying, to be shot by a Vietcong soldier. In frenzy, Michael burns him to death with a flamethrower. As the pigs fight over what may be scraps of clothing or of flesh, helicopters arrive, reuniting Nick and Steven with Michael.

Immediately thereafter, the scene changes to a river, where prisoners are being detained in waist-high water underneath a bamboo hut occupied by their Vietcong captors. One at a time is pulled up, to be forced to play a game of Russian roulette with a fellow-prisoner while the guards place bets on the outcome of each shot. Steven, terrified by the ordeal, receives a flesh wound in the scalp. Together Michael and Nick contrive a ruse by which they kill their captors and escape downriver with Steven whose legs are now severely damaged. Nick is rescued by helicopter, but Michael sacrifices his chance of similar rescue in order to tend Steven.

After a period in the U.S. Army Hospital in Saigon, Nick is invited to watch a game of Russian roulette played by professionals on whom spectators of the game place bets. In suicidal disgust, Nick snatches the gun, holding it at a player's head and then his own, pulling the trigger without mishap. As he flees from the hut, Michael who was in the roulette audience runs after him into the street.

Act III Homecoming.

Michael, having avoided the welcome-home party planned by his friends, returns to his home to find Linda waiting for him. Nothing is known of Nick except that he is AWOL. As he returns to the regular town routine, visiting the steelworks and John's bar, he discovers that Angela is ill, unable or refusing to speak to anybody, and that Steven is in hospital. His attempt to return to deer hunting with his male friends proves abortive. Confronted with the opportunity to kill a stag, he finds himself unable to do so. Visiting Steven in the Veterans Administration Hospital, Michael discovers that he, like Drake in Kings Row, has had both legs amputated and seems to have made the choice of self-incarceration. "I'm going to take you home," Michael tells a protesting Steven.

First, however, he returns to Saigon in the last days of the war, and finds Nick, dazed with drugs, in his new role as "the American," a master of Russian roulette. Facing Nick at the game table, Michael attempts to restore his memory by a repetition of the original roulette incident when they were prisoners of the Vietcong and by allusions to their life in Clairton. "One shot," declares Nick, invoking another memory of Clairton, and laughs as he pulls the trigger to release the fatal bullet.

A television picture of the retreat has the newscaster signing off from "the last chapter in the history of American involvement in Vietnam."

Nick's funeral service is held in St. Theodosius'. After the burial, the mourners sit to have breakfast together in John's bar. Steven is with the group, as is Angela, who can now speak. John gives way to tears as he cooks alone in the kitchen. He begins to sing "God Bless America," and when he returns to the group they all join falteringly in the song. "Here's to Nick" is the toast, and the frame freezes.

———————

Reactions to The Deer Hunter are almost as divided and polarized as those to its ostensible subject, American involvement in Vietnam. If indeed the film is "about" Vietnam, then the war is sufficiently recent and the suffering, not least in terms of a loss of certainty about American self-image, sufficiently severe to explain the virulence with which Cimino's movie has been attacked or, for that matter, the enthusiasm with which it has been received in other quarters. While Wyler's homecoming movie is closer in time to the war against which it is set, there was nothing like the ban on cinematic references to, let alone treatments of, that war which seems to have obtained during and immediately after Vietnam. While the more graphic and detailed scenes of violence in popular American movies set in the United States, particularly in westerns, during the late 'sixties and early 'seventies have been taken as evidence of oblique commentary by filmmakers on an unmentionable subject, the only American movie during the Vietnam period which squarely addressed itself to the war was the insultingly simplistic affirmation of the war's justification embodied in The Green Berets (1968). Francis Ford Coppola's Apocalypse Now (1979) and Karel Reisz's Dog Soldiers (1978) appeared around the same time as The Deer Hunter, indicating publicly that the unvoiced embargo on the war as controversial cinematic subject was now lifted. Of these movies, only the last has been picked out for special censure, as if it were a slightly more sophisticated, and therefore all the more sinister, version of John Wayne's Vietnam movie.

In some respects, the criticism, if not its unusually heated nature, seems justifiable. The selectivity of the Vietnam coverage is noticeable and would seem downright

dishonest to an audience with unhappy knowledge of My-Lai.
For example, in the first Vietnam sequence, we see inno-
cents being casually slaughtered by Vietcong. Immediately
thereafter, their prisoners are used for the sadistic pleas-
ures of their guards. In these Russian roulette sequences,
a prisoner shoots a bullet into his own head and, as blood
spurts from the wound, his captors laugh. Rats move
around the corpses in the bamboo trap farther out in the
river, a trap into which Steven is lowered while still alive.
Thus, it is clearly established that the Americans' violence
is purely that of reaction against unbearable savagery. Michael's burning of the Vietcong grenade-thrower invites the
audience's complicity as does his shooting of all the guards.
Such heroism as is evidenced in the movie is American, the
bestiality is entirely that of the Vietnamese, including, in
the Saigon roulette-game sequences, the South Vietnamese,
unless we count the cynicism and amorality of the French
character who recruits young men for the roulette game as
a comment on the old French imperialism which arguably
led to America's untenable position in Southeast Asia.

        Charges of racial stereotyping would appear justifi-
able, too. The Vietcong are sweaty, grinning, emotionless
automata, whose only impulses are those of cruelty. The
sequence with a South Vietnamese prostitute is instructive
too. Within Saigon's Mississippi Queen bar, a parody of
American bars back home, with Oriental girls dancing almost naked on the bar counter, Nick is picked up by a
Vietnamese girl whom he tries to imagine as Linda. The
grimness of the dirty bedroom, with the girl's baby sobbing
loudly, destroys all hope of such fantasizing and he leaves.
She is rejected by Nick for her evident lack of hygiene and
her evident disregard for her baby. Racial stereotyping is
equally detectable also in Act I. Steven's mother (Shirley
Stoler) is played as a thickly accented caricature of the
Eastern European peasant woman in her heavy boots and
shapeless apparel, particularly when she invades the haven
of male camaraderie represented by John's barroom to drag
Steven out like a naughty schoolboy. Again, the treatment
of the wedding celebrations tends to a folksiness of a sort
that jars with the presentation of Clairton elsewhere.

        At the 29th Berlin Film Festival, the Vietnamese
were sufficiently disturbed by their portrayal in Cimino's
film to ask the Russians to protest on their behalf. Distinguished participants in the Festival, such as Julie Christie, sympathized with the Eastern bloc's hostility to the film,

on the grounds that it is the very portrayal of a foreign nation as "subhuman" which encourages aggressive warfare upon it.  The last sequence, when the group sings "God Bless America, " has added to that interpretation of the movie which sees it as a blindly patriotic and highly political, reactionary attempt to obfuscate the issues with sentimentality.

Cimino's apparently naïve response has scarcely helped his case.  His view that the film is not political seems disingenuous or else foolish, in that he compares it with Gone With the Wind, a movie which may well be read politically as a justification for a slave-owning society.  His critics' certainty that the film constitutes a relatively transparent statement about Vietnam could be thought to be given a firmer basis in such statements from Cimino as, "Vietnam was, after all, the war of my generation, and so I feel extremely privileged to have had a chance to make a major film about something so important ... to make a picture about an event that changed the country for all time."[8]  In an interview, he recognizes that, despite his protestations about the film's apolitical nature, there are bound to be criticisms of the way he set about making it--"and there will be a lot of room to do so!"[9]  Defensive about the dominance of Russian roulette in the Vietnamese sequences, he has taken refuge in statements about reports in Southeast Asian newspapers of "this sort of thing going on, " but seems to have abandoned any claim of authenticity when faced by objectors who have found not a shred of evidence to suggest that this was part of Vietcong practice, changing his stance to a defense for the roulette as a metaphor for the American presence in Vietnam.

Public reaction to the work, as far as it is capable of being judged through newspaper reports, for example, would suggest that it could offer opportunity for a self-indulgent wallow, at once relieving Americans of guilt and allowing a catharsis in the shared sufferings of these "typical" fellow-countrymen.  "The film that could purge a nation's guilt, " ran the headline over Simon Winchester's article on the film from New York, in the Daily Mail of December 19, 1978.  Time magazine on December 9, 1978 claimed that what happens to the men is "a paradigm of what happened to the U.S. "

With all these concessions to their side, there remain nagging doubts about the more strident critics' positions

on The Deer Hunter.    Their case is seriously weakened by
a number of factors.    One is that attention is directed to
merely one "act" of the movie, the Vietnam portion, and
consideration of the lengthier and more lovingly detailed
"acts" concerning Clairton and the deer hunt itself is reduced often to outrage at the apparently dogged patriotism
indicated by the group's singing "God Bless America" in
the last scene.    Moreover, although Cimino has proved one
of the worst spokesmen for his movie and although there is
credible enough evidence of what could fairly be construed
as right-wing audience reactions to it, serious critics, in
order to denigrate this work, have abandoned principles of
film scholarship which were justified and maintained only
with great difficulty a couple of decades ago in the face of
reactionary critics.    One of the great contributions of Cahiers du Cinéma's group of writers in the 'fifties, taken up
and defended by auteurist critics, is surely the refusal to
"read off" meaning, as if it could be extrapolated without
regard to mise-en-scène, signals from, for example, camera angle, camera movement or sound track.    One of the
most significant advances made in turn by the questioning of
the tenets of early auteurism, particularly the questioning of
Romantic belief in the director as sole generator of meaning, was what was elsewhere summed up as "the death of
the author."    However radical that Barthesian formula may
seem, at least it announced the position by which a work
could be viewed without undue--or possibly any--influence
from knowledge of authorial intentionality.    Hitchcock proves
singularly unhelpful as a commentator on his own films and,
in the famous Truffaut interviews with him, remarkably in-
sensitive to the merits that his admirers have discovered in
his movies, and yet faith in the value of his corpus of work
is not thereby shaken.    Therefore, it seems an alarmingly
retrograde step to denounce The Deer Hunter because Cimino
defends it weakly and seems not to appreciate its ambiguity
and complexity.

    Any analysis which would command credibility must
make sense of the greater part of the movie, devoted to
Clairton life, recognizing the ambivalence of the treatment
of both its rituals and those of the hunt.    If Cimino believes
that he has made a film about Vietnam, he also recognizes
that it concerns community, when he describes the end as
"a communal sound, on some level it's like the sacred chord,
a note.    I think it's a lot."[10]    Not all Americans who admired the film necessarily limited their consideration to a
Vietnamese statement either.    For example, one wrote a

letter to the New Statesman, saying of the movie's impact,
"As an American, I am strengthened by the sense of community that can survive even the most shattering of experiences."[11]

The Deer Hunter seems to use at least two specifically American traditions to illuminate each other, one enshrined
in American literature, of the chaste, deer-slaying hero re-
newing himself by emerging from industrialized or regimented
social settings and immersing himself in the world of untamed
nature represented by the wilderness or mountains, the other
(that which the present study is attempting to elucidate) of the
small, caring community which gives meaning to individual
life. It questions and partially subverts both.

Michael is a direct descendant of the highly individual-
istic, assertive, "masculine" heroes of Fenimore Cooper,
Faulkner and Hemingway, [12] who, finding their energies
drained by repetitive, dull reality, restore themselves by
contact with the wild. It is probably not accidental that the
hero who loses himself when exposed to a cruel parody of
the hunt in his Vietnam experience is called by the name of
Hemingway's autobiographical nom de plume, Nick. If the
peculiarly American mythology of the industrial town's young
men finding their masculinity regenerated is celebrated in the
Riefenstahl-like mountain sequences, the fact that Nick, the
hero who most revels in "the trees and mountains," destroys
himself casts doubt on the reality of his earlier perceptions.
Ultimately, it is American myths of masculinity which are
explored, and cast into doubt, by the revelation of their denial of women's personalities and by the men's fear both of
the female and of the expression of masculine tenderness.

In the first section of the film, the hunters' myth of
chastity reveals under scrutiny less attractive aspects, misogyny and homophobia.

The fear or hatred of women in the town's dominant
group is revealed at such moments as when Linda is attacked
by her father. On her first appearance, Linda answers the
coughs and thumping from an upstairs room, and brings soup
to her drunken father. In his rage, he mutters about giving
all the cars in town flat tires and turns viciously upon Linda.
"All bitches--I hate 'em," he snarls as he slaps her. No
explanation is offered for his vindictiveness towards the town
and to its womenfolk. At the wedding celebration, a girl is
struck to the ground by Stanley, her boyfriend, when the

man dancing with her begins to handle her buttocks too freely.  After this outburst, the girl is quickly and happily reconciled with her assailant.  This sort of scene at one level
seems to belong to a tradition of knockabout barroom brawls,
hard, drinking men carousing with sassy, golden-hearted
girls, hiding their sentiments under pragmatic or hard-bitten
exteriors, the tradition of the John Ford Western in particular, but it is this same young man, Stanley, who betrays
sexual insecurity in more obvious ways elsewhere.  For example, on a visit to the bowling alley in Act III, he behaves
in a self-advertisingly masculine manner but seeks approval
from Michael when he asks his opinion of the dumb-broad
character he has brought along for the evening.  Significantly, it is this character's machismo which is most overtly
criticized by Michael after that point in the movie where he
himself proves unable to kill a stag.  Stanley, who has been
firing wildly and who finally kills a deer with the triumphant
cry, "I got one," is discovered by Michael threatening his
companion with a revolver.  Michael challenges him to a
game of Russian roulette.  "How do you feel now, big shot?"
he asks a cringing Stanley before throwing the gun away.

Disconcertingly, some of the fear of women revealed
in the male characters is, as it were, "justified" by the sequence in which Angela spills wine.  Steven is one of the
men about to leave for Vietnam, after all, so that the sym-
bolism of the wine-drinking in the wedding is more powerful
than it would otherwise be.  The bridal couple on the reception-
hall stage drink a cup of wine together.  "If you don't spill
a drop, it's good luck for the rest of your life," they are
told.  Despite their carefulness, a tiny drop of red splashes
the white of the bridal gown, although no character within
the movie notices.  The spot that she drops on her bridal
gown promises Steven's downfall and, as with the Eden myth,
it is the woman who brings about the man's fall from grace.
It is the prostitute, rather than her customer, in Saigon who
invites disapprobation.

Yet, the final section of the movie seems to suggest
a critique of the chaste hunter code which has operated
among the men hitherto.  Linda asks Michael to sleep with
her so that they may comfort each other, but Michael refuses.  "I feel a lot of distance," he mutters.  This sequence contains distinct echoes of Cat on a Hot Tin Roof
(1958), where one of the secrets buried under the hero's
alcoholism and physical disability, relentlessly forced into
the open by his wife Maggie the Cat's goading, is that the

hero Brick's best friend tried to make love to Maggie as a means of becoming closer to Brick. Brick's reaction is to punish Maggie by rejecting her physical advances. Michael and Linda do, however, eventually share a bed in a motel, he fully clothed, she in a towel. Michael, despite his evident compassion for her loss of Nick, seems incapable of responding to Linda in her own right. He treats her as Nick's possession. His sleeping with her is a means of becoming closer to his vanished friend.

Together with inability to recognize the existence of women except as props for uncertain masculine egos goes an inability on the part of the men to express affection for each other, except through rituals or, by proxy, through female possessions of the beloved male.

Misogyny and homophobia are here two sides of the same coin. When masculine comradeship is celebrated, expression of affection is always oblique and even embarrassed. For example, in an early sequence, after the day's work at the steelworks, a siren sounds and the human beings or at least the human personae are permitted to emerge, as the workmen shower, exchange witless locker-room jokes, preen, like Stanley, at the mirror, and engage in a sort of physical roughhouse which permits them to express their sense of comradeship while keeping within the accepted limits of machismo. Again, in the masculine preserve of John's barroom, the men play pool, and dance and sing to the popular song, "Can't Take My Eyes Off You," expressing their affection and sense of comradeship in borrowed words. When a quarrel breaks out between Michael and Stanley over the former's refusal to lend the latter his boots, Stanley attacks Michael by questioning his virility, pointing out that nothing transpires between him and the girls he has been fixed up with.

Ultimately, though, just as Michael demonstrates the inadequacy of Stanley's sense of virility when confronted with the roulette game, he abandons his hitherto constricted code with its denial of manly affection. By saving Steven when his lack of heroism puts his own safety in jeopardy in Vietnam, and particularly in the final Saigon sequence by declaring his love for Nick and risking his life for him, he seems to turn from the myths that sustain the men's precarious sense of masculinity and to break through their general inability to express tenderness for each other except in the indirect form of physical rough-and-tumble.

Still more obviously questioned than the Hemingway-
esque traditions of maleness and heroism is that other strand
of American mythology, celebrating the sustaining value of
belonging to a closely-knit community.  Closely-knit it appears to be, to judge by the public performances of Clairton's
inhabitants.  The joie de vivre of the wedding guests and the
energy released in folk dance and communal song seem to as-
sert the communality of town life.  The wedding might be
taken to offer a reassuring picture of the town's sense of
identity, in the sharing by zestful young and mellow old in
the same rite of passage.  However, to take the boisterous
high spirits of the wedding celebration and the enigmatic
singing after the funeral of "God Bless America" as proofs
of the film's participation in the laudation of the small community seems wrongheaded.

The wedding celebration attempts, for example, to
deny all the factors that occur before it.  The very opening
sequence of the movie, for instance, casts doubts on Clairton's later coziness.  The plangent main theme of the movie's sound track plays through the credits, until a disturbing
introduction to Clairton begins the movie proper.  From beneath a bridge, the camera tracks slowly towards the steelworks on a day of grey weather.  Suddenly, we are taken
within the blast furnace area.  The noise of machinery, fire
and molten metal is overpowering.  Michael and his workmates are scarcely recognizable in their protective gear.
This sequence suggests a greater ambivalence about presentation of the town and its male inhabitants than can be
accommodated by the views of some of the more hostile
critics.  The first shots suggest an inferno, a living hell
from which the men find relief but by which they are shaped
into participating in a particularly limiting kind of camaraderie based on stereotypes of masculine behavior, elevated
into mysticism by the outsider-within-the-group, Michael.
Again, Linda's father unaccountably attacks her before the
wedding in a paroxysm of hatred for the town and its women.
Just before the wedding service, there is a curious exterior
shot of the church--curious for the inclusion of a drunk on
the street corner.

The dubiousness of the ostensible reason for celebration is repeatedly suggested too.  When the bride is first
glimpsed, she is seen to be clearly pregnant.  Moreover, as
the bride and groom enter a waiting car after the celebration,
Steven is anxious to explain something.  "I never really did
it with Angela, Nicky."  We gather that Stanley has been

putting a story about, but Steven's curious new piece of information clarifies little, and the content of Stanley's tale about Angela is never divulged.  What is certain is that the child is not his.

The narrative leading up to the wedding service is, then, far from conventional.  The exploration of masculine friendship and hunt mythology is deepened, the division between man and woman in Clairton widened to embrace that between the fit and young and the discarded old.  Linda's father and the drunk outside the church are different aspects of the same sense of exclusion from the communal, the former expressing impotent rage at forces unidentified.  Steven's reasons for marrying Angela are unclear, as indeed are the trio's reasons for enlisting.  Steven's mother may well ask, as she does the priest, "Why?  Can anyone explain?"  However, in the moment of communality and reassuring church ritual that the wedding represents, doubts melt away, all appears to be affirmation and optimism.

Just as the wedding celebration is rendered uncomfortable or even absurd by these techniques, so the apparent patriotism celebrated at the wedding is held up to examination.  None of the newly enlisted men seems to have any political understanding.  We see a Kennedy portrait in Michael's home, not much differentiated from the other American bric-a-brac (such as Kentucky fried chicken boxes) with which the room is littered.  But the only reason for fighting seems to be that declared by the bunting in the wedding hall--"God and country."  When the Green Beret enters the reception hall to buy a drink, he becomes a sort of specter at the feast.  The motivation for his presence at the bar is shadowy, since the entire hall and bar are given up to the entertainment of the wedding guests and he does not appear to be a local boy.  The three enlisted men share the bar counter with him and begin to express their admiration for him, their desire to get into action.  His only response is an expletive.  "What's it like over there?" he is asked.  He responds with the same expletive.  Angered, the men abandon their attempt to communicate with him.  Economically, the rationale offered by the community for the men's departure to Vietnam is reduced to absurdity by the one character with the knowledge to make that reduction justifiable, the Green Beret.

If Michael, Nick and the others enter the Vietnam conflict because of patriotism, then Clairton becomes the

reason for their decision, and, if Clairton's credibility is
damaged in the course of the movie, so too must the status
of their decision to fight.  Undoubtedly it is, paradoxically,
joy in the sense of home and community that sends these
young men off.  Nick in particular attempts--and fails--to
express this joy.  "I love the trees, you know--the way the
trees are all different in the mountains," he tells Michael.
As the bride and groom drive through town, Michael runs
ahead of them, stripping off all his clothes, running into the
mill area naked.  Nick follows him and covers him with his
jacket.  Michael and he sit exhausted from the exuberance
of the wedding and the final burst of energy.  "I love this
fucking place.  I know it's crazy.  If anything happens, just
don't leave me over there," Nick gasps.  Michael gives his
sacred promise.  When Steven is rendered hysterical with
fear during the Russian roulette torture, Michael advises
him, "Think of something else ... Home!"  Later, as they
escape down river, Steven whimpers, "I want to go home,
Mike."  Even back in Clairton, at the end of Michael's hospital visit to Steven, his last words to him are, "I'm going
to take you home."  And home is the last thought with which
Michael tries to entice Nick away from the suicidal roulette
game.  "Is this what you want? ... I love you ... Come on,
Nicky, come home ... home.  Remember the trees?  The
mountains?  Remember all that?"

Up until the Vietnam sequences, the community has
worked by excluding or suppressing the unacceptable, by
finding rules to fence itself off from meaninglessness.  Their
Vietnam experience makes each of the three friends face, at
least momentarily, what is unacceptable to the community
and what therefore has been unimaginable for them.  Their
contact with the unimaginable casts the community into doubt
and, with it, the meaning of their lives until now.

The clearest illustration of these points may be found
in the sequences in which Nick is a patient at the U. S. Army
Hospital in Saigon and immediately after his discharge from
it.  The hospital is crowded with wounded and raving soldiers.  In the background, rows of coffins are stacked for
dispatch home.  Nick watches the activity below from a
balcony, and then looks at a photograph of Linda.  While
being questioned by a doctor, he retorts angrily to the
query whether his surname is Russian, "No, it's American!"  On further questioning, he breaks down and weeps.
On release, Nick joins a line for telephones and begins to
ring Clairton, Pennsylvania, but instead hangs up.

This moment, when the links with home are rejected at a time of danger because of a sense of moving into a realm which is undreamed of in the security of that home, is echoed in a movie totally unlike The Deer Hunter in every other respect--Brian De Palma's Dressed To Kill (1980), at the point where the Angie Dickinson character, after an afternoon of sexual pleasure with a stranger, telephones to her thoroughly conventional husband but cannot bring herself to address him when she hears his voice. The link between these otherwise disparate works at this point is that the ordinariness of the home environment helps to explain the choice (irresponsible sex with casual pickup/enlisting in a foreign war) which lands the particular character in desperate danger. Because the direct experience of a world denied or suppressed by the original environment casts doubt on the realities of its values and its own credibility, the character in each case can no longer derive comfort from it but is forced to plunge into the forbidden or ignored areas, accepting --in each case--fatal consequences. Nick's choice is to forget the last attempt to make direct communication with home and to move into the crowded streets of Saigon.

The contrast of Act II in its entirety with the Clairton opening is as stark as that of the mellow, possibly maudlin, togetherness and tenderness underlying the group's silence for the Chopin Nocturne with the barbaric cruelty of the immediately following Vietnam episode and the (temporary) abandonment of myths of comradeship to expediency, in Michael's willingness to sacrifice the less "professional" Steven to the survival of himself and Nick. The rapid and all but complete surrender on Nick's part to cynicism and despair in the final sequences must be understood to be due not only to the shock of war's unacceptable realities (human life as a game of chance) but to the impact of that shock on a character cushioned by the limits of his previous world. While Michael's code of honor--the clean, one-shot hunt, his admiration for professionalism in the rule-bound hunt-- seems first to find its fulfilment in the Vietnam experience (even if the rules have to be reversed since he and his companions are now in the place of the stag) at the point where he must eliminate the less heroic Steven from his plans, his subsequent preoccupation with saving him when badly wounded and the final shot in Act II of him running out after Nick argue for a reversal of Homeric values, a more Christian sense of responsibility for the weaker and a more humane interpretation of masculinity. Nick, whose values are shadowy in Clairton, reduced to an inarticulate sense of

delight in mountain scenery and indefinable happiness in being part of the town, has no code which may be altered.
His shock at harsh reality creates a vacuum in him rather
than a modification of a set of values, and his dramatic loss
of faith in whatever he felt to be those aspects of American
life that gave him security seems to result in a vertiginous
glimpse of the void, from which he impulsively retreats in
self-disgust, but into which, in the final section of the film,
he voluntarily launches himself.

The Vietnam sequences, then, occupy a dialectical
position with those centering on Clairton and the mountains.
The one-shot rule for the hunt, the granting of meaning to
chaos by church rituals, are held up to scrutiny against another overwhelming reality. If Cimino believes the Russian
roulette to be a metaphor, it is so paramountly in its commentary on the less deadly games played by Clairton's inhabitants, not, surely, as a metaphor for America's involvement in Vietnam. If Acts I and II are thesis and antithesis,
Act III becomes synthesis. The returning Michael has seen
too much to believe in the rules of the hunt (his own imposi-
tion of order on chaos) or, certainly, in any rules external
to himself, and yet he seems to recognize that Nick's defection is the outcome of this loss of faith in the community's
self-image and its rules for that image's maintenance.
Therefore, he, like those other characters who have glimpsed
the void--Angela and Steven, in particular--suppresses his
knowledge and tries to reconstruct an image, however flimsy, with which his friends can survive, albeit in hiding from
outside reality. This seems to be the meaning of the communal singing of "God Bless America, " despair and solitude
being denied in the borrowing of another man's words to express a simple faith in the great American family that is
the United States, even if each singer suspects the falsity
of the message.

While The Deer Hunter is, in this writer's opinion,
a trenchant exploration of the myths of community and masculinity which, perhaps inadvertently, uses Vietnam as an
overwhelmingly immediate metaphor for the void, the "other-
ness" (to borrow a term from Terry Curtis Fox's useful article on the movie)[13] which the community denies, it still
incidentally makes a statement about the war. If Michael
is trying to insulate Clairton afresh from outside reality and
to keep the town's image alive, there is surely a message
in the movie, that American entry into Vietnam is a manifestation of the isolationism (odd as that may at first appear)

that is with difficulty reasserted in Clairton.  The purblind
patriotism and superficial religiosity of the three heroes' decision to enlist, particularly their inability to grasp that
there may be reason behind the Green Beret's denial of any
point to his war experience, would surely suggest a wider
lack of consideration in national commitment to an imperialist
war, the replacement of political analysis with moral impera-
tives.  While the Vietcong are caricatures and the acts of
bestiality in the Vietnam sequences are entirely of their doing, criticism of America seems undeniably present in the
scenes of the South Vietnamese shut out from the embassy
as the Americans take flight, in the sheer chaos of the departure, but most obviously in the rape of a culture represented in the Saigon scenes, with the city's streets turned
into those of an Oriental Las Vegas, a brutal Americaniza-
tion of the city's nightlife which is very little short in horror of the organized roulette game into which the disillu-
sioned Nick is drawn. [14]

## Notes to Chapter 4

1.  William Wyler, Index, British Film Institute, London,
    1959, p. 17.

2.  The tenuousness of the link between tradition and ac-
    tuality is indicated by the fact that the number of pages
    varies considerably, from 100 to 261 to 434, in differ-
    ent accounts.

3.  See Axel Madsen, William Wyler, Thomas Y. Cromwell
    Co., New York, 1973, p. 266.

4.  A. E. Wilson, in the Star of March 7, 1947, calls it so.

5.  Michael Cimino, "Ordeal by Fire and Ice," American
    Cinematographer, vol. 59, no. 10, October 1978, p. 965.

6.  Ibid., p. 1006.

7.  One of the three male principals returns in a coffin but
    much of the action of Act III can be seen to spring from
    the desire of the community to persuade him to give up
    his sojourn in Southeast Asia and return home.

8.  Michael Cimino, ibid., p. 1032.

9.   Screen International, November 26, 1977, p. 15.

10.  Michael Cimino, quoted in Time Out, no. 462, February 23-March 1, 1979.

11.  Letter from Mark Hayes Danyell, New Statesman, March 30, 1979.

12.  Philip French, in the Observer review of March 4, 1979, discerns particular links with Hemingway's Great War stories, especially "Soldier's Home" and "The Big Two-Hearted River."

13.  Terry Curtis Fox, "Stalking The Deer Hunter," Film Comment 1979, vol. 15, no. 2, p. 23.

14.  A number of articles on The Deer Hunter have been illuminating, notably, Nick Pease, "The Deer Hunter and the Demythification of the American Hero," Literature Film Quarterly, vol. 7, no. 4, 1979, pp. 254-259; Terry Curtis Fox, ibid.; Robert C. Cumbow's review in Movietone News, nos. 62-63, December 1979, pp. 48-49--but the most persuasive and considered judgment of the movie appears in an excellent study by Denis Wood entitled "All the Words We Cannot Say," in The Journal of Popular Film and Television, vol. VII, no. 4, 1980, pp. 366-383. One sentence in this article is particularly informative: "Mike recognizes its [the hunt's] fundamental senselessness, but like the other senseless things in Mike's life--working in the mill and his relations with his friends and going to war--it is something he does, something he does because it is an integral part of the net of traditions that sustains the community by denying its madness." (p. 375)

## 5. ALIEN

"Something evil had taken possession of the town," a voice-
over in the prologue to Don Siegel's Invasion of the Body
Snatchers informs its audience as the movie's hero, Dr.
Miles Bennell (Kevin McCarthy), returns to Santa Mira,
California, from a conference. "I feel almost like a stranger," claims another recent arrival, the movie's heroine
Becky (Dana Wynter), after an absence of five years. Miles
interprets the upsurge in attendance of patients at his clinic,
all claiming that close relatives are impostors, as an outbreak of hysteria in the town. A young boy is brought to
him crying because he has conceived the notion that the woman who claims to be his parent and looks exactly like her
nevertheless is not his mother. It is singularly appropriate
that the solution should be a sedative and that, when it is
administered, the patient should be told by the nurse, "That's
a good boy, Johnny." "Be a good boy," echoes the doctor.
As evil seems in the prologue to be identified with unrest and
apparent neurosis in the hitherto stable and unchanging small
town, so good is equated with acquiescence and sedation.
Becky's sense of strangeness is far less threatening in that
she claims to feel strange to the country as a whole, not the
town specifically, after her stay in England.

If Body Snatchers is normally categorized as a horror
movie, it is remarkably free of violence. The essence of its
horror is that any reassurance offered by the medical, and,
particularly, the psychiatric world--that the breakdown of
confidence in the family and the township may be explained
in terms of neurosis or delusion--is itself demonstrated to
be delusion. Despite the epilogue, which Siegel strongly re-
sisted, with its indication that Dr. Bennell's warning to the
outside world will be heeded, Becky's vague feeling that
America itself has changed would appear alarmingly accurate,
in that the highways beyond Santa Mira are shown to be teeming with lorries carrying the "pods" which explain the townspeople's sense of dislocation.

The explanation for the apparent irrationality in so

97

many formerly placid townsfolk is that seeds have dropped
from the sky, taken root and grown into "pods," similar to
giant, man-sized squash, which eventually burst open to reveal a human shape, distinctive but as yet featureless.  The
last stage is achieved when the human being whom the particular pod replicates is fully assimilated by it.  This final
physical absorption happens during the victim's sleep.  (Hence,
Siegel's disappointment that the movie was not given the title
which he wanted, Sleep No More, instead of the extension of
the title of Jack Finney's novel, The Body Snatchers, a longer version of his serial for Colliers magazine.)1  The new
inhabitants are exact replicas of the originals but affectless,
free of emotion and its concomitant penalties.  "There will
be no more tears," says a pod mother as she brings a baby-
sized pod into her home.  When Miles and Becky struggle to
escape town and to retain their identities, an attempt is made
to persuade them to see the benefits of the new existence.
"There's no need for love.  It never lasts.  Love, faith,
ambition--without them life's so much easier."  Since they
are in love, however, with the lovers' sense of special and
separate privileged status being amply confirmed by their for
once fully grounded conviction that everybody else is emotionally dead, they strive to escape.  Alone in their cave outside
town, Becky is still able to respond to music.  Seconds after,
when Miles returns from a brief reconnoiter, her kiss is
cold, her only desire is to join the crowd, to denounce the
sole remaining individual.  In an unguarded moment, Becky
has succumbed to her exhaustion.  The penalty for this loss
of vigilance, in its most literal sense, is the elimination of
her individuality.

     The central irony of Body Snatchers is that the night-
mare into which the doctor hero is plunged is a reductio ad
absurdum of his own philosophy.  Until he discovers the
truth, he has been disregarding patients' fears, prescribing
sedatives, counselling an unhappy female patient who senses
that her uncle's emotions are now "just a pretence" in a
manner that indicates his comfortable belief that all loss of
faith in family ties can be explained as a symptom of ill
health.  "You'll realize the trouble is inside you," he explains to the bewildered niece. [2]  The doctor's final position
as the only non-pod in Santa Mira, battling against the very
bromides which he administered to his fellow-townsfolk before their absorption, seems poetic justice.  The circle is
closed when the alien is the only man in town who retains a
sense of his, and its, past.  Even in the epilogue with its
promise of containment of the Santa Mira threat, Dr. Bennell

has to suffer the humiliation of the city psychiatrist's conclusion that his story is evidence of psychic disorder.   The
hubris by which individualism and passion are automatically
diagnosed as a threat to community and, because taken as
evidence of neurosis, subjected to "cure" is thus severely
castigated in the reversal by which community is the threat
and individualism the salvation.   The appeal of the small
town as a setting is evident in this regard, for its self-
justification is traditionally rendered in terms of community, of familial values.   The positive value of communality
may however be vitiated by the negative obverse, conformism.   The small town's promotion of the family is persuasive only if the family itself represents fulfilment rather than
repression.

Siegel himself, [3] in describing the town as ill--"The
town is like a cancer growth ... and it's going to spread"--
implies that it was previously well, but the conclusion that
the pod town is an extension and fulfilment of the pre-pod
Santa Mira finds some support in Raymond Durgnat's admission that the "pod people in their final form remind me of
nothing more than the characters in TV's Peyton Place, quiet,
grey, persuasive, reasonable, all individuality dead...."[4]
Viewed thus as a critique of small-town ideology, the movie
is ill-served by attempts to render it as parable, or oblique
political commentary.   Its director states, "The political
reference to Senator McCarthy and totalitarianism was inescapable but I tried not to emphasize it because I feel that
motion pictures are primarily to entertain and I did not want
to preach."[5]   Because the reference is "inescapable" (although Alan Lovell makes the point that the movie could as
easily be taken as an anti-Communist fable), [6] it may be un-
productive to look too far beyond its ostensible subject.   Interestingly, the second version in 1978 [directed by Philip
Kaufman] paradoxically, since it is set in a city, confirms
that the principal address is to questions of community.   San
Francisco is the American city which is most commonly differentiated from all other urban centers by reason of its
beauty of setting and humaneness of architecture and especially for its reputation, enhanced in the late 'sixties, for
tolerance of social deviance.   Though the fictitious Santa
Mira and the mythologized San Francisco are still markedly
different settings and though the second movie purports to
begin where the first "ends, " even to a cancelling of the imposed epilogue--a cancellation implicit in the sequence where
a seemingly demented Kevin McCarthy cries warnings of the
apocalypse to the San Francisco traffic--their common ground

is their lament for the loss of civilized values, once protected in their respective communities.   The first remains
the more disturbing, not only because San Francisco's reputation for peace and love has been repeatedly assaulted since
the 'sixties in any case but because the pods of the Siegel
movie are a logical outcome of normal Santa Mira living.
The pod-seeds were there before the miraculous rain from
heaven.

    Alfred Hitchcock's The Birds (1963) coincidentally
links San Francisco and another California small town again
at a time of crisis and, like Siegel though for different reasons, Hitchcock draws back from the implication that the city
has succumbed to the same forces which have attacked the
town.   His original ending was to have the central "family"
escape the bird-dominated town of Bodega Bay only to find
the Golden Gate bridge covered in predatory birds.   In actuality, the movie ends ambiguously with the car inching its
way through the birds in a lull between their attacks, heading for an uncertain future.

    As the combination of the title and the director's
name, if not knowledge of Daphne du Maurier's short story,
must have indicated in advance to all spectators, this movie
concerns a mysterious outbreak of attacks by birds on human
beings.   In the event, this information turns out to be as useful as hearing that Psycho concerns an old dark house where
horrible murders occur.   The Birds is more unsettling than
Body Snatchers although they share a premise in having "normal" inhabitants of an area becoming possessed by apparently inexplicable behavior patterns which seem to be destructive of the former community.   The fact that the inhabitants
are this time birds, not people, scarcely reassures characters or audience, since it is the reason for the change that
is withheld this time.   While the information that the seeds
fell from the sky to create the pods need be accepted by only those in the audience who are reluctant to engage with
other levels of possible meaning in Body Snatchers, the panic
which afflicts Bodega Bay in The Birds may be communicated
to the audience with particular directness since as little explanation is offered to spectators as to townspeople.   It is a
mark of the crumbling of a society that, in the face of external threat, the very absence of explanation has one human being in an apparently cozy little town blaming another for the
catastrophe.   While the birds behave like alien beings, the
principal outsider is, in actuality, Melanie Daniels (Tippi
Hedren), a sophisticated but vulnerable woman who has come

from San Francisco to Bodega Bay to deliver a pair of love-
birds to Mitch Brenner (Rod Taylor) as a sort of elaborate
practical joke.  The first attack is upon her, but it is quickly followed up by far more violent and concerted invasions
of, for example, a children's party and a school.  The opening of the film in San Francisco not only establishes Melanie's role as brittle sophisticate and the propensity of urban
society to cage, tame and display birds, but supplies a contrast for the small town of which the Brenner family is part
and from which it is separate, being across the bay and
spatially isolated by land.  Explanations for the birds' behavior are so open-ended[7] that ultimately they become unhelpful, and, though the absence of certainty increases the
audience's anxiety, it also helps to displace attention from
the birds to the reactions of particular human beings in particular settings under extreme stress.  If in this sense the
movie's special focus of interest is the family, it is nevertheless a family in a setting, that of Bodega Bay and, somehow, also in a natural setting beyond Bodega Bay.

     After the attack on the school, various local charac-
ters gather in a Bodega Bay diner and offer opinions on the
reasons for the attacks.  The town drunkard complacently
proclaims the end of the world.  A tweedy ornithologist maintains that birds of different species are incapable of such concerted action.  Because the birds are breaking the rules of
ornithology, those who have experienced the attacks are deluded or mendacious.  This reaction parallels the apparently
rationalist attitude of Dr. Bennell to Santa Mira's fears.  The
sequence which follows, where the birds attack when the center of the town is engulfed in flames, has Melanie trapped in
a phone booth, able only to watch but not aid a bloodied victim of the birds, and seems to confirm the isolation and
fragmentation that exist in Bodega Bay, under crisis at least.
When Melanie re-enters the diner, she finds its occupants
huddled silently in a passageway, all confidence evaporated.
Suddenly, a woman who had been listening earlier with growing panic to the various contributions about the bird attacks
from the locals, becomes hysterical.  She claims that the
townspeople told her that the attacks started only after Melanie came to town.  The coincidence of her arrival and the
first attack is too much for her, and presumably for some
of her informants.  "You're evil!" she screams at her.
Most of the characters in these sequences are not seen earlier or thereafter but their reactions are so irrational (the
ornithologist's refusal to countenance reports which run
counter to her study being a manifestation of irrationality
here) or useless that telling points are made against the

notion of the cohesiveness of small-town life, points which
become more significant when the last third of the movie
concentrates on the Brenner family in its increasing independence from the town's protection (just as the town itself
feels dismaying isolation from the nation as a whole in the
newscasts on the crisis).

While it is true that the schoolteacher (Suzanne Ple-
shette) cooperates with Melanie in rescuing the schoolchildren, puts them before herself and finally loses her life by
so doing, she is an earlier version of Melanie, an outsider
who came to the town out of love for Mitch Brenner and who,
by reason of her intellectual superiority and personality,
seems less integrated townsperson than long-term visitor.

Once Mrs. Brenner (Jessica Tandy), Mitch's mother,
has recoiled in shock from the hideous sight of a neighbor's
eyeless corpse and begun to retreat increasingly from responsibility, roughly the last third of the movie concentrates
on the Brenner home, with Mitch taking over the protective,
organizational role traditionally associated with the masculine
and Melanie becoming increasingly supportive, less superficial, more "feminine," a surrogate mother to Mitch's young
sister.  The home becomes the equivalent of the John Ford
homestead under Indian attack.  The touching attempts by
Mitch to reassert order in the chaos of the bird attacks,
whereby he gently takes his mother from her crouching position by the wall to seat her on a chair, simultaneously
mirror and contrast with the diner sequence in which the
inability to combine effectively, the retreat to "safe" habits
of thought and behavior, are more a result of lack of common interests.  At exactly the time that the birds deviate
most markedly from their natural behavior, their "birdhood,"
the members of a family rediscover basic human traits; as
the birds forsake their species and become ever less "natural," the citified heroine learns the need for family and marriage, becomes increasingly "natural."  In this context, Bodega Bay is an artifice, undeniably pretty, but ill-equipped
to adapt for survival, as incapable of cohesive effort as San
Francisco might be expected to prove, as ready to lapse into
witch-hunting and pseudo-rationalization as was Salem.

The precariousness of a civil order which rests, as
all civilization must to some extent, upon the denial of the
natural is epitomized in one of the most ancient of all Greek
myths, concerning the arrival of Dionysiac worship within
Greece.  In the one surviving dramatic treatment (by Eurip-

ides) of this popular tragic story, Pentheus, king of Thebes, attempts to debar the "ecstatic" Dionysiac religion from his kingdom.   Ultimately seduced by the god into spying upon the female votaries of Dionysus, he is recognized by them and torn to pieces.

Dionysus being the god of the elemental, of vegetation and fertility and the irrational, "natural" forces in man, it is almost impossible to interpret the tale other than as a warning against the repression of the instinctive.   The meaning which may be found in the myth is the danger and ultimate hopelessness of denying the elemental by over-stressing order and rationalism in a community. 8

The myth is alive twenty-five centuries later, in literature (especially in the works of D. H. Lawrence, E. M. Forster and Vladimir Nabokov) and in film (The Blue Angel [1930], Theorem [1968], Easy Rider [1969]), and is specially potent in a series of small-town movies dealing with the advent of a stranger with almost magical influence over a previously sleepy, unchanging community.   Many small-town movies are almost self-evidently reworkings, albeit possibly unconscious reworkings, of the myth.   Of these, three examples may suffice:   Joshua Logan's 1956 adaptation of William Inge's play, Picnic; Martin Ritt's 1958 The Long Hot Summer, an adaptation of William Faulkner's novel, The Hamlet, and his tales, "Barn Burning" and "The Spotted Horses"; and the 1962 film version, directed by Morton da Costa, of the stage musical, The Music Man.

All three open with the arrival of a stranger, a mysterious figure with Dionysiac qualities, from somewhere beyond the community in which each is set.   A freight train enters the Kansas town in Picnic in the opening sequence, and Hal, the stranger (William Holden), jumps off.   Behind the credits, he washes in the river and walks between the town granaries towards one of the houses.   The Long Hot Summer begins with a pre-credits prologue in which a barn bursts into flames and what looks like a kangaroo court of outraged locals accuses Ben Quick (Paul Newman) of the crime without proof.   Ben is thrown out of the county.   As the credits roll, he walks down a dirt road, takes a barge downriver, then jumps off to wade ashore and walk to the highway where he is given a ride into Frenchman's Bend by two young women.   The Music Man opens similarly with a sheriff and farmers running the hero--the traveling salesman, Harold Hill (Robert Preston)--out of town.   After a brief

train journey in a plush, red compartment filled with salesmen talking about all the changes with which they now con-
tend, Hill hears the porter yell, "River City--just across
the state line into Iowa--population 212" and gets off.

Having established the shadiness of each man--Hal
the hobo, Ben the barn-burner, Hill the bogus music
professor--the movies begin to explore the towns which they
have entered.

Hal has come to town looking for work with a former
college friend, Allan Benson, but first arrives at the houses
near the railroad tracks, those of Mrs. Potts and Mrs. Owens. Bare-chested as he sweeps up leaves for Mrs. Potts
in return for breakfast, he attracts the interest of Milly
Owens (Susan Strasberg) and the old-maid schoolteacher who
lodges with them, Miss Sidney (Rosalind Russell), both frankly excited by his virility. These two female characters are
indicated to have difficulties in attracting men, Milly because
she is tomboyish and "intellectual" (she has just won a
scholarship to college), Miss Sidney for similar reasons,
with the added burden of now being middle-aged and single.
Milly's beautiful older sister, Madge (Kim Novak), is also
drawn to Hal but veils her interest. At "the other end of
town," significantly, Hal visits the Bensons in their white-
pillared mansion. His career since his college days as a
star athlete is sketched--a spell in the army, a trip to Hollywood with a woman promising him a screen test, work as
a ranch hand, and an unfortunate incident when two women
picked him up and robbed him. Back at the Owens' home,
it is established that Madge is Allan's girlfriend and that
Mrs. Owens wants her to use every wile to gain the security of marriage with him. Miss Sidney's prurience emerges
when she denounces Milly's reading matter, The Ballad of
the Sad Café, as filth, declaring proudly that there was pressure to have it removed from the public library. After a
tour of the Bensons' granaries, Hal and Allan join Madge
and Milly at the swimming pool. In the changing rooms,
the two men step out of their trunks. Next door, the girls
hear their voices and Milly becomes so excited that she
tries to peep through the partition at Hal. The rest of the
day has been set aside for the Labor Day picnic. Hal is
invited and sets off with Milly, while Miss Sidney goes with
her friend ("not a boy-friend but a friend-boy") Howard (Arthur O'Connell), a dull middle-aged bachelor.

In these pre-picnic sequences, the town's mores are

deftly sketched.  The exclusively female households by the
railroad tracks (symbol in small-town movies of modest
means and social disadvantage) preach respectability but
yearn for the first glimpse of virile beauty which is granted
to them, or advise the selling of sexual favors in marriage
for financial security.  The masculine domain of the Bensons'
residence reeks of middle-class affluence and insensitivity,
Allan displaying his empire to his erstwhile college friend,
his father disapproving of Madge as an unsuitable date for
Allan.  Hal begins by feeling need for the safety which the
town seems to offer and particularly for a brake to be applied to his transitory life.  "I gotta get someplace in this
world," he confides to Allan.  While therefore the women
sense the presence of a Dionysiac figure in their midst by
whom they are undisguisedly aroused despite, say, Miss
Sidney's hypocritical postures, Dionysus wishes to turn
Apollonian, to re-enter the accustomed social system represented by the town.  When he confesses that he has never
been to a picnic, the speech indicates his self-exclusion
from all that the picnic (wishfully) represents, a town's
continuity and social cohesion.

　　Ben Quick and Frenchman's Bend in the Ritt film
share a number of features with the Picnic hero and Kansas
town.  The women who pick Ben up on the road are Eula and
Clara, the latter of whom (Joanne Woodward) is an unmar-
ried, lonely schoolteacher.  Eula (Lee Remick) is married
to Jody (Anthony Franciosa), son of Will Varner (Orson
Welles), the man who practically owns the town (he later
talks of "his" courthouse as well as his shops and farms),
Clara is Will's daughter.  She is having an unsatisfactory
relationship with a mother-dominated aesthete but is clearly
interested in the more carnal delights that Ben would seem
to offer.  Later, on the porch of her home with her friend
Agnes (sister to Clara's "friend-boy," Alan), she assents to
Agnes' feeling that life is passing them by.  Both are still
under twenty-five, "for all the good it does us."  Agnes
frankly admits that she longs for marriage, children and
sex.  Clara is hampered by potential suitors' fear of her
domineering father.  The contrast of the women's frustrations with the sound of Eula's shrieks of delight as Jody
chases her through the house makes the reaction to the sight
of the bare-chested Ben even more pronounced.  "The last
desperate resort is strangers," sighs Agnes, with a curious
echo of Blanche DuBois in her voice and words.  Clara, who
evidently sympathizes, counsels tranquillizers.  On Will's
return from hospital (Orson Welles recreating another Ten-

nessee Williams character--Big Daddy in <u>Cat on a Hot Tin
Roof</u>), he is furious with the feckless Jody for allowing a
notorious barn-burner to become one of their tenant farmers.
However, Ben's shrewdness as the salesman for Will's
horses at the local auction impresses him.   Seeing him as
a worthy heir, Will invites Ben for supper.

At that meal, both he and Will find Alan an unworthy
suitor for Clara.  Will wants children and threatens to marry
Clara off to Ben, "that big stud horse," if no progress is
made with the man who has been her beau for the last five
years.   Ben takes up work in one of the Varner stores, increasing Jody's fears that he is being replaced.   After school,
Clara visits him there and succumbs to her desire for him.
When Ben is moved into the Varner's home, Jody is incon-
solable, Clara more easily reconciled.

The elements of spinsterly frustration, of thinly
veiled attraction to the newcomer while he attempts integration into the community, of social division in the town, are
repeated from <u>Picnic</u>.   This time, however, the division between Clara's and Alan's families is less a matter of material differences than of respectability.   While Varner owns
everything, he misses the poise that Alan commands.   Will
Varner has entrepreneurial energy--an energy recognized to
be latent in Ben Quick--but lacks breeding.   If marriage between Clara and Alan offers advantages to both families,
Will is repelled by Alan's faint-hearted wooing, Alan's mother dismayed by any sign of physical intimacy between the
couple.   Clara, a pawn in this game of dynastic marriage,
remains deeply unsatisfied.

In <u>The Music Man</u>, Professor Hill is introduced to
River City--and vice-versa--by means of a satiric, double-
edged song of welcome (with such lines as, "But what the
heck, you're welcome/Join us at the picnic--/You can eat
your fill of all the food you bring yourself"), during which
a farmer and his wife are "accidentally" and quite literally
framed against the background of a church spire to become
the icons of fundamental rural decency which Norman Rockwell so often purveyed.   The principal family in town is that
of Mayor Shin (Paul Ford), whose wife (Hermione Gingold)
constantly attacks the local library for "advocating dirty
books--Chaucer, Rabelais and Balzac."   Her adversary in
the fight for cultural standards is the librarian-cum-music-
teacher Marian (Shirley Jones), a close relation of the
spinster schoolteacher of <u>The Birds</u>, and of Clara in <u>The</u>

Long Hot Summer, but much nearer Milly Owens than Miss
Sidney of Picnic. Hill plays upon the town's professed
morality by whipping up fears of spiritual declension in the
young, thanks to the presence of a pool hall, in the song
"Trouble" ("Those fifteen numbered balls are the devil's
tool") and offering them the remedy of a boys' band. Marian, upbraided by her earthy Irish widowed mother for rejecting the professor's blandishments ("he may be your very
last chance"), finds evidence that he is a charlatan but sup-
presses it when she notices the effect that the advent of the
musical instruments in the Wells Fargo wagon is having on
the whole town, but especially on her younger brother who
has till now been afflicted with a painful stammer. Hill has
worked his magic on the community, appealing to their desire for bogus, "respectable" culture, encouraged by the
mayor's wife, to the extent that they imagine the production
of their boys' brass band as a fait accompli in the song,
"76 Trombones," before either instruments or uniforms have
arrived in town. He diverts the school board from their
feuding and faultfinding by teaching them close harmony when
they thought they were tone-deaf. Gradually, his influence
on Marian herself grows and she accepts his invitation to the
local Ice Cream Sociable. Before setting out with him, she
has to persuade a travelling salesman, looking for Mayor
Shin so that he may denounce Hill, to part with his evidence
against him. During the negotiations, Marian is dismayed
to find that he is supposed to have deflowered one-hundred-
two girls. Though she avoids mentioning this reason for her
concern to him, she accepts Hill's general explanation about
rumor-mongering, that it stems from jealousy. As she
leaves for the Sociable, her mother happily opines that Marian is as affected by the "think system," which Hill oper-
ates, as are the townspeople in the matter of the band or
the school board in their newly found singing ability.

Hill is the most overtly demonic of the three heroes,
able to work magic through his salesman patter (a talent observed to be in Ben Quick's repertory during the horse-sale
sequence) or the persuasiveness of his sheer energy and
earnestness, as much an Orpheus as a Dionysus. He works
on the very hypocrisies of the cultural backwater--repeatedly
reminiscent of Gopher Prairie in Sinclair Lewis's Main
Street in its complacency, its sense of outrage about im-
moral foreign artists, its promotion of the imagined rural
virtues and production of horrendous patriotic tableaux--and
succeeds with Marian who, Pentheus-like, stands out against
the hysteria gripping the town by appealing to her own wish

to be charmed and her underlying need to disregard the evidence of his fakery.

The central event of <u>Picnic</u> is, as in <u>Peyton Place</u>, the Labor Day town picnic. In both films, the picnic fulfils its ostensible function of celebrating the town's humaneness, sense of integration and continuity, but culminates in events which cast doubt on the public postures. Hal is to be offered a job in the granaries, and his companions yearn to see him part of their town. "Wouldn't it be nice if he could join the Country Club?.... There comes a time when a man must stop rolling round like a pinball. Maybe a little town like this is the place to settle down, where people are easygoing and sincere." As the sun sets on the beautifully composed shots of couples at ease, groups of loving friends or relations, and Madge is crowned Queen of the picnic, problems surface. The attraction which Madge feels for Hal is expressed in dance to the music of "Moonglow" in front of Rosemary Sidney, Howard and Milly. Milly, drunk and jealous, tells Madge that she hates her. Rosemary flings herself hungrily at Hal, ripping his shirt, and, when she finds him unresponsive, yells, "You're a fake--not so young--take a look in the mirror."[9] As the group breaks up, Rosemary begs Howard to marry her but he gives no answer. Madge insists on accompanying Hal on his headlong drive away from the picnic site at breakneck speed and tries to reassure him. "You <u>are</u> young and you're very entertaining and you're a wonderful dancer." Hal explains his rootlessness and vulnerability by his mother's indifference to him. Bare-chested again, he clings to Madge and they make love. On her return home, she finds Milly repentant and sober. Hal returns to the Benson house to find two policemen waiting for him with the unlikely charge that he has "stolen" Madge. Once again labelled "a no-good hobo," he flees to Howard's place for refuge.

Next morning, Rosemary at last engineers her wedding to Howard and they leave town in a car with "JUST MARRIED" emblazoned on it. As they drive past the red brick school, Rosemary sticks her tongue out at it. Before jumping on another freight train, Hal asks Madge to join him in Tulsa where he is going to find a waiter's job. "I can't. Don't you see why?" she responds. The sense of loss among the women is immediate. "Everything was so fine, there were geraniums in the windows ... and then he walked in and it was different. There was a man in the house and it seemed good." Milly warns Madge to reconsider, sounding

a little like Allison MacKenzie in Peyton Place: "When I
graduate from college, I'm going to New York and write
novels that will shock people out of their senses.   I'm not
going to live in some dirtwater town. . . .   Go with him,
Madge.   For once in your life, do something bright." And
Madge leaves for Tulsa, deaf to her mother's protestations
about duty.

The town celebration at the heart of The Long Hot
Summer includes a box-supper auction, at which Ben outbids
Alan for Clara's company.   Alone with him, Clara tells Ben
that she is "no trembling little rabbit full of unsatisfied desires" but wants more, that she is not to be given away to
any passing stranger.   She is equally forthright thereafter
with Alan, asking him, "Do you want me the way a man
wants a woman?"   To avoid the disgrace inflicted on his
family by Alan's subsequent decision to call off the engage-
ment, Will flies into the schoolroom to drag Clara out for
marriage with Ben.   Back at the Varner residence, Jody
locks his father in the barn and, crazed with resentment
about his replacement by Ben and his father's indifference
to him, he sets light to it.   Once he has persuaded Jody to
release him, Will feels reconciled to his formerly weak son.
"You got hellfire . . . and redemption in you. . . .   Ah got me
a son again."   A number of reconciliations and a multiple
dénouement follow.   Ben has to flee with Clara when he is
accused by the townspeople of the barn-burning and admits
to her that earlier he took the blame for his father's mis-
deeds.   This time, Will takes the blame for Jody.   As Ben
packs to leave, Clara refuses to allow him to go.   The film
ends with Jody and Eula resuming their play, Clara and Ben
united, Will taking another wife.

The Music Man's Ice Cream Sociable once again
brings the lovers together when Hill admits his feelings for
Marian and she responds by singing "Till There Was You."
As the sheriff spreads the word of his trickery, the town
takes on a vengeful mood, pursuing him with the intention
of tarring and feathering the impostor.   When he is cap-
tured, Marian defends him, declaring that everything which
he claimed was true.   "It all happened . . . in the way that
every kid walked around and behaved this summer."   In the
classroom where Hill is arraigned before the town, Marian
counters the Mayor's ferocity by asking, "Do you remember
what this town was like before he came?. . .   Suddenly there
were things to do."   The boys' band in their ill-fitting uniforms are ushered in and Hill reluctantly conducts.   Their

version of Beethoven's Minuet in G is tuneless and crudely
amateurish but the parents swell with pride and seem de-
lighted with the performance.   The epilogue is a consuma-
tion of the town's collective fantasy.   Skilled trombonists in
smart new uniforms parade through the town square.

       In each film, the repressed or denied breaks through
the surface of gentility or hypocrisy under the influence of a
charismatic stranger.10   Most simply, in the case of the
spinster characters, sexual desire is permitted to express
itself and to find relief.   The honest vulgarity of the Varners and of most of River City's inhabitants replaces the
well-bred ineffectuality which they are tempted to court before the stranger arrives.   Each hero is less a preacher or
active proselytizer than a catalyst who permits those with
whom he makes contact to examine themselves and accept
what they discover.   As the Dionysiac is already part of
man and, especially, it would seem, woman in Greek myth
before Dionysus appears, to release it, so the virility and
energy which Hal, Ben and Professor Hill embody are ideals
which the burghers secretly retain.   In this sense, the stranger is an Americanizer.   This is most obviously true of Ben
Quick, who rids the Varners of their guilt about their success and their entrepreneurial talents, revealing the aristocratic elements in the community as bloodless and insipid,
barriers to the forces of nature, in that Will, Jody and Ben
are all sexually potent and heterosexual, likely to produce
good stock for the continuance of the family, while Alan,
with his "European" sensitivity and breeding, is a mother-
ridden closet homosexual.   In The Music Man, the Mayor's
family, by its attempts to bowdlerize the classics and to impose "tasteful" town entertainments such as the Ladies' Eu-
rhythmic Group which essays a curious revival of Hellenism,
is shown to be much less in touch with the townsfolk's desires than the pool-hall owners.   Hill's ultimate success is
a demonstration of the community's lack of interest in any
"cultural" activities and of the foreignness of such imposi-
tions on the Middle West.   Mrs. Shin's hostility to Chaucer,
Rabelais and Balzac is echoed by Marian's mother's contempt for "Beethoven, Shakespeare and all them high-falutin'
Greeks."   There is a sense in which Marian's own love of
literature and music is shown to be as ersatz--in that it is
treated as an avenue of escape from her true role as a woman and a means to some sort of power over the town through
ownership of the library stock--as that professed by others
in town or that of the pretentious heroine of Main Street.   A
woman's role has nothing to do with the promotion of high

culture unless she is irredeemably on the shelf, and an
American should get on with the breeding of healthy stock
and the pursuit of business success instead of being diverted by questions of class difference or of status.

In such films as those discussed in this chapter, the
visitors to the small town, be they rootless wanderers or
hostile birds, have arrived to remind the inhabitants of their
basic needs, to reassert nature against civilization's inroads
and indirectly to promote the importance of family, child-
breeding and material security. All else is hollow, pretentious or insignificant.

## Notes to Chapter 5

1.  See "Siegel on Invasion of the Body Snatchers," Ciné-
    fantastique, vol. 2, no. 3, winter 1973, pp. 21-23.

2.  A similar belief may be detected in Becky's admission
    that her sense of estrangement was first taken to be
    evidence of a fault in herself. ("I knew something was
    wrong, but I thought it was me....")

3.  Don Siegel, ibid.

4.  Raymond Durgnat, review of reissued Invasion of the
    Body Snatchers, Films and Filming, February 1969,
    pp. 49-50.

5.  Quoted in Alan Lovell, Don Siegel:  American Cinema
    (British Film Institute, revised ed., 1975), p. 54.

6.  Ibid., p. 66.

7.  The sequence of the bird shop in San Francisco, for
    example, could signal that the birds are taking revenge
    on a society which has caged them to relieve its bore-
    dom, but why then is Bodega Bay singled out for attack,
    why do the lovebirds (caged) remain peaceful even when
    other birds are attacking ferociously, why are the at-
    tacks so indiscriminate?

8.  "... the 'moral' of the Bacchae is that we ignore at our
    peril the demand of the human spirit for Dionysiac ex-
    perience.  For those who do not close their minds
    against it such experience can be a deep source of

spiritual power.... But those who repress the demand
in themselves or refuse its satisfaction to others trans-
form it by their act into a power of disintegration and
destruction, a blind natural force that sweeps away the
innocent with the guilty." (E. R. Dodds (ed. ), Introduction to Euripides' Bacchae (Oxford University Press,
2nd ed., 1960), p. xiv. )

9. The decision to cast William Holden as Hal clearly
   necessitated a major change of emphasis in the screenplay. In William Inge's original play, the stranger is
   still young and Rosemary's advance on him is the more
   animalistic. "But you won't stay young forever, didja
   ever thinka that? What'll become of you then?" she
   threatens drunkenly on being rebuffed.

10. The Walt Disney studios produced a remarkable varia-
    tion on the traditional theme in 1960 when the charis-
    matic stranger (Hayley Mills) who transforms the town
    is prepubescent and female, in David Swift's Pollyanna,
    although there is at least one earlier movie, Stuart
    Heisler's Storm Warning in 1951, centering on the up-
    set to an unhealthy town occasioned by the arrival of an
    out-of-town female. In the Disney movie, it is also a
    woman who dominates the town. Aunt Polly Harrington
    (Jane Wyman), disciplinarian, autocratic religious bigot,
    wielding as much power as Will Varner and as much
    influence as the Bensons in The Long Hot Summer,
    sharing a surname with the mill-owner of Peyton Place,
    is the last to allow her hidden warmth and humanity to
    surface under the healing influence exerted by Pollyan-
    na on all with whom she comes into contact. Jane Wy-
    man's performance as Aunt Polly is frequently reminis-
    cent of her playing of the female lead in Douglas Sirk's
    All That Heaven Allows (1956), another small-town movie
    where she must be weaned away from bigotry and re-
    spectability to the acceptance of her loving and "natur-
    al" instincts, this time under the tutelage and influence
    of a Thoreau-esque gardener (Rock Hudson). This lat-
    ter film, incidentally, is Rainer Werner Fassbinder's
    inspiration for Fear Eats the Soul (1973).

## 6.  MISFITS

There is sufficient overlap between the subject of the present chapter and that of Chapter 5 to raise questions about the appropriateness of creating a division between them.  The importation of disorder into an apparently stable social order or the suggestion that chaos is discoverable within that order, as well as, occasionally, the arrival of a Dionysiac character from outside--features common to the films discussed in the previous chapter--reappear here.  The vital difference is that, in the present chapter, the out-of-town catalysts of certain movies are related by blood to the small-town family which sustains the chief impact of the new arrival, and the reinterpretation of, or loss of confidence in, ostensible community and decency is experienced by members of a family, sometimes as a result of contact with an out-of-town relation, sometimes as a result of maturation, but always within the family.  If Melanie Daniels and Ben Quick eventually achieve integration within the small-town family, if Professor Hill revitalizes and becomes part of the town of River City, they all begin as outsiders, altering the town while in turn the town alters the outsider.  Only the birds themselves suggest malaise erupting purely from within the town, though the audacity of that location of the town's destruction is considerably diminished by the marginal relation between non-human inhabitants of Bodega Bay and the township.  If the American small town is deemed to enjoy a privileged relationship with the natural environment--privileged, but often overtly distinguished from it, as in Peyton Place and The Deer Hunter --the examination of small-town values has, however, traditionally concerned itself exclusively with human nature and its potential fulfilment within the relatively closed society of the small town.  The discovery of cracks in the façade and the exposure of isolation and alienation within town and family by members of town and family make specially telling points against the reality of the sense of security and cohesiveness which such towns and families are supposed to promote.

Hitchcock's Shadow of a Doubt, released in the same
year, 1942, as such celebrated small-town movies as Welles'
The Magnificent Ambersons, Brown's The Human Comedy,
Stevens' The Talk of the Town and Irving Pichel's Happy
Land, opens in the seediest of urban settings, after a credit
sequence evoking, with its turn-of-the-century images of
elaborate ankle-length dresses and men in evening dress and
with Lehar's Merry Widow waltz on the soundtrack, a vanished age of elegance.  "Everyone was neat and pretty then,
the whole world, not like the world today," the Satanic hero,
Charlie (Joseph Cotten), later informs the small-town family
that he rejoins in flight from detection.  The world of Charlie, murderer of "merry widows," is that of urban squalor.
He is first seen lying on a bed in a cheap rented room, being informed by his seemingly maternal landlady that two
men have been asking for him.  Indeed, when he looks from
his window down to the tree-lined street below, there are
two men chatting together, clearly awaiting him.  After elud-
ing them, he sends a telegram to Santa Rosa, California--
"lonesome for you all...."  Meanwhile, his niece, Charlie
(Teresa Wright), lies on another bed in another second-floor
bedroom, tired of the dullness and predictability of her family.  "A family should be the most wonderful thing in the
world but this one has gone to pieces.  We go along and
nothing happens."  Uncle Charlie seeks refuge from the ex-
citement of murder and police pursuit with his telegram to
Santa Rosa, his niece Charlie seeks relief from the stale-
ness of domesticity through a (planned) telegram to Phila-
delphia.  The parallelisms and antitheses in the opening sequences of Shadow of a Doubt have been so persuasively detailed by auteurist critics anxious to demonstrate the early
appearance of transference of guilt in Hitchcock's work that
attention has been deflected from equally significant aspects
of these sequences.  If complicity between them is suggested
in the initial positioning of the two characters who share a
name, other interesting speculations are suggested in the
fact that the uncle immediately on arrival takes over the
niece's room and, from that bedroom, looks down on another tree-lined street with two characters chatting.  This
time, Charlie feels no threat.  These are no more than
what they seem, two women in summer dresses passing the
time of day together.  So confident does he now feel that, in
a movie where emphasis is laid on magic coincidence, telepathy and superstitious dread, he defies fortune by flinging
his hat onto the bed.

The principal contrast in the sequences of Charlie

looking out of the windows on similar but sharply differentiated street scenes is between city and village, between
threat and security, seediness and middle-class sufficiency.
However, there is in the credit sequence a sense of falsity
in the almost abstract evocation of period, a wilful nostalgia
(espoused, or simply traded on, by Uncle Charlie?--probably
both) which is bitterly contrasted with present reality in the
credit sequence's end. This leaves the glamorous waltzers
for some tramps by the river and a fade to the city dump,
which in turn casts doubt not so much on Charlie's image of
Santa Rosa as on the family's image of itself and its town.
Uncle Charlie has been fairly described as a figure from the
past, [1] but he is also a figure who is not only a possible victim of nostalgia but also a conscious exploiter of the nostalgia of others. Reunited with his sister, Emma, he joins her
in a sort of <u>folie à deux,</u> a shared memory of gentility, of
youth and beauty, memories which, by excluding Emma's
husband, threaten the happiness of the family in the present
world and hint, vaguely but repeatedly, at incest, until Emma becomes another merry widow, so wrapped up in her desire to relive the past that she closes her eyes to her daughter's peril. The exploration of image, or ideal, and reality
is offered as a theme from the moment when niece Charlie
feels that her family has stopped being what families ought
to be and is explicitly restated when the bogus reporters
seek to interview and photograph the family as "a representative American family" and Emma protests that they are
not typical.

The screenplay of this movie is credited to Thornton
Wilder, Sally Benson and Hitchcock's wife, Alma Reville.
Wilder is believed to have been chosen by Hitchcock because
of <u>Our Town,</u> [2] and Sally Benson's <u>New Yorker</u> stories about
the St. Louis fair of 1903 eventually inspired one of the most
potent celebrations of the American family ever filmed, Vincente Minnelli's <u>Meet Me in St. Louis.</u> The connection of
these writers with the movie would appear to guarantee a
prettification or idealization of the town of Santa Rosa. In
some senses, this expectation is fulfilled. The mother is
sentimentalized and adored by her family, the town is peopled by friendly, paternal policemen and chatty telegraph op-
erators, and, when the nightmare is over with the death of
Uncle Charlie, the detective who has fallen in love with niece
Charlie attempts to negate the uncle's savage (but authentic?)
vision of the world--even the world of Santa Rosa--with the
closing speech, "It's not so bad, but it seems to go crazy
now and then like your uncle Charlie."

Yet, there is a misanthropy, remarked frequently
elsewhere in Hitchcock's works, which runs counter to and
renders problematic the optimism which could superficially
be held to govern the presentation of Santa Rosa. Apart
from Charlie's admission of telepathy, and therefore unusual
mental sympathy between herself and her uncle, there is the
curious behavior of the mother, succumbing to the irresponsible charm of her baby brother, increasingly like the "silly
wives [in the city] that their husbands worked for till they
died." After the second "accident" which befalls her daughter, the camera pans in rapidly to Emma's face and holds it
in closeup as she ponders recent events until, for a second,
she seems to realize the key to the mystery and then wilful-
ly to suppress her knowledge. There is the absorption, albeit playfully and indulgently treated, in the mechanics of
murder shared by Pop and the mother-ridden bachelor, Her-
bert. Most significantly, there is the sequence in which Uncle Charlie reveals to his niece the hidden sleaziness of her
beloved town and therefore of the world. "There's so much
you don't know," he sneers. "You're just an ordinary little
girl living in an ordinary little town ... filled with peaceful,
stupid dreams.... You live in a dream. How do you know
what the world is like? The world's a hell. What does it
matter what happens in it?" It is this description of the
world which haunts niece Charlie to the end of the movie,
when she says, "He thought the world was a horrible place
--he didn't trust people, he used to hate them. He said
people like us had no idea what the world was really like."
If her detective lover reassures her, the audience may find
his comfort hollow when it recalls the ambience in which
Uncle Charlie makes his speech to his niece, a sordid Santa
Rosa cocktail bar, in which an already defeated-looking waitress ("I've been in half the restaurants in town"), once a
schoolgirl in niece Charlie's high school class, gazes hungrily at the ring which Charlie gives back to her uncle, and
confesses, "I'd just die for a ring like that." As the waitress is of the town, so too Uncle Charlie is of the family.
The falsity of the family's image of itself and concomitantly
of Santa Rosa's self-confidence is repeatedly suggested in
the film, above all in the barroom sequence, but also, for
example, in the funeral eulogy ("Santa Rosa has ... lost a
son") which shows that the town retains its sense of safety
and virtue only by being blinded to reality. It does, indeed,
"live in a dream."

In 1959, Minnelli's Some Came Running again takes
the theme of the citified family member who threatens the

stability and complacency of the rest of the family by returning to the small town in which it occupies so prominent a
position, and vastly develops the notion of the squalor of the
town's underbelly.  While Santa Rosa is photographed in a
chaste monochrome appropriate to the later Best Years of
Our Lives, the contrasts in Some Came Running's Parkman,
Illinois3 are much heightened visually by decor, lighting and
use of color.  "I decided to use the inside of a juke box as
my inspiration for the settings," Minnelli reports credibly. 4
Elmer Bernstein's brassy, strident score complements the
garishness of the sets for Smitty's cocktail bar, the transient gambler Bama's home and the spectacular town carnival
at the film's climax.  The lowlife characters are, rightly,
overplayed, becoming parodies, embodiments of the "respectable" townsfolk's worst fears as those townsfolk are in turn
parodies of frigidity and decency, imagined, as it were, by
the lowlife characters.  Dave Hirsh (Frank Sinatra), a writer who has just left the army, enters town with a sluttish
girl, Ginny (Shirley McLaine), in tow.  She soon makes contact with the drifters in town, such as Bama (Dean Martin)
and Rosalie, the stoned-looking brunette who works in the
local brassiere factory, while Dave Hirsh hovers uncertainly
on the periphery of this world.  The casting of Dean Martin
as Bama, a role for which he barely moderates his nightclub persona, and the playing of Ginny by Shirley McLaine,
all smeared lipstick, childish overemphasis and splayed legs,
Rosalie's plunging neckline and fondness for scarlet, together
contribute to the distancing of the audience and the isolating
of Dave Hirsh, underplayed by Frank Sinatra, in a town of
maniacal extremes.  The respectable side of town is housed
in white-pillared domains, with Ideal Home interiors of
marked spaciousness, polished surfaces, winding staircases,
handsome bookshelves, the women as lacquered and groomed
as Ginny is unkempt and tawdry.  Ross Hunter meets Andy
Warhol.  Dave Hirsh's brother Frank (Arthur Kennedy) and
his family hold little appeal for Dave, since Frank had denied him in his youth and now seems vulgar, opportunistic
and hypocritical.  Rather, he is drawn to Gwen French
(Martha Hyer) who leads a tame existence with her father
as a teacher of Creative Writing and Criticism, at Parkman
College.  Gwen, attracted to Dave through admiration of his
writing, succumbs to his advances, her rigorously upswept
hair falling recklessly about her shoulders as, hilariously,
Dave pulls pins from her hair prior to their love-making.
Later, she withdraws from him to the safety of the world of
letters and her asexual life, sharing a home with her father.
"I don't want you to be in love with me.  Don't be, please,"

she begs Dave, as shortly Ginny will beg the opposite,
"Dave, be in love with me." This direct contrast between
Gwen and Ginny, well-manicured, tepid, civilized womanhood versus honest, warm slatternliness epitomizes a wider
contrast between the dull safety of the small town and the
uglier but more life-accepting energy of the world outside,
which has always to be driven underground within a town of
Parkman's hypocrisy. Dave stands uncertainly between the
two, more at ease with the boozing cardsharpers and dumb
broads and yet yearning for the promise of material and
psychological security that Gwen and, to some extent, his
brother's family represent.

Throughout the movie, the town is on trial. At the
moment when Dave consents to marry Ginny, in loneliness
and desperation, a choice is made which is not so much an
affirmation of the charms of the world of honest carnality as
a denial of Parkman's values. The pessimism of Minnelli's
view of the small town is reinforced by Ginny's death. At
the enormous, sprawling carnival which celebrates the town's
centennial, [5] Ginny and Dave pick their way through the
masses at the fair, spatially isolated ("I don't know where
we're going, baby--I just want to get out of Parkman") from
a mob which, while herded together, enjoys no more organic
cohesiveness than any other mob. When Ginny is shot, she
becomes in this context another sideshow for the townsfolk,
and, significantly, her death provides the one moment where
Frank Hirsh and his family come together as a unit. At her
funeral, the divisions are reinforced, with Gwen and her
father together, Dave standing with Bama and Rosalie.

Dave Hirsh, fated to remain an outsider to his own
family, by reason, it is implied, of his superior intellect
and sensitivity, and ultimately estranged from Gwen by her
inability to share his sexuality and honesty, and Uncle Charlie, too unblinkered in his gaze upon the self-limiting town
of Santa Rosa to find peace within it, suggest the smothering
conformity demanded by the small town as its price for integration. These characters arrive in some desperation and
never quite merge into family or town. They must always
alter them or else sacrifice or disguise their own beliefs.
In this respect, the small town becomes a metaphor for the
forces of bourgeois conformism and for all philistine hostility to idiosyncrasy, epitomized romantically in the figures of
the obsessed killer and of the "blocked" writer.

It is this aspect of the small town which Carson

McCullers uses in her book and play, The Member of the
Wedding, filmed by Fred Zinnemann in 1953.  All the principal characters are inhabitants of a small Georgia town,
not outsiders, and yet each suffers some sense of estrangement.  The 12-year-old heroine, Frankie (Julie Harris),
aches to belong to something but seems psychologically unable to fit.  With her crewcut hair, tomboyish clothes and
scraped knees, she is looked upon askance by the young girls
in white dresses and suffers the misery of being passed over
in the election to their "club."  The cook, Berenice (Ethel
Waters), who has looked after her since her mother's death,
patiently explains, "The idea of a club is that members are
included, non-members are not included."  Berenice under-
stands club (town) rules more clearly than anybody.  She is
a one-eyed, frequently-married, black servant whose understanding of Frankie is as perspicacious as it is irksome to
the adolescent.  Mirroring Frankie's loneliness is the even
less focused unhappiness of John Henry (Brandon de Wilde),
the next-door child neglected by his mother, who tries on
Berenice's shoes and handbag or dresses up in an angel cos-
tume.  Frankie and John Henry have as yet failed to learn
the sexual codes necessary for "membership," while Berenice is disqualified from birth, it would appear.

Finding the idea of belonging--to anything--more powerfully appealing as she continues to be excluded, Frankie
becomes obsessed with the approaching wedding of her brother Jarvis to Janice and determines to leave with them, as
"a member of the wedding," for she links staying within the
town with her directionlessness and anomie and leaving town
with freedom and, yet, belonging.  They will be "members
of the whole world," she cries hysterically as she imagines
their departure after the wedding.  Berenice has discovered
more modest ways of surviving.  As Frankie discerns, she
belongs to "the church, the lodge and the colored people."
Yet, she can never be fully part of the town, as she discovers when one of her family, Honey, is thrown into prison.
The belonging which these three characters--Berenice, Frankie and John Henry--may enjoy is together, as a sort of surrogate family, a point made with special clarity and poignan-
cy in their singing of "His eye is on the sparrow."

Rejected by the married couple after the ceremony
and dragged humiliatingly into her home by her father,
Frankie, who has always associated her unhappiness with
being stuck in a town which she hates, runs away.  In rapid
succession, she encounters several unimagined realities, the

sexual desire of a young soldier for her, afterwards the ugliness heretofore hidden from her eyes in the back streets
downtown, and, when she returns home, the final shock of
John Henry's death through illness.   Some time later, these
experiences seem to have transformed her.   She has found a
friend worthy of her ambitions, and has begun to feel attraction to a boy of roughly her age.   John Henry has become
almost unreal, a "little ghost."   Berenice, sitting in the
kitchen which has been the principal set of the movie throughout, waiting to vacate the house for good, is assured by
Frankie that she will visit her but knows that, despite her
good intentions, there will be no such visits.   She is left
alone, crooning in the manner which was first heard with
the opening credits.

This Southern-set movie, like The Sound and the Fury
(1959) and The Heart Is a Lonely Hunter (1968), takes the
maturing of a young lonely girl as its theme and, like these
other works, comments incidentally on the losses involved in
that passage into adulthood and integration, such as the rup-
ture in contact with those adults excluded by reason of color
or mental retardation, the diminution of sensitivity.   The
town is something which beckons and embraces with its reassurance of belonging.   As it delivers its promise and en-
folds the adolescent in its cocoon, it separates her from
those very outcasts which have sustained her hitherto.   The
bitterness, whether intentional or not, which seems incapable
of being forgotten in the apparently reassuring, "healthful"
endings of such movies, comments powerfully on the sacrifices demanded of the individual who wishes to become a
"member."   The James Dean character lays aside the tor-
ments of being passed over by his father and seems to lose
the very qualities to which his brother's girl is drawn as,
at the end of East of Eden (1955), he takes over the head-
ship of the family, stepping into his brother's shoes and
making peace with his dying father so that he may become
"a whole man," confident machismo replacing adolescent
yearning.   Dorothy Malone, hugging the oil-derrick orna-
ment on her father's desk at the end of Written on the Wind
(1957), is the female counterpart to the James Dean character, "maturing" into a place in the respectable family after
giving every indication of temperamental revulsion against
the way of life demanded by family and town.

Delbert Mann's The Dark at the Top of the Stairs
(1960) concentrates on a travelling harness salesman's family in a small Oklahoma town of the early 1920s.   Robert

Preston, playing an earlier, more restrained version of his
Music Man role, is Rubin Flood, paterfamilias in a nuclear
family where his son is unable to defend himself but clings
to his mother (Dorothy McGuire) in fear of "the dark at the
top of the stairs" and where his daughter (Shirley Knight) is
unable to master the arts of sexual attractiveness.  His wife
rejects Rubin's sexual advances so that he is driven to an
attractive widow (Angela Lansbury) who bolsters his ego by
responding to his virility without actually going to bed with
him.

Largely, the film is a drama of the gradual master-
ing of the sexual stereotype and consequent reassertion of
order and happiness within the family, a version of Tea and
Sympathy writ more large, in every way an antithesis to
Theorem, where it is the potentiality of the individual which
is unleashed despite the bourgeois family, rather than the
curbing of individualism achieved in the interests of the family unit.  Rubin's wife, Cora, invites her out-of-town sister
and her sister's husband to visit her so that she can arrange
to leave for their home with her two children.  Gradually,
she learns the truth of their marriage, that because of her
sister's frigidity no sex has occurred for many years.  Meanwhile, her daughter finds another lonely soul to whom at last
she can respond, losing her sense of inadequacy in his affection for her and the tenderness of his courtship.  Her young
admirer is a Jew abandoned by his film-star mother.  He is
ejected from the town's principal family's party on the grounds
of his religion, although additional capital is made of his
date's turning "a nice birthday party into a petting party."
When he is dying after a near-successful suicide attempt,
she rushes to his side to declare her feelings for him, and
a number of changes occur within the family.  Cora discovers her need for Rubin who simply wants his wife to love
him so that he does not have to seek the (remarkably chaste)
solace which the widow has been offering him.  The formerly uncertain mother's boy goes after the school bullies with
a baseball bat and at last earns his father's approval and,
implicitly, his self-respect.

Ultimately, the town's prejudices, which are indicated,
for example, in the gossip which surrounds Rubin's visit to
his widowed friend, are shared by the subjects of the gossip.
The movie seems to reinforce all that stifles the Flood family by apparently equating psychic health and domestic felicity
with the adoption of stereotypical behavior.  Rubin's straying
is seen as a result of Cora's failure to fulfill a wifely role.

"I don't want to lose him," she confides to her apparent
rival, who immediately advises, "Then do your job--pay attention to him." Reenie, the daughter, blossoms into self-
confidence when a young man shows her some understanding
and allows her to feel sexually desirable. The son gains
respect from his parents and, presumably, his schoolmates
when he becomes as aggressive as those who have made his
life miserable. The movie ends with husband and wife re-
tiring to bed together in the daytime, setting the seal of
happiness on their hitherto tortured relations. In this context, the theme of the misfit, potentially present as a major
element in the drama with the inclusion of the young Jew as
a sort of more extreme version of the family members' sense
of disjuncture, becomes tangential, picked up to illustrate
Reenie's sense of ostracization or rather, perhaps, to put it
into perspective, but then casually dropped with his death,
as if his function in the plot has been purely to point up the
good fortune of a Gentile girl to have so much less to fight
against.

While The Dark at the Top of the Stairs seems as if
it has been made not only about a small town but with the
aim of gaining the approval of a small-town audience, with
its final alignment with the small-town ethos, most of the
movies which deal with misfits in provincial families are
sufficiently ambivalent towards these individuals to call the
morality by which they are so deemed into question. As
misfits learn to fit, their characters coarsen or lose the
very qualities to which we were drawn, the standards to
which they conform seem more oppressive. Other misfits
who do not choose to fit or are incapable of so fitting withdraw altogether or are eliminated so that resolution may
take place.

In this respect, the small-town family, like the town
itself, may become a useful metaphor for the constraints
upon individual freedom, a shorthand for all that thwarts
individualism, even that most sacred of values, community,
and nearly all the movies so far examined in this book may
be seen to take as a principal subject the balancing of individual freedom against the solace of "membership." While
the small-town movie may be straightforwardly about the
American small town, it may also be about all that may be
termed "small-town attitudes," about philistinism, puritan-
ism, sexual stereotyping, and so on, and the impact of these
upon the artist, the loner, the deviant. Whether the deviant
withdraws into a shell of sensitivity, with Dave Hirsh, or

finds a way, with the Flood family, to achieve integration, whether provincialism is held up as a force for human happiness or misery, may be less interesting than that the small-town movie lends itself to such manifold explorations of individual and community.

## Notes to Chapter 6

1. By Gavin Miller, in Raymond Durgnat, The Strange Case of Alfred Hitchcock (Faber and Faber, London, 1974), pp. 33-34.

2. See François Truffaut, Le Cinéma Selon Hitchcock (Editions Robert Laffont, Paris, 1966), p. 111.

3. Parkman, Illinois was actually Madison, Indiana, a town interestingly voted "the most typical American small town" in 1941 by the Office of War Information.

4. Vincente Minnelli with Hector Arce, I Remember It Well (Doubleday and Co., New York, 1974), p. 325.

5. Carnivals frequently play a significant part in small-town movies, indicating areas of danger and/or mystery. Thus, the heroine of The Sound and the Fury (1959) is seduced by a carnival worker visiting her town, the hero of East of Eden (1955) first manages to express himself to the heroine when the ferris wheel stops, leaving them suspended high above the fairground. One entire small-town movie, the musical Carousel (1956), is built on the notion of the dangerous lure of the carnival, with its misfit hero, the carousel barker Billy Bigelow, entering the life of a local factory girl with disastrous results until his soul is permitted to revisit earth to put matters aright. The final ballet of the movie records his daughter's bedazzlement by the visiting carnival and the moral outrage of the town's "best families" at such licentiousness. The outrage is out of all proportion to the frivolity of an afternoon at the fairground. Clearly, the carnival represents much more--irresponsibility, carnality, transience, social marginality.

## 7. EPITAPH

Until 1971, American small-town movies cut a swathe through a surprising variety of genres. A large number of them are melodramas (Kings Row, All That Heaven Allows), but many more are comedies (The Bank Dick, It Happened to Jane), musicals (Carousel, The Music Man, Bye Bye Birdie), thrillers (Anatomy of a Murder, In the Heat of the Night) or horror films (Invasion of the Body Snatchers, The Blob). Yet, all of them are united by one element, that the characters consider themselves and their town in relation to the city (Shadow of a Doubt) or to the beneficent countryside (Peyton Place) but never to media representations of the small town or small-town family. None of the films is reflexive, contemplating its place within a series of films on similar themes, and within similar settings, nor are any characters self-conscious, in the sense of comparing their own behavior with that of media representations of similarly placed characters.

When a genre becomes sufficiently aware of itself and its strategies to declare them, it is arguable that its lifespan is approaching its end, and certainly the self-conscious or reflexive movie makes it at least awkward for subsequent directors to return to the "naïve" version when the artifices and conventions of the series have been exposed to its audience.

Peter Bogdanovich's The Last Picture Show was released in 1971 and was greeted by reviewers with almost universal enthusiasm, the approval with which it met never again being matched in critical reactions to work by Bogdanovich. Despite the near unanimity of the favorable press, reviews of the movie reveal a widespread uncertainty as to the choice of approach to it.

If emphasis be placed on the action of the movie, several narrative strands could be selected for consideration.

125

The town of Anarene, Texas, in 1951, contains a number of shabby would-be social centers, the pool hall, a café and, not least, the picture show.   All of these are owned by Sam the Lion, the character who seems to represent the heart of the movie as of the town, not only in being given a central speech detailing the changes in town life, but in acting as a bridge between the younger and older generations of Anarene. The concentration, as far as concerns the younger generation, is principally on three members of the graduating class, Duane (Jeff Bridges) and Jacy (Cybill Shepherd), who in the earlier part of the movie are going steady, and Duane's friend, Sonny (Timothy Bottoms).   The latter, dissatisfied with his tedious relationship with an unattractive high school girlfriend, Charlene, becomes involved with Ruth Popper (Cloris Leachman), the coach's unhappy wife.   Jacy begins to hanker for the more glamorous world apparently offered by an outsider, Bobby Sheen, and, when Duane is used by her so that through her loss of virginity she may become more acceptable to this smart set, he enlists and goes off to Korea after spending his last night at the picture show, watching Red River with Sonny.   Jacy halfheartedly attempts to elope with Sonny but is relieved when parental opposition ends the "romance." Sonny, in the final scene of the movie, revisits Ruth and a sad awareness of their limitations seems to enter their lives. Apart from Sonny, Duane and Jacy, there are other young characters--Billy, a mentally retarded youth who hangs around the pool hall and is eventually killed by a cattle truck, and Joe Bob, the class "creep" who at one point abducts a little girl.   Of the "parental" generation, Sam's waitress, Genevieve, plays an important role on the periphery of the youthful liaisons, but at least as important are the parts of Ruth Popper and Lois, Jacy's mother and her rival for the affection of a local hardhat, Abilene.   Lois has in her early years enjoyed a memorable, but secret, affair with Sam the Lion, whose death, coinciding as it does with the decline in the picture show's popularity, seems to represent the demise of any sense of community in Anarene.

Some reviewers seemed to take Bogdanovich's film as a straightforward, but more truthful, element in the small-town movie series, although most of them were aware of some role played by media in the creation of the movie's meaning.   Thus, P.D. Zimmerman identified Sam the Lion with the town's soul, a link with its frontier past, and saw television as dissolving the "communal bonds which make small towns something more than mere miniatures of the bigger cities."[1]   Pauline Kael considered the movie "a

lovingly exact history of American small-town life. "[2]   When
The Last Picture Show is carefully considered, however,
the most perceptive comments seem to have been made by
Mark Lefanu[3] ("The aim is not, certainly, to produce a
'realistic' picture of small town America.   Bogdanovich
realizes that the cinema is not, in Godard's dictum, the
reflection of reality, but rather, the reality of a reflection
... ") and Charles Champlin[4] ("What Bogdanovich has done,
deliberately I'm sure, is not so much to try to recapture
small town life as to reconstitute a vision of small town
life (usually steamy) as American movies gave it to us under 10, 000 place names in 10, 000 crises. ")

    Bogdanovich's background as film critic, the overt
filmic references in Targets (1968) (Boris Karloff apparently playing himself and commenting on his role within the
film industry), the clear invitation in What's Up, Doc?
(1972) and At Long Last Love (1975) to see them as evoca-
tions of "classic" Hollywood and revivals of such an essentially golden-age genre as screwball comedy, combine to indicate the credibility of viewing The Last Picture Show in
self-consciously cinematic terms.   Furthermore, the focus
of this latter film, as admittedly of the Larry McMurtry
novel from which it was drawn, on the picture show, and
the sequences involving the exhibiting of Red River and
Father of the Bride, must surely help to justify the notion
that we are not presented with a realist treatment of small-
town life but with yet another Bogdanovich evocation of Hollywood.

    Pauline Kael,[5] like Jan Dawson in Sight and Sound's
review,[6] fairly links the film with Peyton Place and, less
fairly, by implication identifies the genre as melodrama.

    The comparison with Mark Robson's Peyton Place is
useful, though Miss Kael's conclusion that Bogdanovich's
film might be considered as a species of, or at least reaction against, melodrama needs fuller investigation.

    Thematically, there is much in common between the
two films.   Both center on the gulf between generations, the
younger being represented by a graduation class, adolescents
about to enter an adult world, deeply involved with the rituals of courtship and to some extent with those attendant
upon graduation, the older being those of all ages who have
already entered that world, against whose mores the young
measure themselves.   Sam the Lion, the accepted arbiter

of town morality, in Anarene, Texas, is simply another version of Peyton Place's Doc Swain or the school principal,
Mike Rossi.   The family as microcosm of generational inter-
action is as central to Picture Show as to Peyton Place.
There are families with missing parents and apparently consequent problems in children's adjustment to their filial
roles.   Allison MacKenzie's and Norman Page's fatherless
homes in Peyton Place are paralleled by Sonny's motherless
home and Duane's lack of a father in Picture Show.   Jacy's
conflict with her dominant and sexually successful mother,
the father being a negligible presence within the family home,
is paralleled by Allison's sexual battles with Constance
MacKenzie.

        The issues facing both sides of the generation gap
seem similar in the two films.   Should Allison (and Jacy)
go on to school after graduation, should girls surrender
their virginity to high-school sweethearts, dare the young
seek fulfilment outside approved liaisons (Allison with bookish, effeminate Norman Page, Sonny with the high school
coach's wife), should unhappy, repressed adults continue
with hypocritical family roles (Constance MacKenzie playing
the gracious widow, to mask her affair in New York and
Allison's illegitimacy, being comparable with Jacy's mother
suffering in her present extra-marital affair, as well as in
obscuring her past, apparently passionate, relationship with
Sam the Lion)?   The young of Peyton Place go off to the
Second World War, Duane to Korea.   If some critics,
prompted by the overtly elegiac nature of the Bogdanovich
films, have discerned a greater preoccupation with death in
it than in the Robson, it may be worth remarking that the
two deaths in Anarene--Sam the Lion's and the retarded
Billy's fatal accident--are arguably less pivotal than Peyton
Place's murder of Lucas Cross, Nelly Cross's suicide, or
Rodney Harrington's death in action.

        If, then, the subject-matter of the two films justifies
their being linked, the question remains whether the Bogdanovich film may then be best understood in terms of melodrama, as another element in the well-established genre or,
more probably, as an implicit critique of it (in the manner
of the British The National Health (1973), where a soap-
opera hospital series for television is juxtaposed with the
more austere images of "reality" in a National Health Service hospital).

        However, it is immediately obvious that the confidence

with which melodrama identifies its problems and their solutions (both predominantly within the family) is missing. As
stated earlier (p. 51), melodrama involves a "tone," attitudes of concern toward its clearly identified conflicts, an
ostensibly straight-faced and sober treatment of love and
death and family. While the themes are all there in Picture
Show, the bewilderment of the characters induces bewilderment in the audience, the casualness and arbitrariness of the
liaisons, the disorienting lack of information about the depth
and "meaning" of, say, Sonny's dalliance with the coach's
wife, or of either Jacy's or her mother's romance with the
same man (Abilene), are light years away from previous examples of the genre, closer to Antonioni than Sirk. It seems
perverse to take it as melodrama. If it is a critique of
melodrama, to what end? The TV comedy series, Soap,
seems an admirable demonstration of the fatuity of guying a
genre whose potential absurdity lies in the seriousness with
which it takes arguably negligible issues, in the inflation of
the domestic to the cosmic. When the seriousness is removed and the audiences are invited to guffaw, the result is
uncomfortably arch. Bogdanovich can scarcely be accused
here of winking at the audience in the Soap manner. If the
irony in his treatment of courtship rituals (the nude swimming parties in Bobby Sheen's house, Jacy's determined bid
to lose her virginity, the high school girls' permission for
petting only above the waist) argues a sophistication in director and audience that would be suppressed or disguised
in a Douglas Sirk melodrama, there is no such detachment
permitted from Ruth Popper's wretched life with her coach
husband or the bitter end to her affair with Sonny, from the
deaths in the film, from the mourning for the end of youth
and the closing of the picture show.

It is misleading to see the relationship of Picture
Show with Peyton Place as a commentary on Hollywood melodrama. Peyton Place may indeed be melodrama, but it is
also the 'fifties epitome of "the small-town movie," a genre
which an extremely small number of Picture Show reviewers
seemed to invoke in their attempt to locate the film. (Thus,
for example, one of this small number, Jim Pines, claims
that the film seems to vacillate between two distinct genres,
the western, and another which he terms "provincial drama."7)

Bogdanovich himself considered that his film was a
retort to Thornton Wilder's Our Town (filmed by Sam Wood
in 1940). As Our Town seems to offer a theatrical summation of all American novels and dramas which stress the

idyllic nature of small-town life and the positive aspects of
small-town values, Peyton Place represents one of Hollywood's definitive affirmations of the small town and may,
since it seems to encompass all aspects of the small-town
movie, usefully be examined in relation to The Last Picture
Show from that angle rather than as a prime example of
melodrama.

Bogdanovich's film opens, immediately after the title,
with a tracking shot from the Royal "picture show," a low,
flat-roofed building, along a deserted, windblown street.
Such trees as are visible are well in the background.   Stark
telephone poles line the street instead.   The only sound is
that of the wind until Sonny's wreck of a truck is audible,
then visible, and country-western music can be heard from
the truck radio.   Through the cracked windscreen as the
truck shudders and jolts on its progress down the street is
seen Billy sweeping the dust off the dirt road.   The two
boys enter a shabby, grimy poolroom.   Sam the Lion is
coughing, Sonny tries to get warm, and the dialogue is well-
nigh indecipherable--not simply because of the Texan accents
but because of the Altman-like, studiedly casual quality of
the sound track.   It would appear that Sam is reproving Sonny
for his sloppy appearance.   When Abilene enters, the still
semi-audible soundtrack yields the information that the local
school ball team has performed wretchedly again.   "Where's
your school spirit?" asks Abilene.   "Don't know," mumbles
Sonny.   When the boys leave the pool hall, a Farrow Oil Co.
truck pulls up, containing some hardhats, including Duane.
As the truck pulls away there is further jeering about the
ball game.

Peyton Place opens with aerial views of the town behind the credits while the sound track swells with the romantic music that is the staple score for this kind of movie
since Our Town.   The color is that of the National Geographic variety, the movie is shot in CinemaScope and the
import of the credit sequence is that Peyton Place has an
organic quality to it, a relation with the changing seasons
and countryside, and a wholeness of town planning.   Thus,
the mills are prominent but architecturally fitting, and the
houses of the town are surrounded by lush greenery of tree
foliage and plant life.

Bogdanovich's decision to use black and white and a
more standard film ratio is not explicable purely as evidence
of a desire for "realism."   His primary concentration on the

picture show itself is significant in the opening sequence because it introduces a dichotomy familiar in the small-town
movie, that of ideal/real, in a new guise--art/life.   The
viewing within the film, of <u>Father of the Bride</u> and <u>Red</u>
<u>River,</u> 8 at the picture show and of TV, is of black-and-
white, standard-ratio work.   While reviewers have usually
contrasted the community feel of the cinema viewing experience with the isolated TV-watching in the movie, there is
little sense of community in the picture show sequences.
The Minnelli work is treated as a make-out movie for a
few awkward teenagers and <u>Red River</u> is an entertainment
for an isolated pair of adolescents.   In both sequences, the
picture show is a means of avoiding reality (the image of
Elizabeth Taylor allows Sonny to forget for a moment that
Charlene is fat and unattractive, the Hawks film fills an
awkward gap in which otherwise good-byes would have to be
protracted).   There is little difference in the experience of
the unhappy Jacy's solitary viewing of the TV show and of
the teenagers, few in number and quite out of contact with
one another, at the picture show.   The opening sequence,
therefore, involves a double contrast.   Firstly, by killing
any sense of wholeness or natural beauty in the town, by
destroying any grasp of the time of year and relegating the
few trees to a dimly perceived background, Bogdanovich denies some of the fundamental qualities of the movie small
town; secondly, by his "neutral" shooting of the empty dirt
road at approximately eye level, he contrasts this grainy,
"uncharacterized" black-and-white view of Texas with the
Hawksian version which heroizes the men in monochrome,
by shooting from below against the skyline, and which links
the separate shots of the individual men engaging in the
same whooping into a sequence whose overall sense involves
an assertion of communal purpose.   Thus, the gulf between
the characters' experiences and the Hollywood presentation
of those experiences to them is explored within a movie
which stands on its head the prevailing conventions of the
small-town movie.   The key element in these endeavors
could be called stylistic, oddly enough (since style seems
so diverse in the variety of small-town movies).   A fairer
judgment might be that this movie appears to recognize the
existence of a rhetoric within the earlier movies, a set of
signals, on sound and visual tracks, that actions and speeches
are "meaningful, " and that there are causes and effects operating throughout the movie, and that the various disparate
personalities and events are somehow united in an overall
order, that of the town itself.   Whereas in the "naïve" movies we are always permitted to know why people take certain

courses of action, the denial of order within the layout of
Anarene, so that it becomes a set of individual buildings
dumped on the landscape with no obviously intended interconnection between houses or between houses and terrain,
is simply one aspect of a denial of patterns of causality in
the lives of the characters.

While the "content" of Picture Show is routine, what
radically alters and subverts it is the casualness and arbitrariness of its treatment.    When Billy, Sam the Lion, Abilene and Duane are introduced, we have no means of knowing whether or not they are background local color or to be
foregrounded, and we can scarcely hear what they are saying.    In Peyton Place, there is a voice-over to signal the
identity of the chief character and we are permitted to move
into town with a newcomer, Mike Rossi, so that the topographical, and thus social position of the land can be grasped
by audience and character alike.    When Allison runs to
school, her route takes in grass and falling leaves, the
cemetery, the local hospital and the town hall.    Then, when
she arrives in school, the ideas for which the town purport-
edly stands and the backgrounds of the principal adolescents
are deftly established in the classroom sequence.

The emphasis in one movie is on an order, whether
good or bad, in the town, on institutions and geographical/
cultural backgrounds and ideals from which all the characters' behavior originates and against which it can be meas-
ured and comprehended.    By removing all sense of wholeness in Anarene with that opening view of one empty road
and by stressing Sonny's bewilderment about any appeal to
such intangibles as school spirit, by the paucity of clues as
to principal or peripheral characters, Bogdanovich creates
a picture of a rootless, anomic society produced more by
geographical accident than design.    Even the Farrow Oil
Company which provides economic viability for the town is
reduced to a passing truck.    The Korean War is no more
or less remarkable--it is neither good nor bad, it offers
employment.    The inaudibility of the sound track is just another aspect of the lack of signposting, the refusal to engage with the significant and the casual or irrelevant.

Thus, while the usual elements are there, their relevance to motivation is seldom clear.    Sonny has the briefest
of meaningless chats with his father at the Christmas dance.
Glances pass between Lois (Jacy's mother) and Abilene, but
the seriousness of their affair is never known by us (or

them?). When Jacy seduces him, we expect a confrontation between mother and daughter of the sort that climaxes Labor Day in Peyton Place and which results in Allison's breakdown and departure. Instead, the impact is dissipated. Jacy comes in, the mother seems to understand what has happened between them and apparently girds herself for battle, Jacy talks about her unhappiness at losing Bobby Sheen to another girl and now whether her mother guesses at or cares about the truth is difficult to judge because she is drawn into a sympathetic discussion. Repeatedly, the casualness and ambiguity of treatment of what would in other small-town movies be key situations disorients the viewer. All the "big scenes" are flattened out by the seldom distinguishable sounds of country-western--the music becomes a syrup which the characters themselves pour over their lives. Sonny courts and breaks up with Charlene, then submits to Ruth Popper and later Jacy with equal unconcern, though his tenderness with Ruth seems genuine. When passions do break out, as in Ruth's coffeepot-throwing tirade in the last sequence, the reaction (Sonny's silent grief) seems to be less to the surface subject than to the consciousness of apparently arbitrary or possibly quite unavoidable behavior. (We may compare the violent fight between Duane and Sonny, where neither seems to have any clue as to Jacy's reasons or their own reactions to her machinations. Also comparable, and consciously so on Bogdanovich's part, one suspects, is the final sequence of Antonioni's L'Avventura, where Monica Vitti strokes Gabriele Ferzetti's head in recognition of the transient nature of love.) School, which provides moral sustenance for the young generation of Peyton Place, sufficient to send them off to war, is simply irrelevant here. The English teacher tries to talk of Keats, but those who listen to the "Ode to a Nightingale" can make no sense of it. The graduation ceremony is casually interpolated, and never alluded to again, a time reference, the marking of a transition in factual terms but of no further significance to the characters. Sam the Lion attempts to muster a town spirit but appears to have no basis on which to construct a code other than basic decency and nostalgia. When he talks to Sonny or Billy, it is of the past. He and his standards seem anachronistic, like his picture show.

And yet there are standards of conduct, largely those created by popular culture, and certain characters--particularly Jacy--respond to media images. The acquired notion of sophistication is particularly evident at Bobby Sheen's

parties where for once country-western gives place to bal-
lads, and Jacy decides the question of her sexual morality
purely on the criterion of her acceptability to this more
glamorous set.  Of all the characters, Jacy is most obviously playing with her externally inspired notions of small-
town behavior when she seduces Abilene and when she persuades Sonny to elope with her by car, and especially when
she falsifies the account of her "loss of virginity."  On the
elopement, she becomes increasingly irritated with Sonny's
eye patch, which interferes with the media image of young
love, and becomes frightened by the thought that her parents will not play their small-town part in her contrived
drama and chase after them to break up this cross-class
romance.

The semiconscious comparisons by the characters of
life in Anarene with the movies' images of behavior are the
most innovative elements in Bogdanovich's movie and may
possibly furnish the reason why Bogdanovich is so generally
lauded for it whereas his later comments on Hollywood's
past are dismissed as trivial.  In the other small-town movies by different directors, there is never a self-conscious
reflection by the characters on their relationship to contem-
porary popular-art depiction of their situations, whereas
here the characters are saturated in the ersatz version of
provincial life contained in country-western lyrics and in
movies or TV artifacts.

Once again, the small-town movie can be explained
as America talking about and to herself.  The Last Picture
Show seems to suggest that, with the small town, even in
one of the fiercely independent states, being now obviously
part of mass society, America feeds upon dead images of
herself and her history which may themselves have been
created by her mass media.  Thus, Sam the Lion's death,
the departure of Jacy and Duane, the closure of the picture
show, do not so much signify the death of community as the
death of the myth of community.

Only two years after the Bogdanovich film, a more
lighthearted but no less elegiac movie, George Lucas' American Graffiti (1973), takes up afresh several aspects of The
Last Picture Show.  In the course of one night, the entire
decade of the 'fifties and of Hollywood's presentation of that
period is acted out and laid to rest in a small-town setting,
with emphasis exclusively upon teenagers.

A film of bright pastel colors appropriate to the
Coca-Cola dream, American Graffiti opens at Mel's Drive-
In while "Rock Around the Clock" plays on the sound track.
This setting is the principal recurring venue and the entire
movie is accompanied by 'fifties rock and the cooler California sounds of the Beach Boys ushering in the 'sixties.
Once again, as so often in the small-town movies, the teenage characters are on the eve of adult experience, having
recently graduated from high school, and once again the exploration of that period of transition is located in summer.
Three local boys--Steve, Terry and Curt--contemplate leaving "this turkey town" for college.   As Steve reminds them,
"You can't stay seventeen forever."   Steve's high school
sweetheart, Laurie, grieved by his desire for greater sexual freedom now that he is leaving home, makes him jealous
by taking up with a hot-rodder but the couple are reunited
after an accident during a hot rod race.   Terry, using the
car Steve has agreed to leave in his keeping during his absence, picks up a friendly blonde, Debbie, attempts to buy
liquor for them, loses the car to a teenage gang, the Pharaohs, and regains it by stealth.   Gradually, the truth of
his inadequacies emerges, but Debbie remains happy with
him and his Vespa, his more usual mode of transport.
Curt, obsessed with a briefly glimpsed blonde who smiled
at him, seeks her in vain throughout the night and, having
at last made contact with her by telephone in the early
morning, becomes the only one to leave town for college.

The story of these three types of love, faithful
(Steve/Laurie), pragmatic (Terry/Debbie) and romantic
(Curt/unknown blonde), like an American version of Ingmar
Bergman's Smiles of a Summer Night (1955), is, unlike the
Swedish film, told against a background of cruising cars,
drive-ins, hamburger stands, and always accompanied by
the hits of the 'fifties and early 'sixties.   The entire town
seems to be overseen by Wolfman, the disc jockey on the
local radio station to whom all the teenagers listen on their
car radios and who arranges the telephone call from Curt's
goddess to him before he leaves town.   Not only are the
images summoned up by American Graffiti those of 'fifties
movies--particularly Nicholas Ray's Rebel Without a Cause
(1955), The Wild One (1954) (for the Pharaohs and the waitress in the threatened town) and the cheap Columbia-
produced rock 'n roll quickies--but the characters see themselves in relation to Hollywood images.   One character without the requisite scholastic achievement to leave town, John,

is modelled on the pop-star image embodied by Elvis Presley and Fabian, and on the James Dean rebel, driving about
in his hot rod, covering his insecurity with his "line" with
girls and his ability to impress the high school boys.    John
disapproves of the Beach Boys, in the belief that "rock 'n
roll has been going downhill since Buddy Holly's death." It
is this character, quintessentially 'fifties and anti-'sixties,
which is extended into that of "the Fonz" in the television
series, Happy Days.    When Terry picks up Debbie, he attracts her interest by telling her that she looks like Connie
Stevens.    (She thought she looked like Sandra Dee, a notion
of the exemplar of feminine pulchritude extended into an entire musical number in Grease, the most commercially successful of all 'fifties pastiches.)    "You're just like the Lone
Ranger," Debbie tells John admiringly when he rushes in to
rescue Terry from the Pharaohs.    The hotrod race, another
element of Grease, is an imitation of the famous chicken-
run sequence in Rebel Without a Cause.

        American Graffiti, after Curt's departure to college,
provides the audience with information concerning only--
maddening to feminists but arguably true to the spirit of the
'fifties movies--the four young men on whom the movie has
centered itself.    Two of them die, Terry in Vietnam, John
because of a drunken driver, while Steve becomes an insur-
ance agent, and Curt a writer living in Canada.

        It would not be stretching the import of the movie too
far to conclude that it suggests the coincidence of the end of
the characters' adolescence with that of America's.    With
grimmer realities than were dreamed of in the late 'fifties
and early 'sixties on the horizon--President Kennedy's assassination, Vietnam and the self-exile of a large proportion
of America's young--the images which the movie's teenagers
seek to embody become quaint, charming but insubstantial,
gone forever.

        American Graffiti makes its points about media im-
ages and the actuality of small-town life in the early 'sixties
while keeping within the period and relegating the future to a
series of titles at the end.    Robert Altman's Come Back to
the Five and Dime, Jimmy Dean, Jimmy Dean (1982), on the
other hand, switches constantly between 1975 and 1955 to
make the most explicit statements of any movie so far about
the relation of small-town life to media images of it.

        A work of sometimes unbearable nostalgia for an

audience which lived through the 'fifties and knew the appeal
of James Dean, Natalie Wood, the hot rods and fan magazines of the time, Jimmy Dean was written by Ed Graczyk,
author of the play of the same name.   It concerns the reunion of the Disciples of James Dean in a hot, dry, decaying Texas township which had known its moment of glory
twenty years before.   This moment coincides with the shooting of Giant, Dean's last film, in a town just sixty miles
away,  and the visit by two of the teenage fans of James
Dean (Mona and Joe) to the town in the hope of landing a
part in the movie.   For twenty years, Mona (Sandy Dennis)
has claimed to be the mother of James Dean's child, the
Jimmy Dean of the title, who was in his childhood put on
public display for the sake of passing tourists.

The destruction of this myth by the one person who
ought best to know, Joe Qualley (Mark Pattin), now in 1975
metamorphosed after "the operation" into a transsexual version played by Karen Black, is only one of the by-products
of the Disciples' reunion, though it is the most important
event.   (It is reserved for last in a lengthy exorcism which
inevitably recalls, with its progressive drunkenness and insistence on facing unwelcome reality, those of Who's Afraid
of Virginia Woolf? and The Boys in the Band.   We learn,
for example, that Sissy's (Cher) much-vaunted breasts are,
since a mastectomy, composed of rubber--"retreads, " as
she defiantly names them--and that Juanita (Sudie Bond) has
falsified the memory of her alcoholic husband by making
him saintly and abstinent.   Here, we are on familiar enough
territory, the sort of terrain commonly explored by, say,
Tennessee Williams.   However, when Mona reverentially
brings out a piece of the false-fronted house erected in 1955
to be the focus of Giant and now decaying as if she were
displaying the Holy Grail and when every significant moment
in the movie is contrasted with the images which the women,
then teenagers, embodied in the 'fifties, we see that the
movie belongs much more closely with Bogdanovich's and
Lucas's meditations of small-town self-perception.

Most interesting of all is the revelation that Joanne
(Karen Black) is the transsexual version of Joe.   Joe Qualley, with his uncertain masculinity, his happiness with the
otherwise all-female gang, his ability to mimic female sing-
ers of the day, epitomizes all the male misfits so commonly featured in the 'fifties small-town movie.   Juanita, whose
husband turns Joe out of a job because of the scandal caused
in town by Joe's masquerade as a female at the school

dance, becomes the embodiment of 'fifties small-town thinking on the matter of misfits.   Joe's answer is to abandon
his gender and to return to the town which persecuted him
full of defiance and a craving for revenge,  with the wish to
confront the town with truths always denied.    What sets this
familiar enough notion apart is that Joe looked like James
Dean at the time.   When the girls study a pornographic photograph of Dean in half-shocked,  half-delighted amazement
in 1975,  the connection between Joe/Dean in the 'fifties and
Joanne/Dean is strengthened.    Just as the real father of
Jimmy Dean is Joe (now Joanne),  so it seems that the real
nature of the star James Dean was suppressed and falsified
to meet the approval of small-town-minded fans.   The spirit
of the 'fifties was the spirit of the small town.  If James
Dean as an image was part of that spirit,  it was at the cost
of his own psyche and sexuality,  the movie seems to say.
And the absorption and packaging of his complex nature to
make him the idol of teenage America did not only destroy
Dean but contributed to the persecution and alienation of every Dean-like youngster.   The laying of Dean's legend,  as
well as of Mona's falsification of her life and its meaning,
to rest proves,  in this movie,  liberating if disquieting.   The
unacceptable has been faced--and accepted.   All that the
small-town ethos denied about itself and its role models has
somehow forced itself upon the consciousness of this ghost
town's most nostalgic denizens.

        In these three movies,  Bogdanovich,  Lucas and Alt-
man seem to inter an area of Hollywood with somewhat dif-
fering sentiments about the interment.   The magic of the
period for the small-town consumers of Hollywood products
is affirmed,  by its re-enactment in the two later movies or
by its power to allow the disenchanted to forget the dreari-
ness of their lives,  in the Bogdanovich movie.   All three
conclude,  however,  that the period and,  less obviously,  all
that was grafted onto it by movie culture can now be considered to be defunct,  memorabilia which cast doubt on
their authenticity even at the time of their greatest potency.


                        Notes to Chapter 7

1.   P. D. Zimmerman,  Newsweek,  October 11,  1971.

2.   Pauline Kael,  New Yorker,  October 9,  1971.

3.   Mark Lefanu,  "The Last Picture Show, "  Monogram
       no. 4,  1972,  pp. 28-29.

4.   Charles Champlin, Los Angeles Times, April 11, 1971.

5.   Pauline Kael, ibid.

6.   Sight and Sound, vol. 41, no. 2, spring 1972.

7.   Jim Pines, Time Out, Issue 109, March 17-23, 1972.

8.   The choice of these two movies to represent Anarene's
     viewing at the end of the period of the cinema's unques-
     tioned dominance is interesting.  Father of the Bride is
     set, not in a small town, but in a suburb, or, perhaps,
     a dormitory town.  The intimate relationship of city and
     home ("father" goes daily to his city office) is unthink-
     able in any of the small-town movies discussed elsewhere
     in this study, but the fact that Father of the Bride's set-
     ting seems to evoke memories of small-town life may
     help to explain the apparent split between small-town
     images and small-town reality:  the American suburbs,
     striving for the appearance of "autonomous" small town,
     for the psychological attractions of the countryside and
     the rural village, but economically parasitic on the cit-
     ies where suburbanites' employment is largely found,
     become far more significant with increasing industriali-
     zation--and particularly from the Second World War
     onwards--than the towns which they seek to emulate.
     Hawks' Red River is a substitution by Bogdanovich for
     the altogether less prestigious Audie Murphy vehicle,
     The Kid from Texas, in McMurtry's novel, while the
     small-town movie viewed in the novel is Stuart Heis-
     ler's Storm Warning.  Bogdanovich's latter substitution
     (of Father of the Bride for Storm Warning) lends cred-
     ibility to Mark Lefanu's view that it is all the Ameri-
     can films of the 'forties and 'fifties, not simply small-
     town movies, which are being contrasted with Anarene's
     experience of life.  It could be argued, however, that
     it is the American "frontier spirit" which is chiefly
     promoted by the westerns and small-town movies of
     these decades as the spirit of America itself, so that
     the grainy, pessimistic Storm Warning is an aberration
     rather than a summation.

## 8.  RESURRECTION?

The confidence (concerning an end to the small-town cycle) which the previous chapter heading may seem to imply requires modification.  To define any genre conclusively is an impossible task, for as long as filmmakers seem to be reworking the material of a particular genre the final definition must remain elusive.  Books which attempt to describe, and to arrive at a synthesis of the principal elements of, a genre[1] must, as the present study must, be content with a description encompassing the movies within the writers' experience and leave the reader with the possibility that even an entirely new direction may be taken after the date of publication.  What can confidently be claimed for the small-town movie is that Bogdanovich and Lucas seem to indicate their belief that they have detected the end of the Hollywood small town and, of course, partly to have effected that end.

Movie genres seldom die, however.  Instead, they usually become television genres.  The earliest signs of a TV small-town genre in the United States was the "continuing story of Peyton Place."  In the 'seventies, the decade of The Last Picture Show, Hollywood's conception of the small town seems to be translated into such TV series as The Waltons or Gibbsville, both of them looking back to an earlier, less industrialized period.  American Graffiti inspires Happy Days, centered on middle-class high school students of the late 'fifties and their hero, the Fonz, played "ethnically" by Henry Winkler against the WASP image of the other youngsters and, with his black leather clothes, motorcycle and tough/tender "alienated" personality, as a loose amalgam of 'fifties Brando and James Dean.

What seems evident is that, whatever the longevity of the more traditionally conceived small town may prove on American television, perhaps fulfilling, like the British Coronation Street, a dream of community most obviously endangered by the very popularity of the viewing in isolation which

141

television-watching normally entails, there is a sense in
which the small-town movies cease to seem viable in the
early 'seventies.  Several hypotheses, not mutually exclu-
sive, could be advanced for this.  Audiences had changed
beyond recognition, leaving adolescents and young adults as
the principal consumers of cinema movies.  The younger
adult population was specially affected by the national loss
of confidence in the image of America consequent on Vietnam and (less relevantly for the films of the previous chapter) Watergate.  Genre itself has arguably become less important commercially, thanks to the popularization of Andrew
Sarris's "auteur theory, " than directorial categorization, so
that well-known modern directors--Bogdanovich, Kubrick, De
Palma, Altman, Scorsese, Spielberg--are "sold" to the public and authorial work becomes in itself a new sort of genre.
These directors also both exploit and subvert their audiences'
expectations of genre so that their films comment on their
less self-conscious provenance.  Thus, Altman's The Long
Goodbye (1973) demands knowledge of the private-eye genre,
Kubrick's The Shining (1980) of the old-dark-house horror
movie, though neither can be compared easily with earlier
components in the respective genres, since the author's
presence, "the marks of enunciation, " seldom escape attention.

        The only recent movie which seems to breathe life
into the small-town genre again as if there had been no intervention by Bogdanovich or Lucas, is The Deer Hunter.
Significantly, what could be argued to be one of the most
recent small-town movies, John Schlesinger's Honky Tonk
Freeway (1981), breaks a cardinal rule of what might tentatively be termed the "classic" small-town movies by setting most of the action outside the chosen small town, here
the Floridian Ticlaw, in urban centers and on the freeway.
The movie reverses the notion of small town as isolated,
for good or ill, from industrialized society, its inhabitants
drawing strength from (or suffering misery through) the autonomy of the town, by making Ticlaw's townspeople fight
all manner of corrupt bureaucracy to establish a commercial
link, its only chance of economic survival, with the outside
world by means of an exit from the freeway.  As in Sirk
and Ritt small-town melodramas of the 'fifties, one man,
played here by William Devane, dominates the business and
cultural life of the town but his influence extends even to the
building which repeatedly expresses, as in the western, the
unity and civilized values of the town--the church.  Religion
and free enterprise are linked in Devane's rabble-rousing

sermon, the townspeople fired by his rhetoric to such zeal
for making inroads into the state's tourist industry as has
been displayed in the past by, say, The Music Man's River
City for its brass band, the symbol of its cultural self-
confidence and determined isolationism.   The theme of the
city's corruption of the small town is already easy to detect
in Schlesinger's 1969 Midnight Cowboy with its inspired prologue of the bus journey from Joe's hick town to Manhattan.
As with the individual Joe Buck, so here the entire town
yearns for its absorption into the ways of the city, feeling
survival itself an impossibility if it cannot batten on the
tourist trade which threatens to pass it by, leaving it as
undisturbed as earlier small towns had prided themselves
on being.

Cimino's and Schlesinger's movies mark a return to
the focussing of movie audiences' attention on the rural village, but there are vital differences which suggest that the
small-town movie can no longer be made in the way it once
was.   Cimino's town is already industrialized, hovering between a sense of playing a part (now rendered increasingly
dubious in real life by the steel industry's overproduction) in
the national economy and of priding itself on its special, separate identity, being close to nature and the deerslayer's natural environment.   Its characters seem increasingly afflicted
with anomie or, in the face of the Vietnam experience, an
enervating sense of absurdity.   Ticlaw is a small town doing
everything in its power to rid itself of the economic handi-
caps apparently attendant on that identity.   Perhaps only this
sort of small-town movie could follow those of the early 'seventies meditations, albeit in totally different modes, on the
possible irrelevance which shelters behind a small town's
pride in its self-containment.   Whether there can be shortly
a return to the more comfortable small-town movie depends
on several factors, not least whether a Reaganite America
can reinvigorate and then maintain a once-potent myth of
self-sufficiency and psychic health in the little communities
of America.

One sub-genre has however begun to represent the
American film industry's entire small-town output, the
small-town horror movie.   The middle 'seventies to early
'eighties by no means originate small-town horror.   Mention has already been made of such notable examples as
Siegel's Invasion of the Body Snatchers and Hitchcock's The
Birds, in Chapter 5, but possibly the greatest single inspiration from the past emanates from The Blob (1958), a movie

which explores the depredations of yet another "thing" from
space on earthlings but whose special significance[2] was in
emphasizing the teenage stratum of town society and its reactions to the invasion.   Several small-town melodramas and
comedies had laid particular store by the community's youth
and the hope that they represented for the future but The
Birds and the more recent horror films set in small towns
generally take teenagers or even children as their objects,
involving them in damaging and often lethal situations.   Concomitantly, the towns themselves, which may once have represented a salubrious environment for their developing lives,
become accretions of past, largely adult, guilt or are seen
as stultifying, harmful communities which at least the sympathetic youngsters must escape to avoid serious, generally
fatal, consequences.

        Thus, for example, two of John Carpenter's horror
films, Halloween (1978) and The Fog (1979), deal with the
visitation of past evil on present-day youngsters.   In the
first example, a young psychopath returns to his hometown
on the anniversary of his first murders and proceeds, now
a teenager, to terrorize the adolescent community, particularly female baby-sitters, since he himself had been neglected by his own baby-sitter.   In The Fog, an entire Cal-
ifornian town is punished for an act of barbarism perpetrated by it a century earlier.   "It's a short story.   A
hundred years ago, a small town in Northern California
maneuvered the wreck of a clipper ship by putting up a
false fire as their lighthouse ... the clipper ship smacks
up against the rocks, killing everybody aboard.   And they
went aboard and stole all the jewels and gold.   Now, a
hundred years later, today, the ghosts come back and haunt
the town as revenge.   And they bring the fog with them,
and the fog is actually a character, sort of like the Blob."[3]

        Drawing upon the earlier small-town movie compo-
nents often to enhance the horror, these later films are
particularly likely to turn the areas of town life most redolent of security and community into the opposite.   Thus,
the prettiest house on the sunniest day in a picturesque
seaside town turns out to contain the moldering corpses of
the leading citizens in Happy Mother's Day, Love George
(1973), set, admittedly, in Nova Scotia rather than the
United States.   The local school becomes a setting for may-
hem in Prom Night (1980).   Bug (1975) opens in a church,
and in the sermon the preacher makes the traditional contrast between life in the village and in the sinful city, at

which point an earthquake shakes the building and any linger-
ing complacency or overconfidence in the innate goodness,
and therefore safety, of rural life.   Towards the end of the
film, a Bible-carrying friend of the scientist hero's wife
dies.   The scientist's literal glimpse of the abyss before
the insects multiply to destroy him is only the most overt
example of the link made throughout the film with the weak
forces of good in town institutions and rationalism and the
unleashing of Satanic power in this complacent, conventionally religious town.   The horrors which permeate Communion
(1976) begin with what seems to be sororicide before a first
communion and continue to the climactic murder of a priest
during the celebration of mass.

        The film, which, possibly by reason of its commer-
cial success, now seems to epitomize the treatment of the
small town in a horror context, concerning itself with the
contrast between conventional small-town-mindedness in religion and high school and the genuinely supernatural, and
centering primarily on the world of teenagers, is Brian De
Palma's Carrie (1976).

        Carrie is the summation of all the misfits who popu-
late small-town movies.   Like Cassie (a name repeatedly
given to her in error by her school principal) in Kings Row,
she is shunned by her schoolmates, like Norman Page in
Peyton Place dominated by a mother of warped personality
and, like the lonely, sensitive spinsters of The Music Man,
The Long Hot Summer and Picnic, she blossoms (briefly)
under the attentions of the most exciting male in the community.   Unlike the pre-'seventies movies, the world viewed
here is exclusively that of the high school.   Even those
scenes set in parental homes relate to the concerns of the
teenagers and particularly their eagerness to attend the
senior prom.   Then, too, while the misfits of earlier films
suggest deeper insight and intelligence than the other townsfolk can appreciate, the power which they exert is that consequent on greater understanding, while Carrie is possessed
of telekinetic force which is enormously augmented as her
suffering becomes increasingly insupportable.

        The movie opens with a basketball game in which
Carrie (Sissy Spacek), the plain, skinny girl at the back,
misses an easy catch and is abused by the other girls.   A
shower sequence follows, shot in languorous slow motion,
with Pino Donaggio's music underlining the voluptuous and
yet serene quality of the visuals.   The relief which Carrie

seems to experience is that refuge seldom explored[4] when small-town misfits are considered, the world of masturbatory fantasy. Even this comfort is denied her, when suddenly, as if in punishment for her caressing of her belly and thighs, menstrual blood begins to flow. The sexually ignorant Carrie, horrified, panics and is mercilessly ridiculed by her more sophisticated classmates who throw sanitary napkins at her, chanting, "plug it up." Their gym teacher, Miss Collins, is angered by the girls' cruelty but also, as she admits to the principal, capable of understanding the irritation which she arouses in them.

Carrie's mother, Mrs. White (Piper Laurie), is first seen striding up to a modern bungalow in a well-tended garden, "on the Lord's work." Her flaming-red hair, overly bright eyes and determined false smile, the embarrassment she produces in the housewife who allows her entry, combine to suggest that she is the local "religious nut," no more accepted in adult society than Carrie is in high school. The movie leaves us in no doubt that the fervor of her religiosity is directly attributable to her self-castigation for her pleasure in sex and, like the prurient hypocrite she gives proof of being by the end of her life, she can see only gross carnality in her daughter. Ridiculed for her naïvety by the girls, Carrie is punished by her mother for the impurity which has caused this first menstrual flow. In self-justification, Mrs. White relates Carrie's experience to Eve's fall, preaching at her that, just as the curse of blood was visited upon Eve for sin, the curse would not have come upon Carrie if she had been sinless.[5]

Misfit personalities are often indicated by misfit homes in small-town movies. The Whites, too, live in a run-down, wooden-framed house with a "For Sale" sign at the front, a sharp contrast with the house glimpsed in the earlier sequence of Mrs. White's missionary work. Sue (Amy Irving), the daughter of this latter house, is as admired by her class as Carrie is despised. Pretty, popular, enjoying the approval of her teachers despite the recent lapse from Miss Collins' favor because of the shower incident, and dated by the handsomest boy in the class, she conceives a plan by which she can compensate for her misconduct. She persuades her boyfriend to take Carrie to the prom. With the fears of her protectress, Miss Collins, allayed and Carrie's own natural disbelief dispelled, Prince Charming does indeed partner Cinderella at the ball, despite a fulminating Mrs. White and the fury of the most vicious of the girls in the class. The physical transformation which manifests itself briefly in the shower scenes, whereby Carrie's beauty was discernible, now reaches fairy-tale culmination as the handsomest boy turns the suddenly prettiest girl round and round on the dance floor in a giddy ecstasy which recalls the endless circling that marks the anagnorisis at the end of De Palma's Obsession (1976).

When the glowing, admired couple mounts the stage to receive the applause of the prom class and its teachers, the course of events suddenly changes. Mrs. White, the malevolent force which tried to prevent Carrie from going to the prom and whose final promise was, "They're all going to laugh at you," and Chris (Nancy Allen), the classmate who most vigorously persecuted the ugly-duckling Carrie, triumph, it appears. A bucket of pig's blood is spilled over Carrie and kills her date for the evening. The silent horror which grips the onlookers is "seen" by Carrie as mocking laughter. Looking like a newborn baby, hair and body coated in blood, her dress clinging like a bloody membrane, Carrie summons up the telekinetic powers of which she has become aware in the sequences involving the indifferent principal and which she has used, mildly, to pin her protesting mother to her bed just before her departure for the prom. Now, by the force of her will, she closes the exits from the hall, causes the electrocution of some teachers, sends objects flying lethally against others and destroys the school in fire. Outside, she destroys the car in which the girl responsible for her humiliation is attempting to escape with her boyfriend (John Travolta). Having eradicated all of the town's "normal" society to which she was drawn and which seemed yet again to deny her, she returns to mother and home in apparently conciliatory fashion. Having washed off the blood in a kind of purificatory ritual, Carrie is murderously attacked by Mrs. White who feels her evil is incurable without death. Before she plunges a knife into her daughter's back, she confesses the pleasure she felt in the one sexual act which she permitted her husband to perpetrate. "I should have killed myself when he put it in me.... Sin never dies.... I should have given you to God when you were born." In desperate self-protection, Carrie calls knives from the kitchen drawers and her mother is repeatedly transfixed in a parody of sexual ecstasy, at last achieving the martyrdom for which she has yearned.

In the final sequence before the surprise which shocks the audience out of its complacency at the end of the film,

Carrie drags her mother into a cupboard and, together with
the corpse and the grotesque St. Sebastian statuette whose
appearance her mother has assumed, she sinks into the
earth in flames.   Life has been unbearable and, rejected by
her community and her mortal mother's womb, she returns
to Earth, pre-Olympian mother deity of supernatural forces.

        Carrie gathers together several themes which seem
to have special potency for 'seventies audiences.   Not least
of these is that of the apparent weakling who takes savage
revenge on a cruel society.   The popularity of Sam Peckinpah's Straw Dogs (1971) and Michael Winner's Death Wish
(1974) surely has something to do with the vicarious wish-
fulfilment offered by these movies, whereby audiences who
feel threatened by callous predators in society and too little protected from humiliation or physical assault by society's appointed guardians may enjoy the magical potency of
telekinesis in a righteous cause, or participate with the
peaceful-man-turned-vigilante in a private citizen's restoration of law and order.   Again, as in Ken Russell's The
Devils (1971), religious zeal is equated with hysteria of a
specifically sexual origin and the psychic damage inflicted
in the name of religion finds violent physical expression.
However, Carrie is also the horror-fantasy version of such
movies as The Chase (where the hero turns his back upon
his town rather than destroying it by fire).   The heroine of
De Palma's film moves from her failed attempt to integrate
within town society to an abortive attempt to reunite with
her mother, followed by a parody of the return to the maternal womb.   The interrelationship of family and town
which is always present in the small-town melodramas thus
reappears, and the themes of the haven, the dream of Utopia and the yearning to belong are powerfully revived.

        At the end of Carrie, the audience reaches for its
coats and umbrellas, comfortable in the generically inspired
belief that the terror is at an end with the disappearance of
the White home into the earth.   Sue visits the blackened site
of the former White residence.   The "For Sale" sign has
taken the form of a cross where a graffitist has continued
the persecution of Carrie with the scrawl, "Carrie White
burns in Hell."   Slowly and reverently, she approaches the
cross and bends down to lay a wreath at its foot.   Without
warning, a bloody arm reaches out from the blackened earth
and grabs her.   Sue wakens screaming and the audience
spills out of the cinema with nerves jangling.   This final
sequence suggests what many of the small-town horror

films also hint at and what most of Carrie signifies--that
there is a price to pay for a dream denied, that America
limits its entry to middle-class happiness at its peril, that
there is an aggrieved spirit abroad in the land which will
take revenge for its exclusion from America's image of her
best self by shaking and even destroying the symbol of that
image, the small town.

## Notes to Chapter 8

1. Examples of such books are: Jim Kitses, Horizons
   West: Studies in Authorship in the Western Film (Secker
   and Warburg, 1970); Colin McArthur, Underworld, USA
   (Secker and Warburg, 1972); Stuart M. Kaminsky, American Film Genres (Pflaum, 1974).

2. Another was the introduction of Steve McQueen to movie
   audiences.

3. "Working with numbers" (Debra Hill talking to Ralph
   Appelbaum), Films and Filming, September 1979, p. 24.

4. Paul Newman's Rachel, Rachel (1968) is an exception to
   this general rule.

5. Mrs. White's fundamentalist theology would logically have
   interpreted the fall in Eden as indicative of the introduction of original sin into the world and would have considered all mankind sinful until washed by the blood of
   the Lamb, Carrie's menstruation simply the penalty for
   female membership of the inevitably sinful human race.
   The insincerity of her missionary zeal is demonstrated
   in her cruel attempt to convince Carrie of personal
   wrongdoing as the cause of menstruation, reinforcing
   the link already suggested in the shower sequence between Carrie's bodily pleasure and the flow of blood.

## 9. A DELINEATION OF THE GENRE

The movies discussed or alluded to in chapters 2-8 provide sufficient data for some attempt to be made at synthesis. At the outset, however, problems must be admitted and faced.

The problems of "defining a genre definitively" are notorious. There is, for example, the circularity of the process by which we examine generic films identified by certain (unenunciated) criteria as belonging to a genre when it is the criteria by which genre is definable that it is our task to discover, or there is the possibility that a genre may take an unexpected direction, a new lease of life, when a writer has attempted to provide a definition.

Then, too, a factor inherent in genre study needs to be asserted and considered. This is the apparent eradication of difference between movies in the bid to arrive at that which is shared, the essence of the generic, when it is quite probably the element of difference which is most fascinating and attractive to audiences. Or, rather, to put it more accurately, it is the tension between the stable, generic elements and the fluid, aberrant tendencies which must be discoverable in every particular example of a genre that should provide the principal interest. If this is so, the present study has attempted to arrive at the stable and common elements after recording the particularities within a particular movie, in order to illustrate this tension, and should not be thought unduly to disguise or eradicate difference until this point. The Deer Hunter is a very different sort of movie from The Best Years of Our Lives and yet they share attitudes to war and home community.

An objection of special relevance to the present study might well be made, however.

This would be that, America being such a huge

country, comprising so many different geographical and cultural areas with manifest geographical and cultural differences, the study of the American small town in movies ought to be a study of different types of American small towns in the movies in, for example, New England, the Middle West, the Deep South.  This objection would have some validity. The New England village is normally depicted as naturally and architecturally attractive, healthful, decorous, a worthy epitome, in modern terms, of the small town as it was originally conceived by the early settlers.  Provinciality of culture and ornateness/vulgarity of middle-class architecture figure with particular prominence in the cinematic depiction of the Middle West.  A sense of decay, of political sores and of social injustice, permeates the small-town movies set in the South.  This writer's feeling is that such a study of subgenres in the small-town movie ought to be illuminating but there is a question which overrides the evidence of differences in the treatment of the small town in these different areas.  Why is it the town, not the city, which so frequently receives attention in these movies?  Why Anarene, Texas or Maycomb, Alabama rather than Dallas or Birmingham?  Why Clairton, Pennsylvania rather than Pittsburgh or Cleveland, Ohio?  Is it not because the town remains a stubborn Puritan ideal in the American psyche, so that the disappointments in Middle-Western life and even the dismay felt at Southern small-town racialism and inequity are particularly poignant in a way that consideration of the Southern big city, for example, would find hard to approach?  If Anarene is so very different from Peyton Place, is not the point of their comparison by writers other than this author that they are two manifestations of a dream of communal living that has never vanished from the American subconscious?

———————

The principal antithesis which emerges, more or less overtly, in every small-town movie is that between ideal and actuality or, perhaps more accurately, between the image of the ideal and a perception of the actuality.  The Kings Row town sign, immediately after the credits, with its promise of the town as salubrious nursery for the young and the immediate contrast with the schoolchildren divided against one another and one young girl's misery, is simply the most economic expression of this universal contrast.  The image of the ideal may be evidenced by the smug self-advertisement of this town or by the almost mystical appeal of teachers or

lawyers to standards of decency which the town is supposed
not only to embody but to "teach." The small town in movies seems forever to be looking upwards at some Platonic
ideal of itself, congratulating itself on its close approxima-
tion to it in actuality or castigating itself for its failure to
match practice with inspiration, and much of the energy ex-
pended in these movies is involved with the dusting off of
long-cherished beliefs, in the seldom enunciated small-town
values of fairness, democracy, kindness, and asserting or
denying their existence in the particular small town under
consideration.

Occasionally, especially in the small-town series dating from the late 'thirties, the ideal, being partly created
and perpetuated by these optimistic works, is confirmed by
the actuality, but the point remains that, even in the Andy
Hardy series, the possibility of a gulf between ideal and
practice is frequently implied though it never does open.
The tension between human frailty and the Carvel "good,
clean town" ideal which is confirmed by its appearance on
the town sign as Andy's train pulls out of Carvel at the end
of Andy Hardy's Double Life accounts for most of the episodic plot, and the match between Judge Hardy's and Abraham Lincoln's profiles in one sequence suggests the bond
between the ideal and the real in this town and its central
family.

This tension between ideal and actuality is exploited
to a greater or lesser extent in a very roughly chronological
line from their coincidence in the Andy Hardy series through
the questioning and doubting of the majority of small-town
movies (the exposure of departures from self-image in
Shadow of a Doubt, Kings Row, Peyton Place, etc., although these aberrations are often weighed ultimately as of
less account than the town virtues and are sometimes purged
by trial or catastrophe) to the deep pessimism about the possibility of salvaging anything of the ideal, in Penn's The
Chase, John Frankenheimer's I Walk the Line (1970) or De
Palma's Carrie, in the last of which the horde of insensi-
tive oppressors and the few with any dim intentions of making a good, clean town are alike swept away to death by the
despairing heroine. Today, the small town is a far likelier
setting for terror than reassurance, but the basis of the terror is still the exploitation of the gap between expectations
of a haven and the discovery of a hell.

The particular application of the ideal/actual explora-

tion varies, but principally there is concern with whether or
not the community's ideals exist at all, and, if they do,
what evaluation may be placed on them in relation to questions of individualism or isolation, which may lead to consideration of further questions, of normality and idiosyncrasy in sexual, social, ethnic or class terms.  Above all,
the small-town movie seems to lay particular stress, in its
exploration of the workings of the community, on the role of
the family which, in turn, is seen as a microcosm of the
town in the sense that again ideal and actuality appear to be
held up for comparison.

## 1) The Community and Its Ideals

The sense of community, or grass-roots participation in the
processes, or at least the symbols, of government and of
national identity is strongly suggested in the small-town movie.  There are the trials at the center of Peyton Place, Return to Peyton Place, Inherit the Wind and To Kill a Mockingbird, the Labor Day celebrations of Peyton Place, the
massive town picnic in Picnic, the much-guyed Fourth of
July celebrations in The Music Man, the Parkman, Illinois
Centennial Festival in Some Came Running.  Coupled with
these are the solemn, ritualistic graduation ceremonies of
Peyton Place and Carousel, the American flags and uniforms
that figure in Shadow of a Doubt and The Best Years of Our
Lives--wartime movies that give sustenance to Mike Rossi's
hopes for Peyton Place and its part in the war effort.  There
is the subtler point of her President's inclusion in the child's
bedtime prayer in Shadow of a Doubt, and the way that man-
agement and labor seem to get along so well on (appropriate-
ly) the Peyton Place Labor Day.

        The rituals and ceremonies themselves, as treated in
these movies, frequently embody a critique of the small
town in relation to the ideals which they purport to cele-
brate.  The trials are sometimes of the town itself, overtly
(Inherit the Wind) or covertly (Selena's terror of town gossip explains much of her aberrant behavior in Peyton Place).
Less obviously, the town celebration, which is intended to
express the community's cohesion, accentuates the divisions
within it.  Dave Hirsh and Ginny are always spatially separated or picked out from the town population at the fair in
Some Came Running, the outsiders are attacked by Chicago
visitor Raymond during the fair, which Minnelli makes gar-
ish and unsettling, and the brief moment of cohesion for
Frank Hirsh's family and, by implication, for Parkman

itself is only when they are spectators of another "sideshow"
--Ginny's death.   Labor Day in Peyton Place is celebrated
with an escape from the town rituals by three couples.   The
central event of Picnic results in the crumbling of carefully
maintained façades, the use of the outsider hero as scapegoat for Rosemary's frustrations and as antidote for Madge's.
The Carousel town clambake ends in attempted armed rob-
bery and Billy Bigelow's death.

        With all the American bunting, uniforms and flags,
there are suggestions that the reality is hollow.   Peyton
Place runs its classroom on democratic lines, with Selena
from the wrong side of the tracks taking as active a part in
school committees as the well-heeled Rodney, but her stepfather, the drunken janitor, claims that nobody learns anything important at school--as soon as they leave, they enter
a dog-eat-dog world.   "Ain't nobody in this here town living
intelligently."   Verification of his beliefs is offered by the
conduct of the penny-pinching school board, dominated by the
same mill-owner who dominates the town itself.

        Movies set in the South are more obviously critical
of the town's political bigotry and social hypocrisy.   The
black cook of The Member of the Wedding, who wants to
vote for a candidate described in vaguely liberal-socialist
terms, is laughed at for her hopefulness, and a member of
her family reports that he has been beaten up by a local
policeman.   The Mockingbird jury returns a guilty verdict
despite overwhelmingly contrary evidence, and the southern
lynch mob makes frequent appearances, for example, in
The Long Hot Summer and Mockingbird. [1]

        The sense of community and of abiding Americanism
that the small town projects is reinforced by the sound
tracks of many small-town movies.   The Music Man has a
score that relies heavily on the conventions of revivalist
hymn-singing and barbershop harmony, Stephen Foster fa-
vorites (particularly "Beautiful Dreamer") are frequently
sung at public events and as community songs (Picnic), and
the "background music" to the melodramas is often strongly
reminiscent of Aaron Copland's "American" themes, [2] and
has the generalized "nationalistic" feel of, say, Elgar's
"Pomp and Circumstance" sounds.   The "Americanism" of
the score can be used for critical or satirical purposes, as
in The Music Man where the hot-gospel rhythms of "Trouble" are used by a salesman playing on the community's
fears to make it buy his message and his goods.   Continuity,

which among other devices community singing of old favor-
ites may signal, is frequently used as a pivot, and not always to offer reassurance.   In The Best Years of Our Lives,
it is continuity which Fred, the wartime captain and peacetime soda jerk, most dreads in his hometown.   In Kings
Row, where insanity is treated as something hereditary and
inevitable, continuity is again the cause of, not antidote to,
insecurity.   The sheer time span of certain small-town movies (Kings Row, The Magnificent Ambersons) and the expression of nostalgia for bygone eras (Shadow of a Doubt) are
further indicators of this notion of continuity.

        Many components of the small-town ideal are indi-
cated by the Kings Row town sign and the Andy Hardy movies
--the promise of community, of decency, morality, normality and sanity, of democratic values, the town as repository
of the fundamental American virtues, a haven of security.
Explicit examples of this conception of the town are easily
found.   There is the explanation from Dr. Tower, in Kings
Row, that man was happier in the twelfth and thirteenth centuries because he had a clearer place in the universe whereas now he breaks down under the strain of a more compli-
cated world.   His retreat to the town with his mentally ill
wife could be taken to indicate his faith in the restorative
power of a sense of belonging in an ordered community.
There is, in Peyton Place, Miss Thornton's speech at the
school dance:   "We're a small town on a small spot on a
great big map.   Peyton Place will be part of you forever.
Make it great by honoring it. "   Mike Rossi, the new principal, has already stated that, if war comes, he wants his
schoolkids to fight for the ideas behind the facts which are
taught at the local school.   The small town as haven is
clearly behind Uncle Charlie's flight to Santa Rosa in Shadow of a Doubt and, even later, when the image is punctured
and called "a silly dream, " the out-of-town detective dis-
agrees. [3]

2) Community/Isolation

By far the most fundamental opposition under the ideal/
actuality heading is that concerning community and its opposite, estrangement and isolation.   Whereas in the Andy
Hardy series, all things work together for and through the
community, most small-town movies involve an examination
of the ideal of community to see whether it exists or not
and, if it does, whether it is in fact of positive value.

The reverse side of community may be conformism, a subjugation of individuality to a majority standard of behavior and culture. The overriding demands on the small town for outward respectability are constantly in evidence, whether as jokes (W. C. Fields' battles with temperance, Andy Hardy glancing anxiously at the neighboring houses as his father appears at the front gate abstractedly pulling a child's toy wagon, the twittering gossips surrounding the Mayor's wife in The Music Man) or as causes of torment (Louise Gordon railing at Kings Row's demands that she deny her sexual longings, the Cross children's inability to seek help in Peyton Place, the horror felt by Cora Flood that the town knows of her husband's visits to Mavis Pruitt in The Dark at the Top of the Stairs, the men outside the courthouse in The Long Hot Summer, the telephone purveyor of (false) information about Allison and Norman in Peyton Place).

The ruthlessness of the community's demands on its individuals generally produces crises in the small-town movies' characters. Invasion of the Body Snatchers has at its center the ruthless extermination of individuality by the "pod people," those passionless, anaesthetized versions of the townsfolk whose view of happiness, exactly like that of Epicurus, is catastematic rather than kinetic, involving freedom from disturbance and pain rather than positive pleasure. The two characters who are pursued by the pod people have been out of town, the hero briefly at a conference, the heroine for several years in England. While the new denizens of Santa Mira are obviously, in context, a contrast with the previous versions (hence, the child running away from his home and "mother"), it is not accidental that the setting is a small town, where community can degenerate into conformism without the intervention of alien forces. Sexual needs ultimately force certain conformist characters to brave the town's contempt. Frank Hirsh, the corrupt establishment figure, dares to have an affair with his assistant in Some Came Running, the spinster librarian of The Music Man at last succumbs to the fraudulent salesman and defends him in the face of town wrath. Sometimes, ironically, it is need for companionship which drives characters to risk groundless accusations of adultery (Rubin Flood in Top of the Stairs).

The ideal/real opposition can be detected again in the frequent existence of an underlying, hidden world of lowlife

and sexual license within the small town, denied or connived
at by its inhabitants but with powerful effect on the lives of
the alienated or ostracized.   Some Came Running is one obvious example.   The respectability beloved by Frank Hirsh
and of such difficult achievement for him with Dave in town,
the artificial, tamely civilized life enjoyed by Gwen French
and her father, are both repeatedly contrasted by decor,
lighting and costumes, with the underbelly of the town, natural habitat of Bama, Ginny and Rosalie.   This sort of
contrast is repeated in The Music Man, where the fake gentility of the mayor's family and its entourage and the safe,
cultivated existence of the lady librarian, are both contrasted
with the lowlife characters represented by the traveling salesman and his friend, Marcellus.   The hidden sleaziness of the
small town is already present in the drinking retreats of
W. C. Fields, and appears repeatedly in small-town movies
usually to indicate truths, about characters or town, which
cannot be faced or which are simply unknown.   There is the
memorable sequence in Shadow of a Doubt where sinister
uncle takes sheltered niece to a local bar.   In The Member
of the Wedding, it is thanks to contact with a hidden hell
that Frankie can return to the comparative safety of her
home with gratitude for its illusions, only to meet another
reality in the death of her playmate, John Henry. 4   Sometimes, it is the other-side-of-the-tracks squalor of certain
shacks in pretty townships that supplies the contrast, as in
the first sight that new arrival Mike Rossi has of Peyton
Place, the filthy Cross shack, where Selena is lusted after
and finally raped by her stepfather, and in which she later
kills him and plans his burial.   These last horrific events
take place in a cleaned-up shack, which, with its decorated
Christmas tree and town-approved cleanliness, has attempted
to take on the more antiseptic look of the MacKenzies' home.
But hell re-emerges even in the improved setting.   In The
Long Hot Summer, the suggestion of an untamed world of
natural lusts underlying the moneyed respectability of the
Varner home and the aristocratic celibacy of Alan's family
(again the opposition of the untamed to both kinds of respectability) is provided by the boys circling the perimeter
of the gardens howling for Eula.

3) Noramlity/Idiosyncrasy

The division of the conventionally viewed integrated community into recognized, respectable, socially acceptable, on the
one side, and ignored, alien, disapproved, on the other, is
exemplified in most small-town movies on a variety of bases.

Since the self-image of the small town is a place of,
among other features, psychic health and "normality, " the
exploration of eccentricity or madness can be undertaken
with particular reference to their social effects, the difficulties engendered by those forms of idiosyncrasy in a community which prides itself on homogeneity.  Kings Row is
the study of a township which rejects the Towers, the un-
conforming recent arrivals in its midst, and, while it is
made clear that mental illness is viewed by Dr. Tower,
with the approval of the hero Parris, as a hereditary afflic-
tion which in time begins to affect his daughter, the pressure
of isolation from other schoolchildren contributes to her deeper withdrawal from town society into her sinister-seeming
family home.

a) Sexual norms:

The Member of the Wedding, by concentrating on, apart
from the black cook, two children both of whom display no
will to learn socially approved, "normal" behavior, is a
particularly apposite example of this component of small-
town movies.  Frankie, differentiated from the frock-
wearing, sedate girls of her age in her clothes and behavior, spends the major part of the film striving to belong to something--anything--and picks upon her brother's
wedding when she is excluded from the club which meets
in the shed behind her house.  Frankie is not excluded so
much because she is too young, though at the end of the
film she "matures" sufficiently to accept more conventional
dress and behavior, as because she has not learned stereotypical femininity but insists instead on tomboy clothes and
deportment, and a crewcut.  On the other hand, her male
playmate, John Henry, emotionally dependent on Frankie
and Berenice (Frankie's surrogate mother, the black cook),
thanks to his mother's neglect, falls easily into the imitation of women, sometimes trying on their clothes.  While
Berenice protects them from the usual consequences of
their indecision about gender roles, town attitudes keep
breaking through.

The Floods' son in Top of the Stairs is mocked and
unfriended by reason of his pacific, unmasculine conduct
and earns friendship only by taking a baseball bat with
which to threaten his bullies, thus falling into the behavior
demanded of him as a boy.  His sister, in contrast with
the sexually aware and socially successful Flirt, is con-
vinced of her unattractiveness and has few social weapons,

such as dancing skill, to deploy.  When she does find a
suitable partner, he is an out-of-towner and a Jew.

In Peyton Place, Norman Page is the recluse--bookish,
over-protected by his mother, awkward at parties, and Allison MacKenzie is the sensitive, uncertain adolescent in contrast with popular Betty Anderson.  The maturity that the
movie seems to suggest results for the two misfits from
their contact with a world war and with New York is indicated in their accidental meeting on a train, where Norman
behaves like a confident paragon of male chauvinism. 5

b) Cultural norms:

The artistic and cultured are often under suspicion of sexual
maladjustment in the small-town movie.  Andy Hardy is surprised to find that "the intellectual goon" in town is a highly
attractive, good-humored coed.  Usually, the female with
intellectual pretensions is an object of pity in these movies,
however.  One of the stock characters is the spinster schoolteacher, afraid of life, taking refuge in books and the care
of young people.  She makes her appearance in film after
film, including Picnic (aging, therefore panicky), Peyton
Place (aged, and so allowed a certain dignity), The Long
Hot Summer, Some Came Running, The Birds and Rachel,
Rachel.  This character may be a lady librarian rather
than a schoolteacher, but she is recognizably close to the
latter in treatment.  Examples may be found in Storm Center (with Bette Davis as the librarian), The Music Man and
Shadow of a Doubt, with its wonderfully economic parody of
a gaunt, tetchy lady librarian.  Related to these ladies is
the plain, bookish girl who appears as a contrast with the
socially successful beauty of a sister.  We have Charlie's
bespectacled, solemn sister in Shadow of a Doubt (she appears again in Hitchcock, in an urban setting, in Strangers
on a Train), Frankie in The Member of the Wedding, the
beauty queen's sister in Picnic. 6  Cultured men are treated
with more respect, but their learning still marks them as
outsiders.  Dave Hirsh, the writer, throws in his lot with
the nomads rather than the town establishment, in Some
Came Running.  Mr. French in the same film and Dr. Tower and Parris in Kings Row are as ambivalent towards the
town as it is towards them.  The town's cultural life is hor-
ribly provincial, as portrayed in The Music Man, a succession of vulgar patriotic tableaux and festivities, and outraged
attacks on "dirty books--Chaucer, Rabelais and Balzac."
Similar points are made about the town's provincialism in

Picnic where the schoolteacher denounces The Ballad of the
Sad Café as filth.

c) Ethnic norms:

Interestingly, ethnic diversity is less stressed in the small-
town movies than in some of the novels on which they are
based.  Those set in the Southern states deal with social
deprivation and political exploitation of blacks (and occasionally poor whites)--To Kill a Mockingbird is the obvious
example--but generally black characters play the menial
roles in the small town (the comic butler in Andy Hardy's
Double Life, the maid or cook in Kings Row and The Long
Hot Summer where black cotton-pickers also appear, the
black train conductor of Shadow of a Doubt).  European origins may favorably distinguish certain sections of the townsfolk, [7] but generally foreign origins are not remarked upon,
although it is noteworthy that Irish origins tend to be connected with simplicity or earthiness. [8]  Discrimination tends
to be only secondarily ethnic, the principal dividing line being between rich and poor (see below) and certain ethnic
groups being of little wealth.  The disapproval expressed by
the mayor of The Music Man for his daughter's suitor seems
to link ethnic and wealth grounds--"His father's one of the
Lithuanians on the south of town. "  The most direct (and
atypical for states not considered Southern) examination of
prejudice is in Top of the Stairs, where a Jew is ejected
from the Country Club.

d) Class divisions:

As sexual eccentricity and departure from general taste test
the communality of the small town, so too it is split by the
division between classes, particularly in the sense of rich
and poor, a division often given physical expression by the
railroad tracks.  Literally on the wrong side of the tracks
are Fred's family in Best Years, Randy Monaghan's in
Kings Row, Selena Cross's in Peyton Place.  The proximity
of the Owens home to the railroad line in Picnic signals the
point of Madge's match with her rich suitor who lives "on
the other side of town. "  The world of the movie small town
is predominantly middle-class, with the financially secure
professional groups as the linchpin of the "town spirit. "

Doctors are key figures in many movies.  In Invasion
of the Body Snatchers, they appear to be arbiters of sanity. [9]
Doc Swain of Peyton Place is not only the arbiter of morality,

in that he has to make extra-legal decisions about the Cross family, but is a principal member of the draft board in the Second World War, personally turning up to bid good-bye to the town's soldier sons.   Therefore, in a context of such reverence for doctors, the irony of Kings Row, that one doctor kills his daughter (to protect her from insanity, admittedly) while the other more established figure enjoys hacking off limbs without anaesthetic, is particularly bitter.

Lawyers play similarly important roles, Atticus being the fount of the town's more humane impulses in Mockingbird.

Newspaper editors, bankers, ministers, tend to be admirably responsible people.

Businessmen are more ambivalently viewed.   Varner in The Long Hot Summer owns the town with all its businesses and therefore the townspeople themselves.   Leslie Harrington, an undemocratic influence too (in that he takes advantage of the local political power gained through his mills, which are the economic basis of Peyton Place's prosperity), is a redeemed character by the end of Peyton Place, thanks to his son's death and his conciliation with the poor-but-honest widow. 10

The lower-middle- and working-class characters tend to be acquiescent, and to confirm the status quo.   Policemen are fair but kindly (the reproving traffic cop in Shadow of a Doubt knows the identity of his offender and shows good humor and respect), domestics, shopkeepers, etc., acquiesce in the prevailing ethos, except for such notable dissenters as Lucas Cross, the janitor of Peyton Place, who finds the school's inculcation of democratic principles totally irrelevant, and nearly all salesmen (hardly ever denizens of the town) who become a byword for slick insincerity and cynical exploitation of the town's ideals (as exemplified in The Music Man) or innocence (as succinctly put by Dave Hirsh's giggling, promiscuous niece in reference to her escort in Some Came Running:   "He's a travelling salesman and I'm the farmer's daughter. ")

If the lower classes seldom question the status quo, the underprivileged frequently recognize the barriers to their happiness constituted by the wealth of others.   Selena, in talking to her budding-lawyer boyfriend, in Peyton Place, uses the term "respectable" interchangeably with "rich" without any apparent awareness. In Shadow of a Doubt, much of the tension in the family after Uncle Charlie's arrival is caused by the mother's return to the sense of her original family's superiority and her husband's feelings of exclusion from the memories which are stirred up by his brother-in-law. Clara Varner is nearly sold off to Ben Quick as a commodity and a biological means to providing her father with a grandson, in The Long Hot Summer, and Madge is nearly sold for different reasons in Picnic.

The gap between classes, which is nearly always in terms of rich and poor, 11 is emphasized by one of the staple situational elements in the small-town movie, the cross-class/cross-culture romance or its converse, the arranged cross-class mating which is challenged by lovers from the same class or of similar outlook. The former is the more frequent version, the tension being created by the rich parent(s) acting in opposition to the wishes of the rich child concerned. Kings Row has Louise Gordon breaking up with Drake, under parental pressure, when he loses his money and respectability, Peyton Place has Rodney's romance with and marriage to Betty Anderson, and there are other examples in Best Years, Written on the Wind, Splendor in the Grass and The Music Man. The parents' hard-headedness is nearly always unjustified and contrasted with the sincerity of the couple's feelings. The Long Hot Summer turns upon a nouveau-riche/aristocratic relationship which fails, Picnic with a cross-class arranged match which backfires.12

4) The Family--Ideal and Actuality

Discussion of the cross-class match acts as a useful transition to an almost inevitable component of the small-town movie, the exploration of the family in this, its most advantageous setting. Often, the small-town movie looks more obviously like a family drama which happens to be set in a small town, but a deeper reading tends to justify the belief that family life is always related to the town environment and to be explained in terms of the town (even if, as in The Birds, the family is contrasted with the town). As with the explanation of the town itself, the principal opposition in this component is that of ideal (or sometimes self-image) and real. Remarkably few families in these movies behave ideally or even wisely, although Andy Hardy's family is constantly paying tribute to itself. No such perfect family appears from the late 'forties onwards. As early as 1943, Hitchcock plants at least one shocking implication in Wilder's

happy family of <u>Shadow of a Doubt</u>, the so-called "typical
family" of the <u>bogus reporters</u> (p. 115), in the mother's inability to move against her brother with whom she is totally
charmed even when he is a threat to her marriage (emphasizing the social divide between herself and her husband) and
then to her daughter's life.

     The malaise which afflicts the family when the typi-
cal roles (bread-winning, dominant father; feminine, acquiescent, supportive wife and mother; dutiful children) are not
or cannot be played is almost constantly present in the small-
town movie.  A stock character, from the time of Fields, is
the domineering wife/mother and her converse, the hen-
pecked husband/son.  The study of the malfunctioning parent
and the consequent tension among the children is aided by the
noteworthy frequency of the absence of one or other parent,
by reason of death or desertion.  For example, of films discussed in the main body of this study, the following center
upon families where only one or neither parent is alive:
<u>Kings Row</u> (Cassie's mother dies, Randy Monaghan lives
with her father, while Drake and Parris are orphans); <u>The
Member of the Wedding; Invasion of the Body Snatchers</u>
(the heroine lives with her father only); <u>Picnic, Peyton</u>
Place; <u>The Long Hot Summer; Some Came Running</u> (Dave
Hirsh was boarded out when brother Frank became head of
the family at the time of their father's death); <u>The Music
Man; To Kill a Mockingbird; The Last Picture Show; Carrie; The Fog</u>.  In <u>Top of the Stairs</u>, the father's constant
absences have produced a situation where the mother alone
decides her children's lives.  The imbalance in mothers'
roles in particular created by a weak or absent husband can
be seen again in <u>Mildred Pierce</u>, <u>The Birds</u>, <u>The Effect of
Gamma Rays on Man-in-the Moon Marigolds</u> and particularly
<u>Psycho</u> (which is difficult to term a small-town movie,
though).  The lack of a mother, whereby the child suffers
psychic damage, is of evident importance in <u>The Member of
the Wedding</u>, <u>East of Eden</u> and <u>Written on the Wind</u>, the
lack of any parents in <u>The Sound and the Fury</u>.

     An implicit critique of the family (or arguably an
affirmation but at least a contrast of the institutionalized
blood-family with a more perfect realization of its potential) is the presence of the happy surrogate family supplying the defects of, or replacing, the blood-family.  <u>The
Member of the Wedding</u> is the best example, with the
grouping of the children in Berenice's arms at the point
where they sing "His eye is on the sparrow, " indicating

the quasi-familial relationships of sentiment.  There is Parris' especially close relationship with his grandmother and
Drake's "parental" relationship with him in Kings Row, the
surrogate daughter of Pollyanna, Dave Hirsh's "parental"
sympathy with Dawn before she returns to her real but
distant-seeming parents in Some Came Running.  The substitution in Billy Wilder's 1964 comedy Kiss Me, Stupid of
whore for wife, wife for whore, is a perfect illustration of
the implicit criticism of actual family relationships in contrast with freely chosen and improved (surrogate) relations.

     Allied with the exploration of the potential and actual
family is the recording of certain formative experiences, the
rooting of present attitudes in retold episodes from the past.
Many of the movies open (and some continue and end) with
voice-overs, usually spoken by women, implicitly or explicitly contrasting the central character's present maturity with
the inexperience of that past time. 13  Growing up is a frequent theme--how sexual initiation or traumatic discoveries
of family secrets or of difficult truths about life and death
catapult the adolescent into a better understanding of himself or herself.  The importance for the character's full
maturity of staying within the town, albeit now more fully
revealed, or at least of returning to face it is stressed in
several films. 14  Characters who have come to an understanding of themselves and their needs do eventually leave
town on occasion, as in Picnic. 15  This aspect of the small
town seems best understood in relation to popularized psychology, with the town standing as the quintessential location
for the operation of the family in community and with the
vaguely Freudian necessity for coming to terms with the
reality of formative experiences to ensure psychic health.
A social or political reading is also possible, though, yield-
ing the suggestion that, whatever the imperfections of the
"system" symbolized by the small town, it is better to stay
within it and ameliorate it than to abandon it in the deluded
belief that some better form exists outside.

## 5) The Small Town and the Natural World--Natural and Urban

The movie small town is viewed in relation to at least two
other areas, the world of nature and the urban world which
is seldom actually glimpsed in the small-town movie.  The
town stands between these two worlds, inclining to one or
other in different movies and yet distinct from both.

        The natural world which is so in evidence in most
small towns is often regarded as a refuge from the conformist pressures of the town, most evidently in the hunt
sequences of The Deer Hunter.  Again, when Cassie is
miserable about her rejection at school, in Kings Row, she
finds momentary happiness with Parris as they swim in a
pond in their underwear.  Equally, Allison and Norman find
a haven in which to discuss their sexual fears in the secret
place above Peyton Place.  Voice-overs frequently refer to
seasons before all else--Allison constantly refers to the
change of seasons as images of the moods of her hometown
(and compare the openings of Mockingbird and The Member
of the Wedding). 16

        The external world of the cities and the citified is
again a contrast, this time usually opposing sophistication
and transience to the small-town values.  A favorite figure
of these movies is the out-of-towner, always disruptive,
whose arrival catalyses some crisis, forces characters to
look at themselves and their environment with new honesty.
Picnic and The Music Man deal with the arrival of a Dionysiac character who forces sexual tensions to the surface and
who energizes the town, only to fall victim to its repressiveness.  Both are not simply urban but transients. 17  In the
small-town movies, urban life is seen to be a matter of im-
permanence and incohesion, in fact.  Townsfolk who have
left town are usually deeply affected henceforth by what in
these movies is seen as a drastic change of environment.
The returning warriors of Best Years and The Deer Hunter
find that a gulf has opened between themselves and their
families and work associates.  Uncle Charlie, returning to
his sister, does not only bring a dark, denied world to
Santa Rosa but shows that it already exists there.  Bad Day
at Black Rock, John Sturges' 1955 movie which most closely
approximates, despite its post-war setting, to a western, interestingly bridges the gap between that genre and the small-
town movie (both genres are recalled, according to Jim
Pines, by The Last Picture Show, too), where the closely
knit community has to reveal unpleasant truths under the
pressure of Spencer Tracy's probing. 18

        While the external world is normally distinguished
from and opposed to that of the town, and is usually unseen,
it would be false to leave the impression that the effects of
external events on internal life are not recognized.  Best
Years, The Deer Hunter, and, to a lesser extent, Peyton
Place and The Member of the Wedding record the impact

of war on the small town, the invention of automobiles is of
crucial importance to The Magnificent Ambersons and Top
of the Stairs, while Mockingbird makes constant reference
to the Depression, and The Music Man opens with the salesmen talking of the new cash-deal pattern whereby credit has
become old-fashioned.  Such economic analysis as is offered
in these works largely restricts attention to local business
ownership, however.

---

A word should be said, before the chapter draws its conclusions, of the role of visual, or "iconographic," elements in
the genre.  Although it is the repertoire of stock characters
(uncertain adolescents, marriage-seeking widows or spinsters,
out-of-town transient catalysts, cynical businessman fathers,
etc.) and themes outlined above which primarily delineates
the genre, there are certainly recurrent iconographic elements, though these never serve alone to identify a movie
as small-town.

        Roads are generally tree-lined, the wooden-frame
houses equipped with white picket fences and lawns with concrete paths leading up to the front doors. [19]  Shadow of a
Doubt's opening sequences play on the contrast between urban
nightmare and provincial dream by making Uncle Charlie look
out on two anonymous men (obviously detectives) on the city
sidewalk on a tree-lined street.  The house visible on this
street is also wooden-frame.  The distinguishing features of
the city street are that skyscrapers can be discerned in the
background whereas Santa Rosa's equivalent is free of all urban architecture, and the foliage of the trees is much lusher
in the small town.  The townswomen in summer dresses
who, in the context (being seen again from Charlie's window), act as the small-town counterpart of the threatening
detectives are essentially small-town characters when located on that particular sort of street at a picket fence.
Civic buildings (schools, hospitals, libraries, for example)
tend to be red brick.  The homes of the rich and ostenta-
tious are also brick, frequently with white pillars.  The
wooden-frame houses always have a porch (occasionally running around three-quarters of the houses) on which the characters sit on summer evenings, for example.  While these
elements serve to differentiate small town from city, it is
almost impossible to separate small-town from suburban
movie on iconographic information alone.  Exteriors of
Meet Me in St. Louis and All Fall Down look just like the
small-town equivalents.

The safest iconographic evidence is probably that of
certain kinds of people (young girls in simple cotton dresses,
boys in open-necked shirts and possibly, in the earlier-set
movies, knickerbockers, middle-aged women in flowery
dresses, men in tidy but never modish business clothes,
none of these likely to be carrying a coat or any other ac-
coutrement--newspaper, attache case, umbrella--other than
schoolbooks in the case of youngsters) in such locations as
leafy-treed sidewalks decorated with picket fences or against
white-painted wooden-spired churches.  The lack of accoutrements emphasizes the simplicity and closeness to home at all
times of the small-town denizen, the choice of clothes--
unelaborate, functional though clean and pretty--would appear
to tie in with the thematics of the small-town movie, a visual external expression of the self-image, that of sensible,
pleasant, friendly people with no time for citified sophistication, a dislike of show or social inequality.  The small-
town inhabitant is wholesome in character, dress and deportment.

Interiors, while following a certain pattern (open-plan
ground floors with partitions capable of being pulled over,
stairs facing or to one side of the main door, telephone generally on table or on wall in hallway beneath stairs, kitchen
with screen door), share much of this with the suburb-set
movies.

Two further useful visual clues to the small-town
movie are the town square, generally with brick buildings
set about it, and a park in the center (sometimes, as in
Invasion of the Body Snatchers, the "square" is a triangle),
and the two-platform railroad station, usually complete with
telegraph office and level crossing in the background, though
it is difficult again to differentiate some of these from the
suburban stations of, say, The Man in the Gray Flannel Suit
type.

As the small-town movie has antecedents, in respect
of its plots, characters, themes, situations, in literature
(both the novel and community sociology) and drama, so in
its visual aspects it relates beyond movies themselves to
popular American magazines and household calendars.  The
"look" which the cameraman strives for in the small-town
movie is often that of calendar art or rather the Saturday
Evening Post front covers, the paintings of Norman Rockwell.
This is particularly true of the picnic sequences of Picnic,
notably that where Kim Novak on her swing and the déjeuner-

sur-l'herbe grouping of the party, with the early autumnal
hues of the leaves, irresistibly recall Saturday Evening Post,
but is also true of many other works, especially Peyton
Place, where the sumptuous natural scenery and particularly
the changing-season montages recall calendar art and that of
the National Geographic, a magazine that specializes when
dealing with North American landscapes in photographs of
nature at her most beguiling--glossy, poster-colored, pano-
ramic views of forest terrains, lakes in autumnal tones, or
pristine, untracked snowscapes.[20] The Music Man is as
bright, clean and sharp-colored as the pages of the National
Geographic but, it must be admitted, the same might be said
of Meet Me in St. Louis or Hello, Dolly!, which are set in
suburbs.

---

It seems to be a doctrine of film studies that the collective
unconscious is mirrored by popular cinema.  How exactly
the mirror reflects, how distorted the reflection may be,
can prove more difficult to determine, but genres are mined,
in this belief, by, for example, sociologists and psycholo-
gists in the search for evidence that may escape more conventional studies.

It is important to stress, though, that the mirror is
held up to the unconscious--in the present case, apparently,
the collective unconscious of the American people--and not
necessarily to any (other) existent reality.  David Thomson
believes that the study of the creation of an image of America by the movies is of particular importance.  His argument is that, America being the first man-made nation in
the world, it is an invented place "where imagined ideals
were invoked as a structure for reality.  It is the product
of artifice, not nature.  No country conscious of its roots
stretching out of sight and knowledge could have the same
confidence in purpose and design.  Whether one regards
America now as an Eden or a Poisonville, it is still a
country concocted from men's imaginations."[21]  A similar
point is made with particular force by Michael Wood: "The
movies did not describe or explore America, they invented
it, dreamed up an America all their own, and persuaded us
to share the dream.  We shared it happily, because the
dream was true in its fashion--true to a variety of American desires...."[22]  He adds to this notion a consideration
of the peculiar importance which "home" has for the American and the curious ambivalence with which it is regarded,

both as a desirable object and something to be dreaded, an
end to individuality and an ideal state of self-fulfilment.
"America is not so much a home for anyone as a universal
dream of home, a wish whose attraction depends upon its
remaining at the level of a wish ... home, that vaunted, all-
American ideal, is a sort of death, and an oblique justification for all the wandering that kept you away from it for so
long."[23] Wood's thesis makes special sense when applied to
that most potent realization of the dream of home, the small-
town movie, and suggests interesting reasons for the variety
of different attitudes to what seems to be the ideal realization of home for Americans.

To some extent, the (anachronistically?) isolated small
town is attractive for its utility in the exploration of certain
themes involving repression and liberation.  The artificially
precise delineation of town boundaries so that community life
is largely contained in a sort of stasis permits the dramatic
concentration which the neo-Aristotelian Renaissance expo-
nents of the "three unities" sought for tragedy.

Primarily, though, the small-town movie would appear
to be a vehicle in which America explores, either to confirm
or deny, certain fundamental, if probably wishful, tenets of
the American way of life.

Evidence for this view of the small town is in the
works themselves.  When America is trying to reassert the
values for which she stands, immediately before Pearl Harbor and throughout the remainder of the war, the most positive image of the small town is offered in the reassuring
series of the period and more small-town movies are made
then than at any other period.  The most damning and unre-
deemed image of small-town corruption, in The Chase,
clearly invites reference to the Kennedy assassination and
its aftermath.  With Vietnam and Watergate, and a deeper
pessimism about the reality of American values, the small
town peters out, or largely becomes (The Deer Hunter being an important exception) a nostalgic fantasy setting of the
American Graffiti variety or a horror-fantasy setting (Carrie).

Easy Rider deals with two hippies who went "looking
for America and couldn't find it anywhere," certainly not in
the redneck township where they paused.  If Americanism
isn't preserved in the small town, it isn't anywhere, these
films suggest, and if it is in the small town, they ask, is
it an ideal worth preserving?  The answers are various, but

again and again these movies touch upon questions concerning the importance of the family, of social integration, equality before the law, of patriotism, setting up comparisons of the founding fathers' ideals with the actuality in what are regularly conceived to be these storehouses of Americanism.[24]

## Notes to Chapter 9

1. The hopelessness of operating the American legal system fairly is again emphasized in The Chase and In the Heat of the Night and the powerful presence of the Ku Klux Klan in a small town is a principal element of Storm Warning.

2. Copland did write the score for Our Town.

3. Roughly 30 years later, the detective's faith persists. When it was known that Peter Bogdanovich was to film McMurtry's novel, The Last Picture Show, a letter (quoted in Rolling Stone, September 2, 1971) was published which said: "Wake up, Small Town America! You are all that is left of decency and dignity in this country."

4. The underbelly of the decent town is seen again in Tea and Sympathy, where the hero attempts to make love to a waitress in the seediest of surroundings and has to flee, still unproven, back to the reassurance of the school grounds and the less physical charms of the housemaster's wife. It is there too in the all-male preserve at the back of the drugstore in Top of the Stairs.

5. A less optimistic view of the mother-dominated recluse is afforded by another Norman, in Psycho.
   The contempt in which the apparently unfeminine woman or unmasculine man is held in the small-town movie is repeatedly exemplified. In The Long Hot Summer, Ben Quick represents a sort of Lawrentian masculine principle to which Clara, for all her overlay of culture, must succumb when she learns that her restrained suitor is (in this context) a pathetic homosexual (at least that seems to be signalled by his willing domination by his mother and by his inability to marry). Other examples of the progress to "normality" by sexually confused young men or women are to be found

in East of Eden (where the instability of the apparently
"healthy" brother is interestingly contrasted with the
disguised strength of the problematic brother), Written
on the Wind, Some Came Running (in each case, an
unhappy promiscuous woman learns self-respect),
Splendor in the Grass.

6. Cassie, though beautiful, seems to use books as refuge
   in her growing isolation, in Kings Row.

7. Special dignity is accorded, for example, to the aristocratic von Eln household in Kings Row, where French
   and German are spoken, and also to the Viennese suc-
   cessors to their property.

8. Examples are the unsophisticated father in Shadow of a
   Doubt who feels ill at ease with the imported wines enjoyed by his wife and brother-in-law, Marian's cheer-
   ful, uncultivated mother in The Music Man, the kindly
   but poor Monaghans in Kings Row.

9. When the doctor enters the City Emergency Hospital in
   the film's prologue, he says, "I'm not insane ... I'm
   a doctor too."

10. Similarly unattractive but ultimately redeemable con-
    trolling families are found in Written on the Wind,
    Picnic and Top of the Stairs, where criticism is di-
    verted from the weak but well-intentioned husband to
    his predatory wife.

11. Sometimes there is a gap between the nouveaux-riches
    and the aristocrats with generations of history and
    breeding. This is true of Kings Row and well illus-
    trated in The Long Hot Summer.

12. Unusually, All That Heaven Allows has a cross-class
    match disapproved by the children.

13. Examples are Allison's commentary in Peyton Place
    and the heroines of Mockingbird and The Heart Is a
    Lonely Hunter talking of their early experiences.
       The frequency and solemnity of high school gradua-
    tions are easily appreciated in relation to this empha-
    sis on maturing.

14. In Kings Row, Parris is attracted to the notion of

leaving his hometown, but realizes that everything that is important to him, including the practice of psychiatry, relates to Kings Row. Equally, Allison and Norman, the misfits of Peyton Place, return with an (unspecified) better understanding of themselves and their hometown, unlike Constance MacKenzie who did return but who cloaked her New York past in secrecy.

An allied, but family-oriented example of the same idea can be discovered in the closing sequences of East of Eden where the James Dean character is urged to make his peace with his dying father or else he will "never be a whole man."

15.    So do characters who despair of the rescue of the town from its blinkered prejudice and provincialism--as in The Chase and Rachel, Rachel.

16.    The contrast of small town and natural world is especially in evidence in Sirk's All That Heaven Allows, on which Griselda Pollock ("Report on the Weekend School," Screen, Summer 1977) writes: "... Ron is not only younger than she [Cary (Jane Wyman)] is, a fact which invites the horrified reactions of her friends and family in the town, but also an outsider and a social inferior, her gardener in fact, who lives outside the town, cultivating trees and living according to the ideals of Thoreau which as Mulvey points out represent a lost American ideal ... the spectator is ... witness to less explicit conflicts of class and to the opposition between the small-town community and the free self-directing individual at one with nature recuperating and living out the lost ideal."

17.    Compare the carnival worker in The Sound and the Fury and the carnival troupe in the last balletic sequence of Carousel, the military types of Some Came Running and Top of the Stairs and the drafted pop star of Bye Bye Birdie.

18.    Tracy performs a similar function as the out-of-town lawyer in Inherit the Wind where he exposes small-town organized religion (encapsulated in Peyton Place by a montage of different denominations' churches on Sunday morning and ridiculed by Uncle Charlie in Shadow of a Doubt) as the embodiment of unthinking prejudice.

Another lawman (this time, a policeman) from out

town who exposes the town's shortcomings is played by
Sidney Poitier in In the Heat of the Night.

19.    These are notable by their absence in that subverter of
       the tradition, The Last Picture Show.

20.    When man's habitat appears, it is harmonious in terms
       of coloring and texture (log cabins on pine-wooded
       slopes by mirror-like pools, and so on).  The conno-
       tations of the photographs are that man and nature live
       peacefully together, complementing each other, mutual-
       ly supportive, free of antagonism, in an ecological
       paradise.  When towns appear in the magazine, they
       are generally the preindustrialized or resolutely unin-
       dustrialized areas of New England, Alaska, etc.,
       rather than the coal-mining towns of Pennsylvania,
       for example.

21.    David Thomson, America in the Dark:  Hollywood and
       the Gift of Unreality (William Morrow and Company,
       Inc., New York, 1977), p. 37.

22.    Michael Wood, America in the Movies, or 'Santa Maria,
       It Had Slipped My Mind' (Basic Books, Inc., New
       York, 1975), p. 23.

23.    Ibid., pp. 40-42.

24.    It is this preservation of Americanism, whether as
       myth or reality, in the small town that is explored in
       Frederick Wiseman's Canal Zone (1977), where the
       American provincial way of life is carefully cultivated
       in the somewhat alien environment of Panama.

# Appendix A: The American Small-Town Movie as a Genre

Richard Collins, in the course of an article[1] in which he attempts to identify the essential elements of genre in "dominant" American cinema, denies that recurrent locations "do more than signal a temporal and geographical context for a film." While this statement must be seen in the context of an attempt to isolate and then order genre components into those that are not only necessary but sufficient to distinguish one genre from another (the distinguishing element being identified by Collins as "a repertoire of key situations"), it has been the present study's contention that at least one location, the American small town, in that it would appear to generate such a repertoire, performs more than the utilitarian function of supplying a geographical context, and even suggests a metaphorical locus for certain recurrent themes, centering on kinship, integration (social, psychological, ethnic) and rites of passage, as well as the more predictable examinations of provincialism and "Americanism."

When the work of establishing that a repertoire of key situations, of recurrent characters, of thematic and iconographic elements, exists in the small-town movie has been done, it may be appropriate to consider what conclusions can permissibly be drawn from their establishment. Principally, it can be asked whether a freshly discovered and thus under-explored genre could be posited on the basis of these elements. The answer depends partly on one's definition of genre. Whether film noir, for example, can be constituted as a Hollywood genre, since the common ground of particular noir works is essentially stylistic, depends on whether "the repertoire of key situations" is taken as the essence of genre. Though such a repertoire has been demonstrated in this study for the small-town movie, it could be taken to be equally affected by another problem in the categorization of film noir. Can a body of work whose essential unity of basis is discovered only some time after the maturity of that corpus be claimed to constitute a genre?

If the very term film noir postdates the movies so labelled,
if the studio thought it was making, and the public thought it
was buying tickets for, romantic melodramas or thrillers or
gangster movies, what relevance is there is now viewing
these same movies in other, generic terms?  Similar questions could be raised about any attempt to claim generic
status for the small-town movie, though some encouragement is afforded by Colin McArthur's statement, "There is
a sense in which all Hollywood movies are genre pieces,
there being in Hollywood a built-in impulse to reproduce a
successful formula. "2

    There is nevertheless some sort of case to be made
in partial answer to the latter question, that involving recognition of the small-town movie contemporaneous with the ex-
hibition of these movies.

    For a start, it could be argued that there would be a
receptivity on the part of audiences to a small-town genre on
the basis of extra-cinematic experience (see Chapter 1).
Moreover, certain directors (e.g., Preston Sturges, Hitchcock, Wyler, Kazan, Frankenheimer, Delbert Mann, Paul
Newman) keep returning to the small-town subject though
they are by no means confined to it, certain cameramen
(especially James Wong Howe), certain players (Betty Field,
Arthur O'Connell, Jane Wyman, Joanne Woodward, Paul
Newman, Gregory Peck), 3 certain composers (e.g., Alex
North, Elmer Bernstein) recur, though none of these can be
primarily, let alone exclusively, identified with the small-
town movie.

    There is, too, evidence both direct and indirect, that
recognition of a small-town movie genre has been made.

    The indirect evidence is partly that of television
which frequently enshrines (as well as creating anew) Hollywood genres.  The long-running series, Peyton Place, though
some years later than the movie, either creates or re-
creates a small-town videodrama at a time when small-town
movies are still being made.  More recent examples are
The Waltons and Gibbsville, and possibly Happy Days, with
its relation to the Hollywood small-town teen-world depicted
in American Graffiti.  Another piece of indirect evidence is
Bogdanovich's filming of McMurtry's novel, The Last Picture Show, to produce a work that relates most obviously
with the image of the small town as created by previous
movies.  It is at once within the small-town movie tradition

and outside, being more reflexive and self-conscious than
any other of these and acting as an epitaph not so much to
Sam the Lion's picture show as to the naïve (with no pejora-
tive connotation) version of small-town life deriving from
Our Town, and largely disseminated through the movies
from the 'thirties onwards. Interestingly, he replaces the
novel's Storm Warning (itself a grainy, though in no obvious
sense self-reflexive, counterimage of the small town) with
an affirmation of domesticity (Father of the Bride), and a
more heroic view of Texas (Red River) is offered rather
than the novel's The Kid from Texas. A movie tradition is
defined by the 1971 movie's commentary.

The direct evidence is meager and largely appears in
the wake of Bogdanovich's work. Before this time, the near-
est approach to the recognition of a tradition is in those
critics who note, or complain of, stereotypical characters
and situations in such works as Picnic. [4] Writing on this
movie, Derek Granger[5] says, "... in essence it is very
much a modern genre piece" but maddeningly he fails to
enunciate the nature of the genre to which he refers, though
the possibility that he is talking of a small-town genre is
increased by his next remark, "There is due emphasis on
topographical background." Apart from this isolated and unexplored suggestion, there is no clear suggestion of a genre
until 1971, when Pauline Kael[6] and Jim Pines[7] refer to it. [8]

If an argument can be made for the generic approach
to such works as Kings Row and Peyton Place, even if explicit recognition of their place in the suggested category occurs only post factum with the work of critic-director Bogdanovich, what is the point of adopting this approach?

Less specifically, we may first ask whether there is
applicability and utility in a generic approach to Hollywood
movies in general. The answer must surely involve the
recognition of the need for pertinent standards of assess-
ment, within which to come to critical terms with the gi-
gantic phenomenon of the Hollywood product. If we are not
to follow the willfully circumscribed habits of those intellec-
tuals, particularly before the 'fifties, who appear to feel
that Hollywood does not require any special discernment on
the critics' part to comprehend its codes, strategies, techniques, then how are we to proceed? Even if we should
condescendingly insist on regarding the phenomenon as worthy of study for no other reason than its profound influence
on the less commonly belabored European cinemas, for

example--and surely this would involve quite unjustified condescension to popular art--we must find, rather than impose,
a system of taxonomies to help us.

The realist criteria wielded by John Grierson, whereby Hollywood films are stripped down to a tiny nugget of
reality usually involving the accurate depiction of manual
work, or by André Bazin, who discovers saving graces in,
for example, the considerable technological advances of Hollywood by means of which increasingly invigorating doses of
reality and ambiguity are permitted to enter the "democratic"
cinema of, say, Wyler or Welles, seem of limited value because they are patently alien standards.   Bazin's realist
aesthetic roots itself in the "essence" of cinema, seeking to
locate its specificity in the mechnical means (the camera)
whereby reality is reproduced.   As the cinema is of all
media the best adapted to render the real (in the sense of
external, visible) world, it is argued, those films which
most neutrally or "ambiguously" photograph the external
world, with as little mediation through the director's personality or perceptions as is possible--and there must always be some sort of re-creating of the real if only by
selection--are most truly cinematic.   Bazin's more catholic (and in some senses Catholic) view of the real is modified by such populist realists as Grierson with his implicit
attribution of superior reality to the world of manual workers and industrial processes.   One of the obvious problems
of the realist approach, even if we leave aside such objec-
tions as that the "neutral" camera is normally focused,
moved, etc., by human agency with certain ends in view and
even if we refuse to explore the validity of claims that Wyler and Welles leave the spectator free, as in life, to discover for himself/herself significance in the deep-focus
frame, is that it must reject, or at least fail to discover
any apparatus with which to evaluate, such non-realist or
anti-realist work as that of German expressionism or the
Hollywood musical, for example, where even the external
world may be re-created.

"La politique des auteurs" was a declaration of war
by certain Cahiers du Cinéma critics against the French
"cinema of quality" and for other directors, including certain Americans, but the principal weakness of the polemic
or rather of its subsequent development into a "theory" by
Andrew Sarris is, again, a measure of inappropriateness.
While certain directors do obviously impose their personalities on their works, more so today as a result of the popu-

larization of authorial concepts, the majority have not done
so. The serious attention focused on certain auteurs was
founded on an implicit assertion of the superior or perhaps
sole value of the individual creator. The Hollywood industry
could thus be viewed in terms largely of those who challenged
or subverted, whether consciously or not, the essentially collective nature of the studios' output. However, this sort of
selection, even if the emphasis on the value of the individual's
working out of his preoccupations in what has traditionally
been discerned to be a communal industrial set-up should be
accepted, leaves us with no methodology whereby the non-
authorial movie may be explored, but simply relegates all
such work to limbo. Moreover, those works which are valued for being shaped by an individual consciousness are frequently explored on the basis of high-art principles. Thus,
some auteur critics determine the value of certain movies
by the degree of subversion of the formulaic or sterile surface movie by, say, metaphysical questionings detectable in
the latent movie or subtext of the superficially uninteresting
studio product.

Both realist and authorial criteria are finally unsatisfactory in relation to Hollywood movies because they do not
fit us to deal with their variety and multiplicity, because
they seem relatively monolithic and to discard or at least to
leave out of serious critical consideration more than they
salvage, and because they mark off movies as a relatively
autonomous area, except in so far as realism relates cinema to the external world, and cinema as a totally autonomous medium.

The generic approach is an attempt to find terms of
reference which are less selective and possibly more valid
because more observant of the facts of production. It takes
as its starting-point the observation that certain broad conventions obtain in Hollywood cinema, that audiences tend to
have built-in expectations of certain sets of movies and that
these expectations may be exploited in the marketing and
promotion of movies, that particular stars, directors, cameramen, build up expertise in certain areas. Rather than
discount these observations as evidence of the sterility or
mindlessness of Hollywood, the genre critic attempts to use
the epithets "formulaic," "typical," etc., neutrally, as descriptions. After all, the broadly formulaic nature of genres obtaining in certain areas of "high art," the usefulness
of knowledge generated concerning, say, Euripides by situ-
ating him against the traditions of Greek tragedy on which

he drew and which he refined and partially subverted, might
be cited to justify the generic examination of art.   (Aristotle,
the first recognizable literary critic of Europe, is also recognizably the first generic critic, despite his normative,
prescriptive side.)  Ephemerality may be accepted for the
individual movie, the less transient aspects being discovered
not in the single work but in the genre where that work may
be located.

        This is not to say that such approaches as the au-
thorial must necessarily be entirely discountenanced.   John
Caughie, for example, has recently reassessed the authorial
approach. [9]  Besides, greater rigor in auteurism's application may be achieved through the generic approach, for example.  If originality is positively valued by the authorial
critic, he or she may the more easily detect it with a solid
understanding of the operations of the particular genre in
which the auteur is working.

        The analysis of the small-town movie may be de-
fended in part on these general lines.   Moreover, if generic
criticism performs work, produces useful knowledge, the
further refining of the already accepted and explored genres
and the defining of fresh genres must obviously aid it to
function yet more productively.  If greater rigor on the basis of generic criticism (although it is certainly not suggested
that generic criticism should be treated merely as an adjunct
to any one other approach, even if a good case has been
made[10] for considering genre in connection with narrative
in general), then surely closer discernment of the factors
which contribute to the (never watertight) compartmentaliza-
tion of individual movies into sets must enhance the rigor
of generic criticism itself.  We might be setting up false
dichotomies if we ask whether Invasion of the Body Snatchers
should be seen in terms of horror film, Don Siegel film,
film noir or small-town movie, or if we imagine that three
Hitchcock works, Shadow of a Doubt, The Trouble with Harry, The Birds, ought to be discussed as either Hitchcock
films (auteurism becoming a subtle form of genre, producing a subgenre of the "thriller" called "the Hitchcock thriller") or thrillers or small-town movies.  Each approach
may have its own legitimacy, but each, at its fullest, requires the information that the others offer.

        Finally, and more broadly, generic criticism has en-
abled us to make relations beyond the cinematic, to the
provenance of particular filmic genres in the theatre, liter-

ature and even painting, [11] and, most importantly, to some
tentative explorations of ideology.


## Notes to Appendix A

1.  Richard Collins, "Genre: A Reply to Ed Buscombe,"
    Screen vol. 11. no. 4/5, 1970.

2.  Colin McArthur, Underworld USA (Secker and Warburg,
    London, 1972), p. 17.

3.  Although any sort of star could be found in a small-town
    movie, the sophisticated urban sort would almost cer-
    tainly be cast as the out-of-town catalyst, the stranger
    in town, or the misfit among the town denizens.    Thus,
    the urban sophistication of Dean Martin is used in Kiss
    Me, Stupid to increase the absurdity of his opposite
    numbers, the Hicksville song-writers; the worldly-wise
    and deeply discontented heroine of Beyond the Forest,
    stifled by her environment and longing for Chicago, is
    played by Bette Davis.
        The image of the small-town inhabitant is that of the
    down-to-earth, well-scrubbed, pretty but "homey" fe-
    male and the solid, dependable, astute and unfussily
    handsome male.    Lana Turner's svelte appearance, her
    artificiality of coiffure and elegance of costume in Pey-
    ton Place help to signal that she has an out-of-town
    past and that she has little of the honesty and direct-
    ness of the more general female type, that she needs
    salvation if she is ever to be a healthy functioning ele-
    ment in the town; the gentlemanly reserve and lack of
    frankness in Joanne Woodward's "suitor" (The Long Hot
    Summer) signal his inappropriateness, his unease, in
    Frenchman's Bend; his Ivy-League handsomeness con-
    trasts with the earthier, and thus more honest, appeal
    of Paul Newman.    The revelation of closet homosexual-
    ity on the former man's part could be taken as a meta-
    phor for the anachronistic and effete quality of the
    landed aristocracy in a modern small town, where en-
    trepreneurial energy and honest vulgarity are demon-
    strated by Newman and parodied by Orson Welles.    In-
    terestingly, it is Newman who turns up as the vaguely
    homosexual and neurotic misfit in Cat on a Hot Tin
    Roof, while Elizabeth Taylor atypically adopts the gutsy,
    beautiful-but-ever-direct persona of the small-town hero-
    ine.

4.  One useful example comes from Gilbert Salachas, "Pic-
    nic," Télécinè 62, December 1965, p. 2: "Tous les
    personnages de Picnic ... semblent donc issus de
    scénarios antérieurs.  Leurs démêlés s'inscrivent dans
    les limites d'une petite ville de province, cadre bien
    connu également des spectateurs de films américains."
    (All the characters in Picnic ... seem then to have
    come from earlier screenplays.  Their problems are
    worked out within the limits of a little provincial town,
    a framework equally well-known to the audiences for
    American films. )

5.  Derek Granger, Financial Times, February 13, 1956.

6.  Pauline Kael, New Yorker, October 9, 1971.

7.  Jim Pines, Time Out, Issue 109, March 17-23, 1972.

8.  To a greater or lesser extent, tentative recognition of
    a genre can be discerned also in Mark Lefanu, "The
    Last Picture Show," Monogram no. 4, 1972; Charles
    Champlin, Los Angeles Times, April 11, 1971; Jan
    Dawson, review of The Last Picture Show, Sight and
    Sound, vol. 41, no. 2, spring 1972.

9.  John Caughie (ed.), Theories of Authorship:  A Reader
    (Routledge & Kegan Paul/British Film Institute, 1981).

10. Stephen Neale, Genre (British Film Institute, 1980).

11. See Griselda Pollock, "Report on the Weekend School,"
    Screen, Summer 1977:  "... the ignorance of the con-
    current development of narrative painting in the nine-
    teenth century, with its particular elaboration of 'mise-
    en-scène' in order to spatialize and render visually
    legible novelistic forms is a serious and puzzling
    omission in the study of film."

Appendix B:  Small-Town Movies Before 1940

The latest movie discussed in this book was released in
1982.  The earliest, however, is a 1940 release.  This
requires explanation.

Firstly, since the book's method rests on the assumption that certain motifs run through the history of the small-
town movie, and since there is no attempt to provide encyclopaedic coverage of all the examples of these motifs but
rather to pick out certain movies for more detailed consideration, as illustrative of general trends, the much greater
difficulties in obtaining the earlier movies for study have
suggested that attention be directed chiefly towards post-
'thirties selections.  However, Michael Wood, one of the
writers who takes as subject the theme of the picture of
America created by the movies, lays special emphasis on
the post-'thirties movies, on the grounds that "the coherent
world of the movies doesn't really assume its full and final
form until about 1939 or a little earlier...."[1]  Robert Sklar
provides particular historical reasons for the consistency
and coherence in efforts at cultural mythmaking before the
Second World War.  "With the rise of Nazi Germany and the
aggressive challenge to democratic ideals, the widespread
doubt about traditional American myths threatened to become
a dangerous political weakness.  In politics, industry and
the media there were men and women, as often of liberal
as of conservative persuasion, who saw the necessity, almost as a patriotic duty, to revitalize and refashion a cultural mythology."[2]

While, then, it is not hard to defend the confinement
of detailed consideration of particular small-town movies to
those of the 'forties onwards, it is important that the significance of the small town as setting for feature movies
from the earliest period of American filmmaking be noted.
"Before 1917," we are told, for example, "more than half
of the American film dramas were played in rustic settings.

Centering around the home and the church, they hymned the
virtues of the simple life and, by contrast, the evils and
perils of the Big City. The heroes and heroines of these
dramas were inarticulate country youths and gingham girls,
the villains 'city slickers.' "[3] It is easy to detect in this
synopsis of the popularity and devices of pre-1917 rural
drama some of the elements that will be so frequently exploited in later small-town movies--the contrast of country
virtue and city vice, the wholesomeness of this ideal setting
for family and religion--but these early films may represent
more than the beginnings of small-town mythology. Eric
Rhode is attracted by Vachel Lindsay's suggestion that the
early cinema provided America with a chance to visualize
herself, so that audiences might be awakened by silent film
to a feeling for their own landscape and a resolve to preserve it in the face of laissez-faire capitalism's enthusiasm
for monstrous cities.[4] The feeling for the actual American
landscape, though not as all-pervasive as this suggests, is
particularly evidenced later in Henry King's Tol'able David
(1921), one of the landmarks in the story of the small-town
movie. The movie is remarkable for its naturalism. King,
according to Kevin Brownlow,[5] was particularly anxious, in
his search for locations, to find "rail fences" (fences constructed by the intermeshing of split logs), and in general
imbued his locale with the precise regional feel of his home
state of Virginia.

     In the teens and 'twenties of this century, the princi-
pal interest of the small-town movies, apart from the awak-
ening of the public to its rural heritage, was however the
idealization of so-called rural virtues. While the evidence
of the times suggested that American values had much to do
with acquisitiveness and consumerism, it was renunciation
and perseverance that were chiefly lauded in the country-set
movies. Tol'able David, if arguably naturalistic in its sense
of locale, appears to embody an idyll, ignoring all those aspects of the setting which relate to the hard grind of agricultural workers' lives in the early years of the century.
David's concerns are universal, the need to prove himself a
man, rather than specific to his position in rural society,
and the atmosphere of idyllic pastoral may well be due to
Henry King's cozy reminiscences of his own Christiansburg
childhood. Likewise, Buster Keaton's pastoral role has been
interpreted to depend for its humor on nostalgia for an
America he never knew.[6]

     Perhaps the most effective way to idealize the rural

community was by painting the impersonality and immorality
of the metropolis in the blackest colors.   Lewis Jacobs describes how some of the earliest movies executed this design.   In The Miller's Daughter (1905), a girl who has been
seduced by an artist from the city returns home, pregnant,
and is taken back into the community when she repents, becomes a church member and marries a local lad in time to
render the baby legitimate.   Similar tales of the dangerous
allure of the city, and the rescuing of fallen womanhood
through the piety of hometown relations and loves were told
in such other pre-First World War movies as In the Firelight, A Country Girl's Peril and First Love Best. 7  In
1920, Way Down East had a simple country-girl heroine
travelling to the city and being seduced by an older man.
Perhaps the contrast between dependable rustic virtue and
the glitter and sham of the city reaches its zenith in Mur-
nau's Sunrise (1927) and City Girl (1930).   The countryside
of Sunrise remains as idyllic as it did in Tol'able David,
but the city has been transformed into a place of magic, an
almost expressionistic evocation of the glamour and seduc-
tiveness of the forbidden urban world, thanks to the talents
of its designer, Rochus Gliese.   The married couple from
the country, threatened by the wiles of the city vamp, for
once rediscover their love for each other not by contemplation of nature but through the delights of the big city.

    It is possible today to see the contrast between coun-
try abstinence and chastity and big-city hollowness and tin-
sel glamour as a means of avoiding a confrontation with a
more disturbing contrast in American society of the teens
and 'twenties--the gap between urban prosperity and rural
poverty, a phenomenon of particular obviousness in the early 'twenties.   By the 'thirties, however, and sterner economic realities, the plight of the farming communities and
especially of migrant workers was sometimes referred to in
Hollywood movies as, for example, in Golden Harvest (1937)
where the industrious farmer hero was depicted as at the
mercy of heartless speculators.   Generally, however, the
more prevalent picture of country life remained that of the
idealized community, a picture given new life by the back-
to-the-land sentiments in the nation at large as a response
to the Depression.   Allied with the revitalized sentiment
about the value of the American small town as it was thought
to be at the turn of the century went a feeling that that period was admirably free of class consciousness and enmity, a
time when individuals counted for something and could either
make their way in the world by their merits or receive help

from those more fortunate than themselves. This feeling, summed up in the term "the fantasy of goodwill," was created particularly by the Saturday Evening Post and was translated into movie terms by Frank Capra in the 'thirties. His Mr. Deeds Goes to Town (1936) centered on Longfellow Deeds's belief in the sharing of his wealth with homeless farmers and agricultural workers to give them a chance to set up for themselves. This movie, like Capra's 1939 Mr. Smith Goes to Washington, suggests a remedy which bypasses New Deal reform and social reorganization, a remedy which posits the saving of a ravaged society by the humane impulses of individuals of sufficient wealth to make their sense of social injustice meaningful.

Such confidence depends on an anachronistic revival of belief in the small-town ethos, in the caring community where individuals have dignity and the rich ensure the survival of the poor by their natural concern with their fellowmen. Nevertheless, in the same year that Mr. Deeds was released, Fritz Lang offered a chilling indictment of small-town bigotry and evasion of reality in Fury, where the community's chief impulse seems to be to conduct a lynching and then shrug off responsibility for that impulse.

There is, therefore, superficially at least, some sort of progression in the small-town subject of the pre-'forties movies, from the wish to advertise and promote the American landscape in the early years to the 'thirties eagerness to mythologize the small town and what it was wishfully taken to stand for. The idealization of the ways of the small town was as frequent, however, in 1905 as it was in 1936, and the less obvious, but nonetheless detectable, counter-strain of small-town movies, suggesting its provincialism and narrowness of outlook, keeps turning up as a counterbalance. What is fascinating about the chronological study of the small-town movie is the discovery of the sheer tenacity and even ossification of its treatment. Since there is no consideration of the earlier movies in the main body of this book, it may be instructive to note how many of the motifs discovered there are already present in silent movies and early talkies.

In Chapter 2, Peyton Place relegates New York City to a vague place "out there," of dubious morality and even of uncertain reality. The contrast between city and country has already been noted for the earlier movies, finding its apotheosis in Sunrise. There are innumerable other exam-

ples among the movies of the 'twenties.  In the 1923 movie
of Booth Tarkington's Gentle Julia, the heroine is lured to
Chicago by a suitor who proves to be already married, and
returns to marry her hometown beau.  The Boy Friend
(1926) shows the folly of the heroine's dissatisfaction with
her small-town life in envy of a friend who writes glowing
accounts of city life from New York.  The friend returns
to disillusion her about the city and the heroine marries
her loyal suitor.  Why Girls Go Back Home (1926) speaks
for itself.  The young farmer hero of Broadway Madness
(1927) is rescued from his infatuation with a big-city gold
digger by a hometown sweetheart who embodies more ster-
ling virtues.  Harry Langdon, in Long Pants (1927), falls
for a city vamp also, but on discovering that she has murdered her husband is grateful for the security represented
by his faithful Priscilla.

        Chapter 5 explores the frequently recurring motif of
the alien, usually from the city, who disrupts or even ce-
ments potentially fragmenting small-town life.  Often this
urban alien is the sort of swindler later epitomized, in The
Music Man, by the bogus Professor Harold Hill.  The Flirt
(1922), Dollar Devils (1923) and The Confidence Man (1924)
all concern the exploitation of country innocence by unscrup-
ulous or phoney salesmen.  In Battling King (1922), a town
which is controlled by a gang is restored to liberty by a
boxer who happens to be stranded in it.  An interesting va-
riant is offered in The Town Scandal (1923), where it is the
hypocrisy of the town, with its Purity League, which is ex-
ploded by the arrival of a Broadway chorus girl who knows
much more about the natures of the leading male citizens
than they wish to be made known at home.  An equally unlikely savior of town society is the flapper heroine of Bare
Knees (1928) who, undiverted by the male townsfolk's preoccupation with her physical charms and apparently daring
attitudes, patches up a marriage and settles down with a
husband of her own.

        Closely connected with the figure of the alien is that
of the outsider-within-town, discussed in Chapter 6.  In The
Conquest of Canaan (1921), a young man who is shunned by
the town because of his unconventional attitudes and his desire to expose the town's political leaders, proves himself
as a lawyer and is reintegrated within it, becoming mayor
of Canaan.  Miss Lulu Bett (1921) deals with a spinster who
is first pitied, and then the subject of gossip, before she
finds salvation in marriage to a local schoolteacher.  Main

Street (1923), the curiously altered movie version of Sinclair
Lewis's classic novel, has the heroine and the Swedish Erik
Valborg victimized by town gossip.   In Welcome Stranger
(1924), it is a Jew that is driven from a small New England
town by local hostility but who is welcomed back to the community when the project in which he has been persuaded to
invest money proves beneficial to it.   In Down Upon the
Suwannee River (1925), the hero is ostracized because of
his atheism, and the woman whom he leaves behind when he
escapes town hostility is wrongly stigmatized as an unwed
mother.   His travels convince him of the rightness of religious doctrine and he and the heroine are restored to each
other and to the approval of town society when he becomes
a member of the church.   In Blondes By Choice (1927) and
The Girl in the Glass Cage (1929), depressed women are restored to the bosom of the community by the loving care of
a member of the upper class.

These two figures, the out-of-town catalyst and the
inside-town misfit, usually set off examinations of the small
town as a place of repressiveness, which it seems sometimes to be in the silent movies and early talkies too.   D.W.
Griffith's Way Down East (1920) centers upon Anna Moore
and her suffering, through small-town prejudice because she
is an unwed mother, a constant victim who is eventually
turned out into a New England blizzard.   Another heroine
who has experienced rejection, in A Noise in Newboro
(1923), goes to New York to make a name for herself, and
returns seven years later to expose the true nature of her
former boyfriend and local corrupt politicians to the townspeople.   Gossip is the chief sign of the town's narrowness
and cruelty.   In The Slanderers (1924), a family which is
the victim of gossip gains respect through the return of the
older son as a war hero.   The town of Dr. Bull (1933) gossips about the morals of the widow who regularly entertains
the doctor hero.   Much of the action of Broken Homes (1926)
is concerned with the heroine's need to protect her private
life from the unsympathetic scrutiny of the locals.   Probably
the most savage exposure of small-town bigotry and hypocrisy is, however, Fritz Lang's Fury (1936) (see p. 186).

If the town is not quite the cohesive community that
its depiction normally includes, one of the principal causes
of tension, as in the later movies, is the thwarting of lovers' eagerness for marriage by parents impelled by motives
of snobbery or of desire for material security for their
children.   Keeping Up With Lizzie (1921) details the dis-

astrous result of a youthful romance being broken up by
parents' concern with social class.   Lizzie returns from
her European tour with a "Count" anxious to marry into
money.   The trouble caused by the bogus aristocrat results
in permission to the original couple to marry.   In A Certain Rich Man (1921), the heroine's father forces her to
marry a man who will save his business and the sweethearts have to wait twenty years before their longed-for
marriage may take place with the death of the first husband
in a railroad accident.   Romance Road (1925) deals with the
melting of parental opposition to a girl's marriage with a
young soldier when he makes good, while Risky Business
(1926) demonstrates the wisdom of the heroine's choice of
a country doctor for husband rather than the worthless rich
man chosen by her mother.   In The Medicine Man (1930),
the heroine escapes the loveless match arranged by her
father thanks to the quick wits of a recently arrived medicine man with a travelling troupe, who marries her instead.
Parental domination which features prominently in all these
stories and is found again in so many later movies is particularly evident in The Sap (1926) where, like Norman Page
in Peyton Place, the boy coddled by his mother becomes a
war hero in direct reaction.   Her Unborn Child (1930) concerns the damage inflicted on young love by the domination
of the hero by his possessive mother.

Another frequent betrayal of the small town at its
utopian best is perpetrated regularly in the small-town movie by the undemocratic influence of a rich man or boss over
town affairs.   It takes the determination of a young lawyer
newly arrived in Owasco, Michigan, to awaken the town to
the need to topple the lumber king who dominates its affairs
and prevents the realization of justice, in The Yellow Stain
(1922).   Bing Bang Boom (1922) concerns the fight of a duped
recent arrival, with the help of the local newspaper editor,
against the village boss.   In Jazzland (1928), a local coun-
cilman is discovered to be in league with big-city businessmen attempting to force a nightclub upon a small New England town.

Just as most of the usual negative elements are found
in small-town movies before 1940, as regularly as after, so
those elements which permit the town to be thought of as a
Utopia (see Chapter 3) are also discoverable in the earlier
movies.   The innocent triumph in small towns by virtue of
that innocence, as in Grandma's Boy (1922), where Harold
Lloyd as Blossom Ben manages to beat the town bully and

win the girl.   The good doctors who play such a large part
in the utopian series of the late 'thirties and early 'forties
can be found in the story of the good, but poor, country
physician of <u>Risky Business</u> (1926).   In John Ford's <u>Dr. Bull</u>
(1933), Will <u>Rogers</u> is not only invariably right in his diag-
noses, but proves to be a pillar of the church and the pro-
moter of small-town decency and fair play.   Henry King's
<u>The Country Doctor</u> (1936), though set in Canada, is worthy
of consideration since it generated the Dr. Christian series
(see p. 52 ff. ).

        This catalog of themes and characters of small-town
movies ought to show how analysis of the small-town movie
in some detail may profitably be undertaken with reference
to selections from more recent movies.   The only type of
small-town movie dealt with in the main body of this book
which is not found in the pre-'forties movies, the self-
reflexive examination of small-town life (<u>see</u> Chapter 7) is
not discoverable before the 'seventies in <u>any</u> case, so that
there need be no sense that vital information is denied us
by concentration on the later decades.


                            Notes to Appendix B

1.   Michael Wood, <u>America in the Movies, or 'Santa Maria,</u>
     <u>It Had Slipped My Mind'</u> (Basic Books, Inc, New York,
     1975), p. 12.

2.   Robert Sklar, <u>Movie-Made America:   A Social History</u>
     <u>of American Movies</u> (Random House, New York, 1975),
     p. 196.

3.   Richard Griffith, Arthur Mayer and Eileen Bowser, <u>The</u>
     <u>Movies,</u> revised and updated edition (Simon & Schuster,
     New York, 1981), p. 110.

4.   Eric Rhode, <u>A History of the Cinema from its Origins</u>
     <u>to 1970,</u> (Penguin, Harmondsworth, 1978), p. 32.

5.   Kevin Brownlow, <u>The Parade's Gone By</u> (Secker and
     Warburg, London, 1968), pp. 106-7.

6.   Eric Rhode, <u>ibid.</u>, p. 241.

7.   See Lewis Jacobs, <u>The Rise of the American Film</u>
     (Teachers College Press, New York, 1939), pp. 72
     and 142.

# Appendix C:  A Selection of Small-Town Movies

1913  The Reformers, or The Lost Art of Minding One's
      Business (D. W. Griffith)

1918  Little Women (Harley Knowles)

1919  True Heart Susie (D. W. Griffith)

1920  Pollyanna (Paul Powell)
      Way Down East (D. W. Griffith)

1921  A Certain Rich Man (Howard Hickman)
      The Conquest of Canaan (R. William Neill)
      Garments of Truth (George D. Baker)
      Keeping Up With Lizzie (Lloyd Ingraham)
      Miss Lulu Bett (William C. De Mille)
      Tol'able David (Henry King)

1922  Battling King (P. D. Sargent)
      Bing Bang Boom (Fred J. Butler)
      Boy Crazy (William A. Seiter)
      The Danger Point (Lloyd Ingraham)
      The Flirt (Hobart Henley)
      Free Air (E. H. Griffith)
      Grandma's Boy (Fred Nemeyer)
      The Yellow Stain (Jack Dillon)

1923  Alice Adams (Rowland V. Lee)
      Dollar Devils (Victor Schertzinger)
      Gentle Julia (Rowland V. Lee)
      Main Street (Harry Beaumont)
      A Noise in Newboro (Harry Beaumont)
      The Town Scandal (King Baggot)

1924  The Confidence Man (Victor Neerman)
      Sherlock, Jr. (Buster Keaton)
      The Slanderers (Nat Ross)
      Welcome Stranger (James Young)

1925       Down Upon the Suwannee River (Lem F. Kennedy)
           The Dressmaker from Paris (Paul Bern)
           Private Affairs (Renaud Hoffman)
           Romance Road (Fred Windemere)
           Stella Dallas (Henry King)

1926       The Boy Friend (Monte Bell)
           The Broadway Boob (Joseph Henabery)
           Broken Homes (Hugh Dierker)
           Risky Business (Alan Hale)
           The Sap (Erle Kenton)
           Why Girls Go Back Home (James Flood)

1927       Blondes By Choice (Hampton Del Ruth)
           Broadway Madness (Burton King)
           Long Pants (Frank Capra)

1928       Bare Knees (Erle Kenton)
           Jazzland (Dallas M. Fitzgerald)
           Manhattan Cocktail (Dorothy Arzner)

1929       The Broadway Hoofer (George Archainbaud)
           The Carnation Kid (E. Mason Hopper)
           The Girl in the Glass Cage (Ralph Dawson)

1930       Embarrassing Moments (William James Craft)
           Her Unborn Child (Albert Ray, Charles McGrath)
           The Medicine Man (Scott Pembroke)
           Tom Sawyer (John Cromwell)

1933       Dr. Bull (John Ford)
           Little Women (George Cukor)
           State Fair (Henry King)

1934       It's a Gift (Norman Taurog)

1935       Ah Wilderness (Clarence Brown)
           Alice Adams (George Stevens)

1936       Fury (Fritz Lang)

1937       A Family Affair (George B. Seitz)
           They Won't Forget (Mervyn Le Roy)

1938       Adventures of Tom Sawyer (Norman Taurog)
           Judge Hardy's Children (George B. Seitz)
           Love Finds Andy Hardy (George B. Seitz)
           You're Only Young Once (George B. Seitz)

1939      Andy Hardy Gets Spring Fever (W.S. Van Dyke II)
          Meet Dr. Christian (Bernard Vorhaus)
          What a Life (Jay Theodore Reed)

1940      Andy Hardy Meets a Debutante (George B. Seitz)
          The Bank Dick (Eddie Cline)
          The Courageous Dr. Christian (Bernard Vorhaus)
          Dr. Christian Meets the Women (William McGann)
          Judge Hardy and Son (George B. Seitz)
          Our Town (Sam Wood)
          Remedy for Riches (Erle Kenton)

1941      Andy Hardy's Private Secretary (George B. Seitz)
          Cheers for Miss Bishop (Tay Garnett)
          Henry Aldrich for President (Hugh Bennett)
          Life Begins for Andy Hardy (George B. Seitz)
          Life with Henry (Jay Theodore Reed)
          The Little Foxes (William Wyler)
          Nice Girl? (William A. Seiter)

1942      The Affairs of Martha (Jules Dassin)
          Andy Hardy's Double Life (George B. Seitz)
          The Courtship of Andy Hardy (George B. Seitz)
          Happy Land (Irving Pichel)
          Henry Aldrich, Editor (Hugh Bennett)
          Henry and Dizzy (Hugh Bennett)
          The Human Comedy (Clarence Brown)
          I Married a Witch (René Clair)
          Kings Row (Sam Wood)
          The Magnificent Ambersons (Orson Welles)
          Moontide (Archie Mayo)
          Shadow of a Doubt (Alfred Hitchcock)
          The Talk of the Town (George Stevens)

1943      Henry Aldrich Gets Glamour (Hugh Bennett)
          Henry Aldrich Haunts a House (Hugh Bennett)
          Henry Aldrich Swings It (Hugh Bennett)
          Johnny Come Lately (William K. Howard)

1944      Andy Hardy's Blonde Trouble (George B. Seitz)
          The Curse of the Cat People (Gunther von Fritsch,
                    Robert Wise)
          Hail the Conquering Hero (Preston Sturges)
          Henry Aldrich, Boy Scout (Hugh Bennett)
          Henry Aldrich Plays Cupid (Hugh Bennett)
          Henry Aldrich's Little Secret (Hugh Bennett)
          Miracle of Morgan's Creek (Preston Sturges)
          The Sullivans (Lloyd Bacon)

1945    A Medal for Benny (Irving Pichel)
        Mildred Pierce (Michael Curtiz)

1946    The Best Years of Our Lives (William Wyler)
        Boomerang (Elia Kazan)
        Colonel Effingham's Raid (Irving Pichel)
        Love Laughs at Andy Hardy (Willis Goldbeck)
        The Strange Love of Martha Ivers (Lewis Milestone)
        The Stranger (Orson Welles)

1947    Magic Town (William Wellman)
        Summer Holiday (Rouben Mamoulian)

1948    Another Part of the Forest (Michael Gordon)
        Deep Waters (Henry King)
        June Bride (Bretaigne Windust)
        Little Women (Mervyn Le Roy)

1949    Angel in Exile (Allan Dwan, Philip Ford)
        Beyond the Forest (King Vidor)
        Chicken Every Sunday (George Seaton)
        Cover Up (Alfred E. Green)
        Intruder in the Dust (Clarence Brown)
        Our Very Own (David Miller)

1950    Fancy Pants (George Marshall)
        Stars in My Crown (Jacques Tourneur)

1951    Bannerline (Don Weis)
        Has Anybody Seen My Gal? (Douglas Sirk)
        A Place in the Sun (George Stevens)
        Storm Warning (Stuart Heisler)

1952    Come Back, Little Sheba (Daniel Mann)
        Wait 'Til the Sun Shines, Nellie (Henry King)

1953    The Affairs of Dobie Gillis (Don Weis)
        All I Desire (Douglas Sirk)
        It Happens Every Thursday (Joseph Pevney)
        Meet Me at the Fair (Douglas Sirk)
        The Member of the Wedding (Fred Zinnemann)
        Small Town Girl (Leslie Kardos)
        Take Me to Town (Douglas Sirk)

1954    Bad Day at Black Rock (John Sturges)
        Bad for Each Other (Irving Rapper)
        Suddenly (Lewis Allen)

The Wild One (Laslo Benedek)
Young at Heart (Gordon Douglas)

1955    East of Eden (Elia Kazan)
        The Rose Tattoo (Daniel Mann)
        The Trouble with Harry (Alfred Hitchcock)

1956    All That Heaven Allows (Douglas Sirk)
        Carousel (Henry King)
        Invasion of the Body Snatchers (Don Siegel)
        Picnic (Joshua Logan)
        Storm Center (Daniel Taradash)

1957    The Pajama Game (George Abbott, Stanley Donen)
        Peyton Place (Mark Robson)
        Written on the Wind (Douglas Sirk)

1958    Andy Hardy Comes Home (Howard Koch)
        The Blob (Irving Yeaworth)
        Brain Eaters (Bruno VeSota)
        Handle With Care (David Friedkin)
        Home Before Dark (Mervyn Le Roy)
        Hot Spell (Daniel Mann)
        The Long Hot Summer (Martin Ritt)
        Some Came Running (Vincente Minnelli)

1959    Anatomy of a Murder (Otto Preminger)
        The Fugitive Kind (Sidney Lumet)
        It Happened to Jane (Richard Quine)
        Li'l Abner (Melvin Frank)
        Rally Round the Flag, Boys (Leo McCarey)
        The Restless Years (Helmut Kautner)
        The Sound and the Fury (Martin Ritt)
        A Stranger in My Arms (Helmut Kautner)
        A Summer Place (Delmer Daves)

1960    The Bramble Bush (Daniel Petrie)
        College Confidential (Albert Zugsmith)
        The Dark at the Top of the Stairs (Delbert Mann)
        Desire in the Dust (William F. Claxton)
        The Devil's Partner (Charles M. Rondeau)
        Home from the Hill (Vincente Minnelli)
        Inherit the Wind (Stanley Kramer)
        Pollyanna (David Swift)

1961    By Love Possessed (John Sturges)
        The Ladies' Man (Jerry Lewis)

Return to Peyton Place (Jose Ferrer)
Splendor in the Grass (Elia Kazan)
Summer and Smoke (Peter Glenville)

1962     Follow That Dream (Gordon Douglas)
The Music Man (Morton Da Costa)
Sweet Bird of Youth (Richard Brooks)
To Kill a Mockingbird (Robert Mulligan)

1963     The Birds (Alfred Hitchcock)
Bye Bye Birdie (George Sidney)

1964     Kiss Me, Stupid (Billy Wilder)

1965     Bus Riley's Back in Town (Harvey Hart)
Joy in the Morning (Alex Segal)

1966     Boy, Did I Get a Wrong Number (George Marshall)
The Chase (Arthur Penn)
The Russians Are Coming, The Russians Are Com-
ing (Norman Jewison)
This Property is Condemned (Sidney Pollack)

1967     Hurry Sundown (Otto Preminger)
In the Heat of the Night (Norman Jewison)

1968     Did You Hear the One About the Traveling Sales-
lady? (Don Weis)
The Heart Is a Lonely Hunter (Robert Ellis Miller)
Rachel, Rachel (Paul Newman)

1969     Angel in My Pocket (Alan Rufkin)
The Gypsy Moths (John Frankenheimer)
The Molly Maguires (Martin Ritt)

1970     I Walk the Line (John Frankenheimer)
The Lawyer (Sidney J. Furie)
Rabbit, Run (Jack Smight)
... tick ... tick ... tick (Ralph Nelson)

1971     Billy Jack (T.C. Frank [Tom Laughlin])
Brother John (James Goldstone)
Cold Turkey (Norman Lear)
The Last Picture Show (Peter Bogdanovich)

1972     The Effect of Gamma Rays on Man-in-the-Moon
Marigolds (Paul Newman)

1973     The All American Boy (Charles Erdman)
         American Graffiti (George Lucas)
         The Crazies (George A. Romero)
         Happy Mother's Day, Love George (Darren McGavin)
         The Legend of Boggy Creek (Charles B. Pierce)
         Tom Sawyer (Don Taylor)
         Welcome to Arrow Beach (Laurence Harvey)

1974     Buster and Billie (Daniel Petrie)

1975     Bug (Jeannot Szwarc)
         The Giant Spider Invasion (Bill Rebane)
         The Killer Inside Me (Burt Kennedy)
         Smile (Michael Ritchie)
         Vigilante Force (George Armitage)

1976     Baby Blue Marine (John Hancock)
         The Born Losers (T.C. Frank [Tom Laughlin])
         Carrie (Brian De Palma)
         Communion (Alfred Sole)
         Eat My Dust! (Charles B. Griffith)
         Martin (George A. Romero)
         Misty (Joe Sarno)
         Ode to Billy Joe (Max Baer)
         A Small Town in Texas (Jack Starrett)

1977     The Car (Elliot Silverstein)
         Kingdom of the Spiders (John "Bud" Cardos)
         Rolling Thunder (John Flynn)
         The Town That Dreaded Sundown (Charles B. Pierce)

1978     The Deer Hunter (Michael Cimino)
         Halloween (John Carpenter)
         Hill's Angels (Bruce Bilson)

1979     Beneath the Valley of the Ultra Vixens (Russ Meyer)
         Breaking Away (Peter Yates)
         The Evictors (Charles B. Pierce)
         The Fog (John Carpenter)
         Norma Rae (Martin Ritt)
         The Runner Stumbles (Stanley Kramer)
         The War at Home (Glenn Silber, Barry Alexander
              Brown)

1980     How to Beat the High Cost of Living (Robert Scheer-
              er)
         Motel Hell (Kevin Connor)

        Popeye (Robert Altman)
        Prom Night (Paul Lynch)

1981      The Boogens (James L. Conway)
        Ghost Story (John Irvin)
        Halloween II (Rick Rosenthal)
        Honky Tonk Freeway (John Schlesinger)
        The Raggedy Man (Jack Fisk)

1982      Come Back to the Five and Dime, Jimmy Dean,
           Jimmy Dean (Robert Altman)

Selected Bibliography

ADAIR, Gilbert.  Hollywood's Vietnam (Proteus, 1981)

ALTHER, Lisa.  Kinflicks (Penguin, 1977)

ANDERSON, Sherwood.  Winesburg, Ohio (Viking Press, 1964)

BAZIN, André.  What Is Cinema?, 2 vols. (California University Press, vol. 1, 1967, vol. 2, 1971)

_____.  "William Wyler" in Qu'est-ce que le cinéma?, vol. 1 (Les Editions du Cerf, 1958), pp. 149-173

BELLAMANN, Henry.  Kings Row (Jonathan Cape, 1941)

BROWNLOW, Kevin.  The Parade's Gone By (Secker and Warburg, 1968)

CAUGHIE, John (ed.).  Theories of Authorship: A Reader (Routledge & Kegan Paul/British Film Institute, 1981)

CIMINO, Michael.  "Ordeal by Fire and Ice," American Cinematographer vol. 59, no. 10, October 1978, pp. 965 ff.

COLLINS, Richard.  "Genre: A Reply to Ed Buscombe," Screen, vol. 11, no. 4/5, 1970

CONNERY, Donald S.  Small Town (Eyre Methuen, 1973; pub. 1972 in USA under title One American Town)

COOK, David M. and SWAUGER, Craig G. (eds.).  The Small Town in American Literature, 2nd ed. (Harper & Row, 1977)

COSGROVE, John.  "Revisiting Kings Row," Screen Facts no. 9, vol. 2, no. 3

DAVIDSON, Bill.  The Real and the Unreal (Harper, 1957)

DODDS, John W.  Everyday Life in Twentieth Century
     America (B.T. Batsford, Ltd., 1965)

"Dossier on Melodrama." Screen, vol. 18, no. 2, summer
     1977

DURGNAT, Raymond.  The Strange Case of Alfred Hitchcock
     (Faber and Faber, 1974)

FOX, Terry Curtis.  "Stalking The Deer Hunter," Film
     Comment 1979, vol. 15, no. 2

GRIFFITH, Richard, MAYER, Arthur and BOWSER, Eileen.
     The Movies, revised and updated edition (Simon &
     Schuster, 1981)

Halliwell's Filmgoer's Companion, 6th edition (Hart-Davis,
     MacGibbon Ltd., 1977)

HARDY, Forsyth (ed.).  Grierson on Documentary (Faber,
     1972)

HARRIS, P.A. and LASKY, M.S.  The Films of Alfred
     Hitchcock (Citadel Press, 1976)

HIGHAM, Charles and GREENBERG, Joel.  "Vincente Min-
     nelli" in The Celluloid Muse:  Hollywood Directors
     Speak (Angus and Robertson, 1969)

INGE, William.  Four Plays (Heinemann, 1960)

JACOBS, Lewis.  The Rise of the American Film (Teachers
     College Press, 1939)

KAMINSKY, Stuart M.  American Film Genres (Pflaum,
     1974)

_____.  Don Siegel:  Director (Curtis Books, 1974)

KITSES, Jim.  Horizons West:  Studies in Authorship in the
     Western Film (Cinema One series, Secker and War-
     burg, 1970)

KRACAUER, Siegfried.  Theory of Film:  The Redemption of
     Physical Reality (Oxford University Press, 1965)

LEWIS, Sinclair. Main Street (Jonathan Cape, 1921; reissued 1973)

LINGEMAN, Richard. Small Town America: A Narrative History 1620-The Present (G. P. Putnam's Sons, 1980)

LOGAN, Joshua. Josh: My Up and Down, In and Out Life (Delacorte, 1976)

LOVELL, Alan. Don Siegel: American Cinema, revised edition (British Film Institute, 1975)

LYND, Robert S. and LYND, Helen Merrell. Middletown, A Study in Modern American Culture (Harcourt, Brace and World, Inc., 1929)

McARTHUR, Colin. Underworld USA (Cinema One series, Secker and Warburg, 1972)

MacCANN, Richard Dyer (ed.). Film: A Montage of Theories (Dutton, 1966)

MADSEN, Axel. William Wyler (Thomas Y. Cromwell, 1973)

MAST, Gerald and COHEN, Marshall (eds.). Film Theory and Criticism, 2nd edition (Oxford University Press, 1979)

METALIOUS, Grace. Peyton Place (Frederick Muller, 1957)

MINNELLI, Vincente with ARCE, Hector. I Remember It Well (Doubleday and Co., 1974)

NEALE, Stephen. Genre (British Film Institute, 1980)

PEASE, Nick. "The Deer Hunter and the Demythification of the American Hero," Literature Film Quarterly, vol. 7, no. 4, 1978

PERKINS, Victor F. Film as Film (Penguin, 1972)

POLLOCK, Griselda. "Report on the Weekend School," Screen, vol. 18, no. 2, summer 1977

RHODE, Eric. A History of the Cinema from its Origins to 1970 (Penguin, 1978)

ROCHE, Catherine de la.  Vincente Minnelli (New Zealand
     Film Institute, 1959)

ROTHA, Paul.  The Film Till Now, revised and enlarged
     edition (Vision Press, 1949)

SARRIS, Andrew.  The American Cinema (Dutton, 1968)

_____.  Hollywood Voices (Secker and Warburg, 1971)

SCHICKEL, Richard.  "Vincente Minnelli" in The Men Who
     Made The Movies (Atheneum, 1975)

SCHORER, Mark (ed.).  Sinclair Lewis (Prentice-Hall, Inc.,
     1962)

SCHRAG, Peter.  The Vanishing American (Victor Gollancz,
     Ltd., 1972); U.S. title, The Decline of the WASP

SHERIDAN, Bob.  "Invasion of the Body Snatchers--a cri-
     tique," Photon no. 22, 1972

"Siegel on Invasion of the Body Snatchers," Cinéfantastique
     vol. 2, no. 3, winter 1973

SIMSOLO, Noël.  Alfred Hitchcock (Editions Seghers, 1969)

SKLAR, Robert.  Movie-Made America:  A Social History of
     American Movies (Random House, 1975)

SOLOMON, Stanley J.  Beyond Formula:  American Film
     Genres (Harcourt Brace Jovanovich Inc., 1976)

STEIN, Maurice R.  The Eclipse of Community (Harper &
     Row, 1964)

THOMAS, Tony.  "Sam Wood: A Master of His Craft" in
     The Hollywood Professionals:  King, Milestone, Wood
     (Tantivy Press, 1974)

THOMSON, David.  America in the Dark:  Hollywood and
     the Gift of Unreality (William Morrow and Company,
     Inc., 1977)

TRICHAUD, François.  Vincente Minnelli (Editions Robert
     Lafont, 1966)

TRUFFAUT, François and SCOTT, Helen G.   Hitchcock
(Secker and Warburg, 1968)

VIDAL, Marion.   Vincente Minnelli (Editions Seghers, 1973)

VIDICH, Arthur J. and BENSMAN, Joseph.   Small Town in
Mass Society (Princeton University Press, 1968)

WALKER, R. H.   Everyday Life in the Age of Enterprise,
1865-1900 (Batsford, 1967)

WHITAKER, Sheila.   The Films of Martin Ritt (British Film
Institute, 1972)

WILDER, Thornton.   Our Town (Longmans, Green and Co.
Ltd., 1969)

William Wyler.   Index (British Film Institute, 1959)

WILLIAMS, Christopher (ed.).   Realism and the Cinema
(Routledge & Kegan Paul, 1981)

WOOD, Denis.   "All the Words We Cannot Say," The Journal of Popular Film and Television, vol. VII, no. 4,
1980

WOOD, Michael.   America in the Movies, or "Santa Maria,
It Had Slipped My Mind" (Basic Books, Inc., 1975)

WOOD, Robin.   Hitchcock's Films (Castle Books, 1969)

ZINMAN, David.   Saturday Afternoon at the Bijou (Arlington House, 1973)

# INDEX

Titles are capitalized. Underlined pages represent most complete treatment of topic.

ADVENTURES OF HUCKLE-
  BERRY FINN, THE  10
Aeschylus 65n.
AFFAIRS OF DOBIE GILLIS,
  THE  51
AGAMEMNON  65n.
AH WILDERNESS  1
Aldrich, Henry  53-54, 60
ALL FALL DOWN  24n., 167
ALL I DESIRE  21
ALL THAT HEAVEN ALLOWS
  21, 48, 112n., 125, 172n.,
  173n.
Allen, Woody  17
Alther, Lisa  15
Altman, Robert  130, 136, 138,
  142
AMERICAN GRAFFITI  1, 134-
  136, 141, 170, 176
ANATOMY OF A MURDER  125
Anderson, Sherwood  11, 12
ANDY HARDY COMES HOME
  65n.
ANDY HARDY'S DOUBLE LIFE
  55-59, 153, 161
ANDY HARDY'S PRIVATE SEC-
  RETARY  59
ANNIE HALL  17
Antonioni, Michelangelo  129,
  133
APOCALYPSE NOW  83
Archer City, Texas  18
AT LONG LAST LOVE  127
AVVENTURA, L'  133

BACCHAE  111n.
BAD DAY AT BLACK ROCK
  166
BALLAD OF THE SAD CAFE,
  THE  104, 161
BANK DICK, THE  125
BARE KNEES  187
"Barn Burning"  103
Barthes, Roland  86
BATTLING KING  187
Bazin, André  30, 67, 72, 178
Beach Boys, The  135, 136
"Beautiful Dreamer"  155
Bellamann, Henry  12, 15, 16,
  27
Bensman, Joseph  7, 8
Benson, Sally  115
Bergman, Ingmar  135
Bernstein, Elmer  61, 117, 176
BEST OF EVERYTHING, THE
  51
BEST YEARS OF OUR LIVES,
  THE  18, 19, 48, 67-79,
  117, 151, 154, 156, 161,
  163, 166
BEYOND THE FOREST  21, 48,
  181n.
BING BANG BOOM  189
BIRDS, THE  100-102, 106,
  143, 144, 160, 163, 164,
  180
BIRTH OF A NATION, THE
  63
Black, Karen  137
BLOB, THE  125, 143
BLONDES BY CHOICE  188
BLUE ANGEL, THE  103
BODY SNATCHERS, THE  98
Bogdanovich, Peter  18, 23n.,
  47, 125, 126, 127, 128,
  129, 130, 131, 133, 134,
  137, 138, 139n., 141, 142,
  171n., 176, 177

BOY FRIEND, THE  187
BOYS IN THE BAND, THE  137
Brando, Marlon  64, 141
Brautigan, Richard  15
BREAKFAST AT TIFFANY'S  17
British Film Institute  1
BROADWAY MADNESS  187
BROKEN HOMES  188
Brown, Clarence  114
Brownlow, Kevin  184
BUG  144-145
BYE BYE BIRDIE  125, 173n.

CAHIERS DU CINEMA  86, 178
Camden, Maine  18, 39
CANAL ZONE  174n.
"Can't Take My Eyes Off You"
    89
Capra, Frank  186
CAROUSEL  52, 123n., 125,
    154, 155, 173n.
Carpenter, John  144
CARRIE  1, 21, 145-149, 153,
    164
CAT ON A HOT TIN ROOF
    88, 106, 181n.
Cather, Willa  9
Caughie, John  180
CERTAIN RICH MAN, A  189
Cahmplin, Charles  127
CHASE, THE  1, 16, 64, 148,
    153, 170, 171n., 173n.
Chicago  77, 154, 181n., 187
CHOEPHORI  65n.
Christian, Dr.  52-53, 54, 60,
    190
Christie, Julie  84
Cimino, Michael  79, 80, 81,
    83, 85, 86, 94, 143
Cincinnati, Ohio  18, 71, 80
CITY GIRL  185
Cleveland, Ohio  24n., 80, 152
Collins, Richard  175
Colusa, California  18
COME BACK, LITTLE SHEBA
    (movie)  48
COME BACK, LITTLE SHEBA
    (play)  22n.
COME BACK TO THE FIVE AND
    DIME, JIMMY DEAN, JIMMY
    DEAN  136-138
Comedy, New  48
COMMUNION  145

CONFIDENCE MAN, THE  187
Connery, Donald S.  6
CONQUEST OF CANAAN, THE
    187
Cooper, Fenimore  87
Cooper, Jackie  53
Copland, Aaron  155, 171n.
Coppola, Francis Ford  81, 83
CORONATION STREET  141
COUNTRY DOCTOR, THE  52,
    190
COUNTRY GIRL'S PERIL, A
    185
COUPLES  15
COURAGEOUS DR. CHRISTIAN,
    THE  52-53, 54
Cowley, Malcolm  11
Curtiz, Michael  48

da Costa, Morton  103
DARK AT THE TOP OF THE
    STAIRS, THE (movie)  1,
    120-122, 157, 159, 161,
    164, 167, 171n., 172n.,
    173n.
DARK AT THE TOP OF THE
    STAIRS, THE (play)  22n.
DAVID HARUM  9
Davis, Bette  160, 181n.
Dawson, Jan  127
De Palma, Brian  93, 142,
    145, 147, 148, 153
Dean, James  45, 120, 136,
    137, 138, 141, 173n.
DEATH OF A SALESMAN  65n.
DEATH WISH  148
Dee, Sandra  136
Deep South  18, 152, 155
DEER HUNTER, THE  1, 41,
    79-95, 113, 142, 151, 166,
    170
Deland, Margaret  9
Depression, The  5, 6, 7, 9,
    54, 60, 61, 64, 167
Devane, William  142
DEVILS, THE  148
Dickinson, Angie  93
Dionysus  102-103, 105, 107,
    110, 111n., 113, 166
Disney, Walt  59, 112n.
DOG SOLDIERS  83
DOLLAR DEVILS  187
Donaggio, Pino  145

DOWN UPON THE SUWANNEE
    RIVER  188
DR. BULL  188, 190
DR. STRANGELOVE  59
DRESSED TO KILL  93
du Maurier, Daphne  100
DUMBO  59
Durbin, Deanna  60
Durgnat, Raymond  99

EAST OF EDEN  45, 48, 120,
    123n., 164, 172n., 173n.
EASY RIDER  103, 170
Edwards, Blake  17
EFFECT OF GAMMA RAYS ON
    MAN-IN-THE-MOON MARI-
    GOLDS, THE  164
Eggleston, Edward  9
ELECTRA  65n.
Elgar, Sir Edward  74, 155
Epicurus  157
Euripides  65n., 102-103, 179

Fabian  136
FAMILY AFFAIR, A  54
Farrow, Mia  27
Fassbinder, Rainer Werner
    112n.
FATHER OF THE BRIDE  20,
    127, 131, 139n., 177
Faulkner, William  23n., 87,
    103
FEAR EATS THE SOUL  112n.
Ferzetti, Gabriele  133
FIDDLER ON THE ROOF  81
Field, Betty  53, 176
Fields, W. C.  157, 158, 164
film noir  175-176, 180
Finney, Jack  98
FIRST LOVE BEST  185
FLIRT, THE  187
FOG, THE  144, 164
"Fonz, The"  136, 141
Ford, John  30, 88, 102, 190
Forster, E. M.  103
Foster, Stephen  155
Fox, Terry Curtis  94
Frank, Elizabeth  70
Frankenheimer, John  17,
    24n., 153, 176
Frederic, Harold  10
French, Philip  96n.
FURY  186, 188

Gale, Zona  9
Garland, Hamlin  10
GENTLE JULIA  187
GENTLEMAN FROM INDIANA,
    THE  22n.
GIANT  137
GIBBSVILLE  141, 176
GIRL IN THE GLASS CAGE,
    THE  188
Gliese, Rochus  185
GLORY FOR ME  68
"God Bless America"  83, 85,
    86, 90, 94
Godard, Jean-Luc  127
GODFATHER, THE  81
GOLDEN HARVEST  185
Goldsmith, Clifford  53
Goldwyn, Sam  67
GONE WITH THE WIND  64,
    85
GOODBYE, MR. CHIPS  28
Graczyk, Ed  137
GRANDMA'S BOY  189
Granger, Derek  177
GREASE  136
GREEN BERETS, THE  83
Grierson, John  178
Griffith, D. W.  188

Halliwell, Leslie  1, 15
HALLIWELL'S FILMGOER'S
    COMPANION  1
HALLOWEEN  144
HAMLET, THE  103
HAPPY DAYS  136, 141, 176
HAPPY LAND  51, 114
HAPPY MOTHER'S DAY, LOVE
    GEORGE  144
Hardy, Andy  54-59, 60, 153,
    156, 157, 160, 163
Hawks, Howard  131, 139n.
Hayes, John Michael  27
HEART IS A LONELY HUNTER,
    THE  120, 172n.
Heisler, Stuart  112n., 139n.
Hellman, Lillian  16, 64
HELLO, DOLLY!  169
Hemingway, Ernest  87, 90,
    96n.
HENRY ALDRICH FOR PRESI-
    DENT  54
HER UNBORN CHILD  189
Hersholt, Jean  52

Hiroshima 75
Hitchcock, Alfred 35, 45n.,
    48, 86, 100, 114, 115, 116,
    143, 160, 163, 176, 180
Holden, William 103, 112n.
Holly, Buddy 136
Holt, Paul 70
HOME BEFORE DARK 48
HOME TOWN 9
HONKY TONK FREEWAY 142-
143
HOOSIER SCHOOL-MASTER,
    THE 9
Hopkins, Miriam 64
Howe, E. W. 10
Howe, James Wong 35, 176
HUMAN COMEDY, THE (book)
10
HUMAN COMEDY, THE (movie)
1, 114
Hunter, Ross 117

I WALK THE LINE 153
IMITATION OF LIFE 51
IN THE FIRELIGHT 185
IN THE HEAT OF THE NIGHT
125, 171n., 174n.
Inge, William 16, 22n., 103,
112n.
INHERIT THE WIND 154,
173n.
INTRUDER IN THE DUST 48
INVASION OF THE BODY
    SNATCHERS (Kaufman) 99
INVASION OF THE BODY
    SNATCHERS (Siegel) 1,
    24n., 97-100, 125, 143,
    157, 161, 164, 168, 180
IT HAPPENED TO JANE 51,
125

Jacobs, Lewis 185
JAZZLAND 189
Jewett, Sarah Orne 9
Jewison, Norman 81

Kael, Pauline 23n., 47, 126,
    127, 177
Kantor, McKinlay 67-68
Karloff, Boris 127
Kazan, Elia 176
Keaton, Buster 184
Keats, John 133

KEEPING UP WITH LIZZIE
188
Kennedy, President 64, 91,
    136, 170
Kerr, John 44
KID FROM TEXAS, THE 139n.,
    177
KINFLICKS 15
King, Henry 52, 184, 190
King, Martin Luther 64
KINGS ROW (book) 12-14, 15,
27
KINGS ROW (movie) 1, 19, 21,
    27, 28-35, 38, 39, 40, 41,
    43, 44, 47, 48, 50, 52, 55,
    59, 60, 82, 125, 145, 152,
    153, 156, 159, 160, 161,
    162, 163, 164, 165, 166,
    172n., 177
KISS ME, STUPID 165, 181
Korngold, Erich 30
Kubrick, Stanley 59, 142

Lang, Fritz 186, 188
Langdon, Harry 187
Las Vegas 95
LAST PICTURE SHOW, THE
    19, 23n., 47, 125-134, 141,
    164, 166, 171n., 174n., 176
Lawrence, D.H. 103, 171n.
Lee, Harper 60
Lefanu, Mark 127, 139n.
Lehar, Franz 114
Lejeune, C.A. 70
Lesser, Sol 27
Lewis, Sinclair 6, 9, 10, 11,
    12, 13, 107, 188
LIFE WITH HENRY 54
Lincoln, Abraham 59, 153
Lindsay, Vachel 184
LITTLE FOXES, THE 48
LITTLE WOMEN 51
Lloyd, Harold 189
Logan, Joshua 103
Lone Ranger, The 136
LONG GOODBYE, THE 142
LONG HOT SUMMER, THE 48,
    103, 105-106, 106-107, 109,
    112n., 145, 155, 157, 158,
    160, 161, 162, 163, 164,
    171n., 172n., 181n.
LONG PANTS 187
Los Angeles 59, 77

Lovell, Alan  24n. , 99
Loy, Myrna  68, 69
Lucas, George  134, 137, 138,
    141, 142
Lydon, Jimmy  54
Lynd, Helen and Robert  6, 7

MacLaine, Shirley  117
Madison, Indiana  18, 123n.
MAGNIFICENT AMBERSONS,
    THE  48, 114, 156, 167
MAIN STREET (book)  6, 10,
    11-12, 13, 15, 107, 110
MAIN STREET (movie)  187-188
Malone, Dorothy  120
MAN IN THE GRAY FLANNEL
    SUIT, THE  168
Mann, Delbert  120, 176
Martin, Dean  117, 181n.
Marx, Karl  50
Masters, Edgar Lee  11
Mayer, Louis B.  54, 59
McArthur, Colin  176
McCarthy, Kevin  97, 99
McCarthy, Senator  99
McCullers, Carson  118-119
McMurtry, Larry  127, 139n. ,
    171n. , 176
McQueen, Steve  149n.
MEDICINE MAN, THE  189
MEET DR. CHRISTIAN  52
MEET ME IN ST. LOUIS  19,
    20, 24n. , 45, 115, 167, 169
melodrama  47-51, 125, 128,
    129, 142, 144, 155, 176
MEMBER OF THE WEDDING,
    THE  18, 19, 23n. , 48,
    119-120, 155, 158, 159,
    160, 164, 166
Menzies, William Cameron  27
Metalious, Grace  12, 14, 15,
    16, 27, 38
Middle West  14, 18, 110, 152
MIDDLETOWN, A STUDY IN
    MODERN AMERICAN CUL-
    TURE  6
MIDDLETOWN IN TRANSITION
    6
MIDNIGHT COWBOY  143
MILDRED PIERCE  48, 164
Miller, Arthur  48
MILLER'S DAUGHTER, THE
    185

Minnelli, Vincente  19, 20, 44,
    45, 47, 49, 51, 115, 116,
    117, 118, 131, 154
MIRACLE OF MORGAN'S
    CREEK, THE  51
MISS LULU BETT  187
"Moonglow"  108
Motion Picture Alliance  28
MR. DEEDS GOES TO TOWN
    186
MR. SMITH GOES TO WASH-
    INGTON  186
Mulligan, Robert  60, 61
Mulvey, Laura  173n.
Muncie, Indiana  6
Murphy, Audie  139n.
MUSIC MAN, THE  1, 103,
    106-108, 109-110, 121, 125,
    143, 145, 154, 155, 157,
    158, 160, 161, 162, 163,
    164, 166, 167, 169, 172n. ,
    187
musical, the  20, 178
My-Lai  84

Nabokov, Vladimir  103
NATIONAL HEALTH, THE  128
New England  2, 3, 4, 5, 6,
    14, 16, 18, 27, 39, 41, 43,
    44, 152, 174n. , 188, 189
New York City  17, 18, 20, 37,
    41, 42, 43, 51, 55, 56, 60,
    74, 77, 109, 128, 160, 186,
    187, 188
New York state  7
Newman, Paul  103, 149n. ,
    176, 181n.
NICE GIRL?  60
NIGHT AT THE OPERA, A
    27-28
1941  59
NOISE IN NEWBORO, A  188
North, Alex  176
Nowell-Smith, Geoffrey  49

OBSESSION  147
O'Connell, Arthur  104, 176
"Ode to a Nightingale"  133
O'Donnell, Cathy  68, 69
OLD CHESTER TALES  9
O'Neal, Ryan  27
ORPHEUS DESCENDING  22n.
Oswald, Lee Harvey  64

OTHER SIDE OF MIDNIGHT,
    THE  51
OUR TOWN (movie)  1,  27,  28,
    130,  171n.
OUR TOWN (play)  10,  27,  129,
    177

PAJAMA GAME, THE  51
Peck, Gregory  61,  176
Peckinpah, Sam  148
Penn, Arthur  16,  64,  153
Pentheus  103,  107
PEYTON PLACE (book)  12,
    14-15
PEYTON PLACE (movie)  1,
    19,  27,  36-43,  45n.,  47,  48,
    50,  52,  60,  65n.,  108,  109,
    112n.,  113,  125,  127-133,
    145,  153,  154,  156,  157,
    160,  161,  162,  163,  164,
    166,  169,  172n.,  173n.,  177,
    186,  189
Pichel, Irving  114
PICNIC (movie)  19,  21,  48,
    103-105,  106,  107,  108-109,
    145,  154,  155,  160,  161,
    163,  164,  165,  166,  168,
    172n.,  177,  182n.
PICNIC (play)  22n.,  103
Pines, Jim  23n.,  129,  166,
    177
PLACE IN THE SUN, A  48
Poitier, Sidney  174n.
Pollock, Griselda  173n.,  182n.
POLLYANNA  112n.,  165
Presley, Elvis  136
Preston, Robert  103,  120-121
PRODIGAL PARENTS, THE  9
PROM NIGHT  144
PSYCHO  45,  100,  164,  171n.

RABBIT, RUN  15
RACHEL, RACHEL  149,  160,
    173n.
RALLY ROUND THE FLAG,
    BOYS!  51
Ray, Nicholas  135
Reagan, Ronald  27,  143
REBEL WITHOUT A CAUSE
    135,  136
RED RIVER  126,  127,  131,
    139n.,  177
Redford, Robert  64

Reisz, Karel  83
RETURN TO PEYTON PLACE
    27,  154
Reville, Alma  115
"Revolt from the Village" the
    11,  12
Rhode, Eric  184
Riefenstahl, Leni  14,  87
RISKY BUSINESS  189,  190
Ritt, Martin  103,  105,  142
Robinson, Casey  27
Robinson, Edward Arlington  9
Robson, Mark  43,  47,  127,
    128
"Rock Around the Clock"  135
Rockwell, Norman  106,  168
Rogers, Will  190
ROMANCE ROAD  189
Rooney, Michey  55,  65n.
ROSE TATTOO, THE  48
roulette, Russian  82,  84,  85,
    88,  89,  92,  94,  95
Russell, Harold  68
Russell, Ken  148

Saigon  82,  84,  88,  89,  92,
    93,  95
San Francisco  51,  99,  100,
    101,  102,  111n.
SAP, THE  189
Saroyan, William  10
Sarris, Andrew  142,  178
SATURDAY EVENING POST  8,
    9,  16,  168,  169,  186
Schlesinger, John  142,  143
Schrag, Peter  8,  16
Scorsese, Martin  142
"76 Trombones"  107
SHADOW OF A DOUBT  48,
    55,  114-116,  125,  153,  154,
    156,  158,  160,  161,  162,
    163,  164,  167,  172n.,  173n.,
    180
SHINING, THE  142
SHOWBOAT  64
Siegel, Don  24n.,  97,  98,  99,
    100,  143,  180
Sinatra, Frank  117
Sirk, Douglas  48,  49,  51,
    112n.,  129,  142,  173n.
Sklar, Robert  183
SLANDERERS, THE  188
SMALL TOWN  6

SMILES OF A SUMMER NIGHT
   135
SOAP 129
SOME CAME RUNNING 48,
   116-118, 154, 157, 158,
   160, 162, 164, 165, 172n.,
   173n.
SOUND AND THE FURY, THE
   48, 120, 123n., 164, 173n.
SPELLBOUND 35
Spielberg, Steven 59, 142
SPLENDOR IN THE GRASS
   21, 163, 172n.
SPOON RIVER ANTHOLOGY 11
"Spotted Horses, The" 103
Springdale 7, 8
Stanley, Kim 61
Stevens, Connie 136
Stevens, George 114
STORM CENTER 160
STORM WARNING 21, 48,
   112n., 139n., 171n., 177
STRANGERS ON A TRAIN 160
STRAW DOGS 148
Sturges, John 166
Sturges, Preston 176
SUMMER AND SMOKE 22n.
SUMMER PLACE, A 48
SUNRISE 185, 186
Swift, David 112n.

TALES OF NEW ENGLAND 9
TALK OF THE TOWN, THE
   114
TARGETS 127
Tarkington, Booth 9, 187
Taylor, Elizabeth 131, 181n.
TEA AND SYMPATHY 44,
   121, 171n.
THEOREM 103, 121
THIN MAN, THE 71
Thomson, David 169
"Till There Was You" 109
TO KILL A MOCKINGBIRD
   (book) 60
TO KILL A MOCKINGBIRD
   (movie) 23n., 60, 61-64,
   154, 155, 161, 162, 164,
   166, 167, 172n.
TOL'ABLE DAVID 184, 185
TOWN SCANDAL, THE 187
Tracy, Spencer 166, 173n.
Tragedy, Greek 48

Tragedy, Renaissance 48
"Trouble" 107, 155
TROUBLE WITH HARRY, THE
   180
TROUT FISHING IN AMERICA
   15
Truffaut, François 86
Twain, Mark 10, 16

Updike, John 15

VALLEY OF THE DOLLS 51
Van Doren, Carl 11
Vidich, Arthur J. 7, 8
Vidor, King 48
Vietnam 41, 80, 81, 83, 84,
   85, 86, 87, 88, 89, 91, 92,
   93, 94, 95, 136, 142, 143,
   170
VIEW FROM THE BRIDGE, A
   65n.
Vitti, Monica 133

WALTONS, THE 141, 176
War, Cold 5
War, Korean 5, 7, 126, 128,
   132
War, Second World 5, 7, 13,
   41, 51, 60, 67, 128, 139n.,
   162, 183
Warhol, Andy 117
Washington, D.C. 55, 76
WASP, the 8, 16, 73, 141
Watergate 142, 170
WAY DOWN EAST 185, 188
Wayne, John 83
WELCOME STRANGER 188
Welles, Orson 48, 105, 114,
   178, 181n.
WEST SIDE STORY 17
Westcott, Edward 9
Western, the 20, 83, 88, 129,
   139n., 142, 166
WHAT A LIFE! 53
WHAT'S UP, DOC? 127
WHERE LOVE HAS GONE 51
WHERE'S THE REST OF ME?
   27
WHO'S AFRAID OF VIRGINIA
   WOOLF? 137
WHY GIRLS GO BACK HOME
   187
WILD ONE, THE 135

Wilder, Billy  165
Wilder, Thornton  10, 16, 27,
   115, 129, 163
Williams, Tennessee  16, 22n.,
   105-106, 137
Winchester, Simon  85
WINESBURG, OHIO  11, 13
Winkler, Henry  141
Winner, Michael  148
Wiseman, Frederick  174n.
Wood, Michael  160, 170, 183
Wood, Natalie  137
Wood, Sam  27, 28, 129
Woodward, Joanne  105, 176,
   181n.

Wright, Teresa  68, 114
WRITTEN ON THE WIND  48,
   120, 163, 164, 172n.
Wyler, William  48, 67, 68,
   72, 79, 80, 83, 176, 178
Wyman, Jane  112n., 176

YELLOW STAIN, THE  189
YOUNG AT HEART  48
YOUNG SAVAGES, THE  17

Zimmerman, P.D.  126
Zinman, David  54
Zinnemann, Fred  119